A Football Man

The Autobiography

A Football Man

The Autobiography

JOHN GILES

With Declan Lynch

HODDER &
STOUGHTON

First published in Great Britain in 2010 by Hodder & Stoughton
An Hachette UK company

1

A CIP catalogue record for this title is available from the British Library

ISBN 978 1 444 72096 9

Typeset in Galliard by Palimpsest Book Production Limited

Printed and bound in Great Britain by
CPI Mackays, Chatham ME5 8TD

Hodder & Stoughton policy is to use papers that are natural,
renewable and recyclable products and made from wood grown
in sustainable forests. The logging and manufacturing processes are expected
to conform to the environmental regulations of the country of origin.

Hodder & Stoughton Ltd
338 Euston Road
London NW1 3BH

www.hodder.co.uk

To my mother and father, and all my family

Acknowledgements

I would like to thank PJ Cunningham and Tim O'Connor for all their help and encouragement.

Photographic Acknowledgements

The author and publisher would like to thank the following for permission to use inside photographs in *A Football Man*.

Getty: section 1, p4
Sportsfile: section 2, p6
Colorsport: section 1, p6 (both photos); section 2, pp4, 5 & 7
RTÉ photo archive: section 2, pp6, 7, 8
Mirror Pix: section 1, p7

A special thanks for Bernard Spain for the photo in section 1, P2, top image.

The author and publishers have endeavoured to contact all copyright holders. If any images used in this book have been reproduced without permission, we would like to rectify this in future editions and encourage owners of copyright not acknowledged to contact us.

Contents

PROLOGUE

EAMON DUNPHY got me into television. By 1986, I had finished in football management and I had no plans for the future. Eamon, who had been a part of RTÉ's coverage of the major championships for eight years, believed I could be an asset to the panel for that year's World Cup in Mexico. So over a few drinks he urged RTÉ producer Mike Horgan to approach me. But Mike was reluctant, and with good reason.

When I was manager of the Republic of Ireland, and I had to deal with the media, I felt that the less I told them, the better I had done my job. Ideally, I would have told them nothing, but some form of communication was necessary, so when I did the pre-match and post-match interviews, I always erred on the side of caution. I now realise that I was over-cautious, but, at the time, I thought it was justified. As a manager, I felt that my primary duty was to the players, not to the journalists. If a journalist suggested that we were a bit loose at the back, I would reply in a non-committal way, because if I agreed with him, I felt that my defenders might regard it as a criticism of them – and I needed them to trust me, more than I needed the journalist to think I was a great guy.

I had seen the bond between the manager and the players destroyed by careless criticism in post-match interviews, and I didn't want to make that mistake. Which, as far as the media was concerned, made me a nightmare.

So I can understand why RTÉ might have thought, What's the point in getting John? He's not going to say anything.

But Eamon persevered with Mike Horgan and, at the last minute, RTÉ decided to take a chance. However, their reticence made me reluctant to travel to Dublin from my home in Birmingham. I had dreamed since I was a small boy of becoming a professional footballer, but I had never had any ambition to be a television pundit. But Eamon persevered with me too. I had a very casual approach to it all and saw it as a one-off assignment. I played golf on the day of a match and came into the studio at the last minute, with little or no preparation. I treated it more as a holiday than work, and I certainly didn't see it as a long-term career.

Indeed from that day to this, I have never felt nervous on the RTÉ panel. I just regard it as talking football, and I am comfortable with that. I didn't fully appreciate at first, that I had already done most of the preparation and training I would need on the football fields of Dublin and Manchester and Leeds and beyond.

In the 1980s, RTÉ wasn't a serious rival to the much more popular coverage put out by the BBC or ITV, and the station's viewing figures for the Mexico World Cup were as modest as before. Apparently, I had made no real impact.

But the RTÉ people were surprised that I had been so forthcoming in my contributions. Despite my relaxed approach, I had still felt an obligation to give an honest opinion. Having watched football coverage over the years as a player and as a manager, I had found it mostly bland, mostly dishonest, mostly, in fact, ridiculous.

I'd hear the pundits saying that a team 'scored too early', which implies that the manager should have warned his team not to score until a more appropriate time. 'They'll have to keep it tight for the first fifteen minutes', was another favourite – as if you don't have to keep it tight for the last fifteen minutes. And 2–0 could be 'a dangerous lead'. To which I could suggest only one solution – don't score the second goal.

They were always talking about 'tactics' – in fact, they still are. Even in 2010, Gary Lineker was attributing England's failure in the World Cup to Capello getting his 'tactics' all wrong, because, apparently, nobody plays four-four-two these days. Frankly, if you're going to play Emile Heskey up front, if you leave your goalkeepers wondering if they are playing until the last minute, if Gerrard and Lampard are playing badly, and everyone else is passing the ball badly, your tactics fade into insignificance.

The best tactic there has ever been, is to find really good, honest players, who will train hard and look after themselves. If the manager plays the best players in their best positions, he is then in the happy position of only needing to employ the oldest and most successful of all tactics since the game was invented – when his team has the ball, every player is obliged to use it as constructively as possible and when his team doesn't have the ball, every player makes an honest effort to get it back.

Sometimes, this means that the big centre-half has to clear the danger if he is under pressure. That is as positive as he can be in that particular situation. In almost every other situation, players have a responsibility to use the ball constructively.

It sounds sensible enough, yet when the television pundits get going, 'tactics' can have all sorts of meanings. If a team was losing 3–0 at half-time, the panellists would be reluctant to attribute the score to silly individual errors, preferring to talk about tactics and formations – about four-four-two and four-three-three and all that stuff. They can still be heard holding forth about the losing manager needing 'to get more players in the box'. But how can you get more players in the box if the opposition has the ball? And if the right-back has the ball in a deep position, you can get plenty of players into your opponent's box, but is it the correct thing to do? The full-back might need someone to pass the ball to, but he can't if they're all in the box.

Alternatively, the manager 'will have to push the full-backs forward'. Again, where is the ball? Do they still go forward when the opposition has the ball or do they go forward at times when the correct thing to do, is to come deep and get possession of the ball?

'Getting more players in the box', or 'pushing the full-backs forward', or 'putting an extra player in midfield' might make the pundits sound knowledgeable, but the fact remains that the ball is the most important thing on the pitch, that good players will take up correct positions in relation to it, while bad players will continue to take up poor positions, regardless of tactics or formations.

Apart from the lack of real analysis, there had rarely been any effort to differentiate between the good players and the bad players. Let alone between the good players and the great players. Which not only did a disservice to the viewers, it did a disservice to the good players and the great players.

Having felt so strongly about this from way back, I started to think that there might be more in this television work than just a bit of fun every four years on World Cup assignments. I had no definite plans to do anything else and I had a young family to support – football had certainly not left me in any position to retire. I was aware that RTÉ were doing live matches in England, and they didn't have a co-commentator. So I went to see Tim O'Connor, then Head of Sport in RTÉ, and who was also a good friend of mine. Tim took a gamble on me as a co-commentator, giving me one piece of advice, which I have cherished over the years, 'Don't talk unless you've got something worthwhile to say.' Even if it means nothing is said for five or six minutes of a game, it is the right thing to do.

The commentating led to some work in the newspapers. I started writing a column for Vincent Browne in the *Sunday Tribune*, and Eamon again paved the way for me to do a column in the *Evening Herald*, one that continues to this day. I was also recommended to the *Daily Express* by the outstanding sports journalist Jim Lawton, with whom I had become friendly when I was managing in Vancouver. Jim and I would have a successful partnership doing a column over a twenty-year period, before parting company a couple of years ago.

As I was now officially becoming a pundit on television and in the papers, I felt the time had come to make a big confession. In the eyes of the general public, I had the image of being a creative player, which was true. But because I was rarely in trouble with referees, and was sent off only once in my entire career, I also had the image of being a lot more innocent of wrongdoing than I actually was. In the game, I had a darker reputation, not as one of the clichéd 'hard men', but as a more dangerous type. I could look after myself in a very professional way, as they say.

I took the decision that if I was to embark on a career in which honest comment was essential, in which I might have to condemn bad tackles, for example, then I would have to come clean about my well-earned reputation among my fellow professionals. It was pretty embarrassing, having to tarnish my own image in the *Daily Express*. Some of my friends thought I was mad to do it and warned me that, in future, I would be known only for the bad tackles, that the creative play would be forgotten. To a large extent, this has happened, but I still think it was the right thing to do, and it meant that I could never be accused of double standards when I was passing comment on others.

If I wanted to get into punditry properly, I would also have to cut any links with the dressing room, so that I wouldn't be protecting players or managers who were pals of mine. Even today, I can still see this malaise in a lot of television punditry, with ex-players going to great lengths to keep the viewer in the dark about any unique insights they might have. Not only are they not doing what they're supposed to be doing, they are doing the direct opposite.

So when Jack Charlton became manager of the Republic of

Ireland in 1986, I found myself in the strange position of commenting on someone who had been both an old pal from the dressing room at Leeds United, and a rival candidate for the Ireland job. To some, Jack was my friend; to others, my enemy. You could get yourself really tangled up there, which again demonstrates that, in this game, you're better off just giving it straight.

Of course I knew Jack.

One cold Monday morning in Yorkshire, a long time ago, the Leeds lads were sitting around after a hard training session when Jack picked up his newspaper, wrapped a towel around himself and announced that he was 'off for a crap'. The toilets were outside, opposite the dressing rooms, and were open-topped. When we knew that Jack was settled in across the way, Allan Clarke and I went outside, found the big drum used for gathering the kit, emptied it and filled it with freezing-cold water. There was a skip outside the open-topped toilet where Jack was ensconced and we quietly lifted the drum onto it, and then got up there ourselves. Peering down into the toilet, we could see that Jack was totally engrossed in his newspaper. We couldn't miss him. We lifted the drum and let him have it. I can still hear his gasp of shock as the cold water lashed over him. We ran back to the dressing room and began to look as innocent as we could. Jack burst in, angrier than we'd ever seen him. He picked me out and said, 'You fucking little Irish bastard, I know it was you.'

He was right, but he couldn't know for sure – and he never got an admission from me, until now.

'Jack it wasn't me,' I said in injured tones. 'You don't know who did that and still you're blaming me.'

Allan Clarke, who wasn't Jack's favourite person, began to say something, perhaps the start of a confession. But Jack was too angry now, and he interrupted, 'Don't you start, you skinny bastard.' And as he stood there, his wet hair stuck to his head, his towel dripping, and the newspaper in his hand soaking wet,

Jack declared defiantly, 'I wouldn't mind, but you missed me anyway.'

Then he slammed the wet newspaper on the dressing-room table and, looking around the room, gave us this warning, 'No one . . . and I mean no one . . . will have a crap in peace again as long as I've anything to do with this club.'

Yes, I knew Jack.

He could be a grumpy bugger, but he had qualities of honesty and decency which outweighed that. He was also the best centre-half in England between 1963 and 1972, and I am always delighted to see him at our Leeds reunions. We did have basic differences about how the game should be played. So when Jack was managing the Republic in his way, and I was starting to criticise him in my way, really it was just like old times.

Jack's main emphasis in the game was to 'put them under pressure' when the opposition had the ball. Football is about time and space, and clearly the less time and space you give the opposition, the more chance you have of getting the ball back. I agreed with that. But I totally disagreed with Jack's lack of emphasis on using the ball constructively when his team was in possession. The way I see it, the more you keep the ball, the less you need to be winning it back in the first place.

When Ireland qualified for Euro '88 and then Italia '90, this basic philosophical difference between myself and Jack was being aired on RTÉ at a time when a lot of people just wanted to celebrate the Republic's success – and it was worth celebrating. That success could partly be attributed to Jack's leadership, his absolute belief in what he was doing, and his ability to communicate that to the players. But if we were to do our job properly on the RTÉ panel, we also needed to point out that we now had an outstanding collection of players – better than England's at that time – and that this tabloid notion that Jack was taking a bunch of journey-men and somehow enabling them to compete at the highest level, was just not right.

Amidst the growing euphoria of Italia '90, Ireland played a dire, scoreless draw with Egypt in Palermo, after which Eamon was seen to throw his pen across the table in frustration, declaring, 'I am ashamed of Irish football today.' The press mischievously turned this into Eamon declaring that he was ashamed to be Irish and, for a while, he became a scapegoat – they couldn't turn on Jack or the players, so they turned on Eamon, whose car was surrounded by an angry mob at the airport as he arrived back from Italy. Mercifully, the guards arrived, and advised him to get out of there quickly, to take the long way home via Portmarnock. Yet despite all the ructions – and maybe because of them – Italia '90 was probably the making of the RTÉ panel.

While I would not agree with some of Jack's philosophy, I was delighted at his success in popularising the game in a way that had never been seen before in Ireland. We were getting huge audiences and even amid all the madness of that time, I think viewers could see that we weren't like the others on the BBC or ITV, who just said what everyone wanted to hear.

Today, we have a pool of about ten panellists and presenters for the World Cup, back then there was just Eamon, Bill O'Herlihy and myself broadcasting from a tiny studio in Montrose, covering all the games. Our life was studio to bed to studio, eating on the run. We had no time to read the papers and had no real contact with the outside world, so we weren't aware of our growing popularity. We went a bit mad with the scratchpad when Frank Rijkaard spat at Rudi Völler, and Eamon traced the trajectory of the spit from the Dutchman's mouth to the German's head, a special moment.

Then, as now, Bill had to hold it all together. Eamon and I had to know our own minds, but Bill had to know the minds of the viewers, and the questions they'd want him to raise, a job he has always done brilliantly.

We found out people were out there impersonating us. We used to say, 'Hold it there', when we were using the scratchpad, and that became a catchphrase for comedians. The scratchpad itself was an innovation I had seen first in Canada, used by an ex-player called John Madden to illustrate the finer points of American football. I told Tim O'Connor about it and he brought one in for Euro '88. It is a cliché that football is a simple game. In fact it is very complex, and, like most things in life, it only appears simple when it is done properly. The scratchpad helped to simplify some of the complexities for viewers, just as John Madden's scratchpad had taught me about the moves leading to a touchdown.

Long before I arrived, Eamon's contribution had been immense. When he began in 1978, the ground rules for this sort of programme were already established. The producers were the bosses and the panellists had little or no influence in deciding what segments of a game should be analysed. But Eamon changed that. He felt that the former players were the professionals, which, of course, in matters of football, they were. And his judgement was backed by Tim O'Connor and Mike Horgan, all of which meant that our programmes were 'driven from the floor', a phrase that is now synonymous with Eamon in RTÉ.

Eamon and I have had one horrible and well-known dispute, during the Saipan fiasco. Eamon supported Roy Keane. I tended to side with Mick McCarthy. I think Eamon felt that this was the same old FAI nonsense that we'd both been fighting against all our lives and, as a result, he may have expected me to support Keane.

And, of course, there *were* elements of the old FAI nonsense in it. But I still felt Keane himself was in a bad place at the time, that he was probably being oversensitive, that he should have waited until after the World Cup and then created a storm. Eamon and I had a fundamental difference of opinion which mirrored the split in the nation, and it damaged our relationship at the time. Millions of Irish people were caught up in the fever of Saipan, and we were feeling it too.

It was difficult for us, trying to do the programmes when we weren't on speaking terms, either off-air or on-air, but it was even more difficult for Bill O'Herlihy and others who worked around us, trying to make the best of it. The rapport we used to have just wasn't there for a while, which affected the programme as a whole, quite apart from what it was doing to Eamon and myself. We had known one another since we were kids, and now it had come to this, over something that happened between other people, on another continent.

It took us a while to make up, but we did, and it's all right now.

There was no dramatic summit meeting between us. I think that time just healed it, as it does for most people. And things were happening that confirmed the absurdity of it all. Keane accepted employment at Sunderland from Niall Quinn, one of his former arch-enemies. Keane and McCarthy shook hands as rival managers. And Keane has been quoted as saying that he now realises he wasn't playing for Mick McCarthy but for Ireland.

Eamon and I were actually together in RTÉ when we heard the stunning news that Keane was joining Quinn – or 'Mother Teresa' as he had called him – as Sunderland's new manager.

'Imagine we fell out over those guys,' I said.

We are also well-known for making that distinction between good players and great players. I feel it is important to draw that line for a few reasons. First of all, it is just better to be accurate in the words you use. If you're saying that everything is great, it all becomes meaningless. After all, if everything is great, ultimately nothing is great.

And in my view, football is entitled to the same set of standards as books or films or the theatre. In all these areas, serious efforts are made to try to establish who the true greats are, the ones whose work will stand the test of time.

Football has its own men of genius, as important in their own way as any of the great writers or painters – arguably, they are more important because their genius is accessible to everyone. Basically, football makes more people happy than almost anything else out there. So it should be taken seriously, and its great practitioners should be honoured in the right way.

I was lucky enough to play with and against some of the great players of the game, and to watch some of them as a pundit. Players like Pelé, Garrincha, Beckenbauer, Jairzinho, Carlos Alberto, Cruyff, Zidane, Bobby Charlton, van Basten, Gullit, John Robertson, Kenny Dalglish, Roy Keane and Paul McGrath. They set the standards by which great players should be judged.

So when it comes to assessing Eric Cantona or Cristiano Ronaldo, I would say that they have done some of the things that great players do, but they have also done some things that the great players would never do. For example, Ronaldo does not always work for the benefit of the team, but for his own glorification. He remonstrates with his team-mates, even when he is at fault and he seldom, if ever, makes the effort to chase back and to regain possession of the ball when his team has lost it.

Like Cantona he is an extraordinarily talented lad. He is a star – and the game needs stars. A player may have great ability, but there are five other criteria for someone to be what I would regard as a great player.

1. Whatever abilities the player possesses must be used for the benefit of the team. This requires honesty of effort.

2. Moral courage is needed to take responsibility in accepting the ball, no matter how important the game and regardless of the score.

3. An honest effort must be made to regain possession when the other team has the ball.

4. There must be no public remonstration with team-mates.

5. A player must have the intelligence and humility to play the simple pass when that is the right thing to do.

Broadly speaking, all the great players have all of these virtues. And it diminishes their achievements when they are placed in the same bracket as players who are just extremely gifted. Television and television pundits are mainly responsible for raising a certain type of player who shouldn't really be there, to the very highest rank. My own father, Dickie, who had a real knowledge of the game, towards the end of his life was watching *Match of the Day* with me. 'That Glenn Hoddle . . . great player,' he said with an air of certainty.

Dickie was always totally convinced of his own rightness in football matters, to the extent that he was once sitting in the company of my Leeds team-mate Norman Hunter, and Norman was holding forth on the game, only to be told by Dickie, 'Norman, son, you don't know what you're talking about.'

Now, as we watched *Match of the Day*, in his eyes Glenn Hoddle had suddenly become a great player. Growing up, I had always deferred to my father's knowledge of the game, but now I had had my own career, and had developed my own knowledge, so when he started on the greatness of Glenn Hoddle, I felt it was time to pull rank on him.

'I played against Glenn Hoddle loads of times. And I can tell you he's not a great player,' I said. I explained that Hoddle had excellent technique and was a wonderful distributor of the ball, but that he never really delivered in a way that the great players did. I felt this was because he lacked the real sharpness and aggression which top midfielders possess. When he had the time and space, he could have a series of matches in which he was outstanding. But this would lead to closer marking and because of this lack of sharpness in tight situations, he couldn't lose his marker. So he would become anonymous for a few games, at which point opponents relaxed a bit, giving him the freedom and space to show his class. And so it went, which helps to explain why Hoddle could have fifty caps for England, and was still widely regarded as 'promising'.

'And another thing you're forgetting,' I said to my father. '*Match of the Day* is a highlights programme.'

Even Dickie Giles, who had seen countless thousands of football matches, was tending to ignore the fact that *Match of the Day* was leaving out a lot of things. That the camera, in this case, was lying.

I never thought I'd end up in front of those cameras one day. But I'm very glad that I did.

I have been so lucky in life. My mother said I was 'born with the caul', which is a sort of hood that covers some newborns, and is said to be a sign of good luck. In fact, she insisted that one of the nurses made off with the caul, and perhaps even sold it – ships' captains would keep a caul on board, and it was generally regarded as something of great value. Many things have happened to me, which would confirm that I was 'born with the caul', and very high up there is the fact that I had the privilege to know some of the greatest footballers of the past fifty years.

I hope that we will always be able to name the great players, and to revere them. I hope that this book brings back a lot of memories for people who love football. And I hope it's of interest to younger people who see this grey-haired old man on television, and who may not be aware that I used to play this game.

John Giles
September 2010

1

THE GIFT

RIGHT FROM the start, I could kick a ball correctly. I was not aware of this in any abstract or technical way, I could just feel the joy of it.

From the time I was about three years of age, I knew that I was kicking it the right way because of the enormous satisfaction it gave me. I would be kicking it around with my grandfather, known as 'Darkie', who would play football with me for as long as I wanted, which was for ever. After I had started to feel this joy, just from kicking a ball, and kicking it the way it's supposed to be kicked, every hour that passed without a ball at my feet was an hour wasted.

I realise it was a gift. And I also realise that I had done nothing to deserve this gift – I'd made no great sacrifices to feel this satisfaction.

I had not worked hard to develop it, I just had it.

I can no more take the credit for it than I can take the credit for receiving a present on my birthday. But, as I got older, I would also be lucky enough to have the awareness that I needed to do everything I possibly could to honour this gift. To make it my life, not just a pastime or a job. I knew I had an obligation to use this gift in the right way and to be as good a professional as I could. To get the respect of my colleagues, not just to appeal to the crowd. To be selfish in getting the most out of what I'd been given, and unselfish in doing it for the team.

But as a very small boy I hadn't developed that awareness and whatever I put into it, at the age of three, I would get back just by kicking that ball, again and again.

I'm sure a golfer feels the same way, when he swings a club for the first time and realises that he's able to do it properly, for no apparent reason except that it's meant to be. People marvel at the way that the amateur golfer hardly ever bothers to practise, while the professional, with so much more natural ability, never seems to stop practising.

In one way it's all a mystery and in another way really there's no mystery to it. The player who can kick a ball correctly just loves kicking it. Whatever it is – timing, co-ordination, just some raw instinct – he can make the ball do what he wants.

I know that feeling because it flowed through me even when I was kicking a 'bouncer', which wasn't even a proper football, but a rubber ball about twice the size of a tennis ball and which cost around a shilling – not that I was concerned about that as I kicked it around Ormond Square with Darkie, my old pal. I guess he got a kick out of it too. He could see what it meant to me to have this gift, he could see that I was lucky.

There wasn't a lot of luck going around in 1940, the year I was born. Looking back, it seems that I'd got most of it around our way. But that's only looking back.

We don't live our lives like that, we live them day by day, and we look forward. We have the reality and we have the dream. The reality, in my case, was a corporation building at Ormond Square, near the fruit markets and the fish markets, just down from Christchurch, between Capel Street Bridge and Merchant's Quay Bridge, and around the corner from the Four Courts in the heart of the city. The reality was number 7A, which had just two rooms and a pantry where nine of us lived. The dream was football.

The eight people apart from myself who shared our home

were my two grandparents on my mother's side, the aforementioned 'Darkie' and Mary-Ann; my older sister Anna, my younger
sisters Kay and Pauline and my brother Christy who was the
youngest in the family; my father who was also called Christy,
but who was known as 'Dickie', and my mother Kate.

There were times when I saw my mother crying, reduced to
a state of absolute despair by the constant struggle to put food
on the table. But mostly I didn't pay much attention to the hard
facts of life in Dublin of the 1940s. Nor did I lose sleep about
whatever Hitler was doing to the wider world outside Ormond
Square and outside Ireland, in which the Second World War was
known simply as 'The Emergency'. I shared a bed with my grandparents and my brother, and actually I can't recall a time in my
life when I slept better. The Germans dropped bombs on the
North Strand when I was about six months old, and that wasn't
far away from us, but I slept through it. And when I was old
enough to play football, I continued to sleep soundly at night,
exhausted after playing till dark.

The realities of war and poverty didn't keep me awake at
night, probably because the dream was far more powerful than
any reality. The dream was happening every day in games of
five, six, or seven-a-side that would go on for hours, in all
weathers, on the 'pitch' that was Ormond Square. And at its
most perfect, I would play in Ormond Square and dream of
playing for Manchester United, which was my team. I had
pictures of United players like Jack Rowley and Stan Pearson
all over my bedroom wall. I would cut pictures of United players
out of the paper and put them into a United scrapbook, and
dream.

It was the same dream that most of the kids had at that time.
What I didn't realise was that my dream would come true.

My father always gave the appearance of being bigger than he
actually was. And it wasn't just the trilby that he wore, which

seemed to give him a few extra inches. It was the fact that he had a large personality, that he was, as they say, a character.

He was much more of a character than I was, or would ever be. I was shy and sensitive, more like my mother, who couldn't read or write but who was a pretty good judge of people. My father wasn't too strong in that department, at any stage of his life, but there is no doubt that he was an exceptionally good judge of football.

Dickie was a football man.

By this I don't mean that he was a man who loved football the way that a lot of other men love football, I mean that football, to him, was a complete obsession, it was the meaning of life.

He had played for Bohemians and Shelbourne in the League of Ireland, and for Distillery, then a well-known Leinster League team. He was a midfielder, an inside-forward as they called it back then. When his playing career was cut short by a knee injury at the age of twenty-seven, he moved into management with some success at Distillery and Drumcondra. And when he realised that I could play the game, my father was able to nurture whatever abilities I had, because of that deep knowledge of his.

I don't know where he got it from. There were other footballers in our extended family such as my cousin Christy, who had played for Doncaster Rovers and Ireland, but playing the game and knowing the game can be two different things. To know the game is an innate thing, an instinct in itself. José Mourinho or Arsène Wenger have become great football men, in their different ways, even though neither of them played the game with any distinction. So it's a mysterious ability to have, and, apparently, it can come from anywhere. But wherever it came from, my father had it.

Throughout my career both as a player and as a pundit, I have been able to draw on aspects of that knowledge. And it gave me a confidence, a belief in my own judgement, that I mightn't otherwise have had. I never doubted his wisdom when it came to football.

In fact, he probably knew the game better than he knew himself, and better than he knew me or my mother, or anyone else for that matter. He was eccentric in ways that he didn't realise. When I look back through the years, I can remember times when this highly intelligent man – my mother called him, among other things, the mad professor – seemed to be completely lacking in what you might call basic common sense.

But I wasn't complaining about that the day he gave me my first pair of football boots.

I was eight years old and it remains one of the happiest days of my life.

And Dickie being Dickie, these were no ordinary football boots. He was on a trip to Belfast and was window-shopping in the city when he saw this specially made pair of boots, for display purposes only. They were miniatures and not for sale. Except Dickie somehow managed to persuade the shop assistant to take the little boots out of the window and to sell them to him.

So it was that he brought back these beautiful boots for me. In the 1940s, they didn't actually make football boots for young kids – you had to wait until you were nearly in your teens before you could wear a proper pair of football boots. There wasn't the choice between Adidas or Nike either. There was basically one type of boot, in one colour, with a toe-cap that would now be regarded as a deadly weapon. Maybe that was part of the reason why eight-year olds couldn't have them. When I put them on, it was a magical moment. I was able to try them out immediately on the grass area of Ormond Square and get used to them.

They fitted me perfectly.

If you set out to create the ideal circumstances in which to develop a young footballer, you could not come up with anything better than Ormond Square as I knew it. With so little room in the flats, the parents would send their children out to play as much as possible, and had no anxiety about doing this, as parents would today. They were happy to get us out there, because there was nothing for us to do indoors anyway, and no books apart from school books, which I hated.

In fact, I hated everything about school. Even today, I hate having to bring up the subject and I would like to pretend that it didn't happen at all. But then I must accept that school was another of those realities – probably the harshest one – that makes the dream all the sweeter.

My grandfather Darkie, when he wasn't kicking a ball around with me, had the unhappy task of bringing me to school at Halsen Street, or George's Hill as we called it. I was scared stiff of the nuns and most of the other teachers too, not necessarily for anything they did to me, just for their general crankiness. I was at George's Hill from the age of four to the age of seven, when we made our First Holy Communion, and Darkie brought me there every morning, despite my tears and protestations, and collected me in the afternoon.

But when that ordeal was over for another day, it was all foot-ball for me, and for all the other kids on the Square. There would always be enough lads – including my younger brother Christy, and my cousins Jimmy Redmond and Georgie Waller – to start a game, with a lamp-post and a coat serving as the goals.

I was part of the gang, but I hadn't always been. I had had to earn my place.

I lived on the side of the Square known as The Flats. The other side was known as The Cottages, and was regarded as being slightly more posh than the flats. But the hard part for me, when I was about five years old, was the fact that I had no kids to play with on my side. And there were loads of kids on the other side, such as Eamon O'Brien, Mickey Farrelly, Johnno Quinlan and Shay O'Brien, who was the leader of the gang.

So I would be playing on my own and my mother would be

telling me to go over and join the other kids and, while I desperately wanted to be part of the gang, I was also tormented by
shyness. The more my mother would force me to go over, the
worse the torment. I wasn't afraid of them physically because we
were all roughly the same size, which was generally on the small
side, but I just couldn't bring myself to make friends with them
properly. So I'd be looking at them playing football and the ball
would come to me, a tennis ball or maybe a bouncer, and I would
kick it back to them. But I wouldn't be part of their game.

Still my mother made me go over. And so it went until the
day that Mickey Farrelly started to bully me, pushing me a few
times, knocking me over onto the kerb and giving me a bang on
the elbow. Blinded with rage, I lashed out at him, giving him a
right good whack on the nose, which caused his nose to bleed.
His mother came out and was flying into a rage against me when
Shay O'Brien, like a hero, said his piece, 'That's not right,' he
said to Mrs Farrelly. 'It was Mickey's fault.'

Shay had stuck up for me. I was in the gang now. I could play
ball with them for life after that. And in this case, life meant life.
Shay moved to New York in 1959, but I kept in touch with him
until the day he died in 2007.

We gang members may have been a danger to ourselves from
time to time, but we were safe in the sense that there was no
traffic. Though there were threats of a different kind hanging
over us. The Square was surrounded by railings with spiked tops
which would burst our bouncer. And while that would be hugely
disappointing for us, we could at least accept that it was an accident. By contrast, there was an old woman whose home was
right behind one of the goals, who would burst the bouncer
just for spite. In fact, she would leave her door ajar in the hope
that it would fall into her clutches, and she could ruin our sport.

I remember the madness of it, the excitement and the noise
of all those kids, but I also remember those quiet times when I
would be alone and I would kick the ball around, feeling that

satisfaction of kicking it the right way, time after time trying to hit the number 7 outside our house.

Because the bouncer was smaller and harder to control than a normal football, it helped me to develop skills, such as ball control, balance, spatial awareness and correct positioning, something for which I would be grateful later in my football life. Even the way it bounced off the kerb helped me develop a sense of anticipation.

When my father was manager of Drumcondra, we would occasionally get a proper ball which had been discarded by the club, and one of the lads would somehow sew it up so we could play with it. But a new one would have been far too expensive for us, at a time when we would be stealing apples and pears from the market stalls, or raising a half-penny or a penny by collecting and returning jam jars and lemonade bottles to a shop. Another way we had of getting the odd penny or half-penny was selling pig feed to a woman who reared pigs for slaughter in a yard nearby. We would arrive with bags of potato skins and other waste food, knock on the window and show her what we had, sometimes with paper stuffed underneath it to bulk it up, praying she wouldn't check it out. But when we had got enough pennies together, we might go to the pictures.

Dubliners often reminisce fondly about these old picture houses, the Maro, the Tivo and the Pheno, but I remember them as complete dumps. And I have the distinction of being thrown out of all three of them for making too much noise and messing about in general. I remember during a film in the Maro one day, a big block fell from the roof and crashed down into the aisle. No one paid any attention to it, they just kept watching the film. But if the block had fallen in the wrong place, at least six to eight kids would certainly have been killed.

I especially loved the movies *Samson and Delilah* and *Shane*.

I also heard a lot of good music because my mother always

had the radio on in the kitchen. She had had a battered old thing until she got a new one on the never-never from a guy who came to the door. And it meant so much to her, to be able to hear these beautiful sounds drifting into the room from England and America. We all had our favourites – my mother loved Frank Sinatra, my father was a big fan of Bing Crosby, and Flanagan and Allen. My grandfather loved the songs of Gracie Fields, especially 'Sally', which had helped the Allied troops through the war – and helped at least some of the Irish through the Emergency. I listened to all that stuff, but I was particularly taken by the voice of Nat King Cole. In fact 'Nature Boy' by Nat King Cole was the first record I ever bought.

We had hoolies in the house at Christmas and other times of the year too, at which the elders would do their party pieces. My mother would sing 'How Are Things In Glocca Morra?' from '*Finian's Rainbow*', and 'Don't Laugh At Me Cos I'm A Fool' by Norman Wisdom. My father would do 'Underneath the Arches'.

We may have had the music and the movies but, for me, the truly great stars were English footballers, such as Wilf Mannion, Raich Carter and Peter Doherty. They lived in my imagination, in another country, but I could actually see my Irish heroes for real. My father would bring me to international matches in Dalymount Park in the years after the war, which meant that I could see Jackie Carey, Bud Ahearne, Tommy Eglington, Peter Farrell, Con Martin, Davy Walsh, Alf Ringstead, Arthur Fitzsimons and Paddy Coad.

I have vivid memories of waiting outside St Peter's Church in Phibsboro for my father, with the match about to start and still no sign of him. Carey and Eglington and Coad would all be playing, but I never got to see them playing a full match, because Dickie was always late. Always.

Usually, the matches would be on a Wednesday, which meant that as well as seeing the stars, there was the indescribable joy of getting a half-day off school. I still have a deep emotional attachment to Dalymount Park, and I can still feel the excitement that I felt back then, standing outside St Peter's, seeing my father rushing towards me at about 3 o'clock.

'How many?'

My grandmother would greet me with this same question every Sunday, when I came home from playing for our team in the Sodality League.

'How many?' she would insist when I was slow to oblige her with a response.

Because she wasn't asking me the number of goals we had scored, or the extent of our winning margin. Quite the opposite, in fact. I think we lost every single game we played for a year. And yet the fact that we were actually playing in this league, every week, meant that we were in an almost constant state of elation.

We called our team St Columbus. It's not that the lads in the Square had any particular devotion to that saint, but the Sodality League was run by the Catholic Church and we must have thought it would do us no harm to have a name with a religious ring to it.

There were other conditions attached to playing in the Sodality League. We had to go to Church devotions on Thursdays, and to mass on Sunday morning in Dominic Street. If we didn't, we weren't allowed to take part – the term 'pray to play' comes to mind.

But the rewards were great.

We would be playing every Sunday on a proper pitch, in a team strip, in an organised league. This was the next stage of the dream for me, and I was mad with excitement at the prospect. I had devised my own personal fitness programme, which involved jumping off the high wall at the back of our house, thinking it would strengthen my legs for the glorious football career which I was certain now stretched ahead of me. We were managed by Joe O'Brien, who was a bit older and therefore a natural authority figure. A lot of my pals were on the team, including Tony Guy, the aforementioned Shay O'Brien and his younger brother Eamon. Shay was our most enthusiastic player, without being good. Eamon was a classical sort of player, but gentle. The other lads on the team came to the Square from across the river, around Winetavern Street. They included Paddy McManus, a tricky little midfielder, and our best player Joe McMahon, or 'Joe Boy', a bigger lad who played left-back. We also had the Byrne brothers Joe, Johnny and Tony, all of whom were excellent players. Joe was a midfielder, a good tackler, always captain of the team, Johnny was a very good centre-forward, and Tony, who was a year younger than me and very keen, would come out with us every Sunday, though he would only get to play one match that year. The three brothers would all eventually play for Shamrock Rovers, with Tony getting an FAI Cup winners medal when he replaced Frank O'Neill in a final replay. Johnny also became a top player with Transport and collected numerous honours. Joe's promising career was, I believe, hampered by knee problems.

So we seemed to have a decent enough side, in theory. But there were two slight complications. First we had to get a set of jerseys, which we couldn't afford. We held several collections to raise the money but we never got enough, so we went for second-hand jerseys instead. They had once been red, but had now faded to pink because they'd been washed so much. We consoled ourselves with the thought that whatever colour they were, they were all the same colour, so we were still a proper team.

I was the other slight complication. I would have qualified to play for an under-8 team, but the youngest level of organised football at the time was under-14. So I was playing against boys who were nearly twice my age, which, without boasting, is probably a measure of the potential I was showing in those days. In fact, the whole team was too young, which is probably the main reason we got beaten all the time, given the fact that a few of us were pretty useful. And I was easily the smallest, smaller even than most kids of my own age. But out on the pitch, I was still able to do my stuff.

My mother could not be convinced, and had this terrible fear that one of the older, stronger boys would break my leg. In her mind, that was the worst thing that could ever happen – a broken leg. In fact she could never bring herself to watch me playing even when I became an established professional, still fearing that one day, my leg would be broken.

She did all she could to protect me, by feeding me even when I didn't want to be fed.

And she really was a terrific cook, which I didn't appreciate at the time. I would be playing a lot at the weekend, so Sunday dinner would usually be a roast with cabbage and potatoes. I'd tell her I didn't want any dinner, that I just wanted the ball, to go out and play, but she wouldn't let me, because I hadn't eaten enough.

Eventually, she took me to the doctor, even though there wasn't much wrong with me in any obvious way, and he asked her what I was eating.

'Chips, bread and butter, bread and butter and jam, beans, eggs, dripping on bread, and tomato on bread,' she said

'That's fine,' he said.

She was amazed, but she accepted what he said, and it helped her to cope.

My mother was like many women of that time, completely tied to the home to a degree that now seems almost unbelievable. I started to realise this before I went to England, to accept that I had been very cheeky to her when I was younger, unable to understand how hard she had had to work, how hard everything had been for her. Apart from us children, she was looking after my grandmother Mary-Ann who was bedridden for several years, and who passed away in the house. My grandfather Darkie too was in poor health after suffering a stroke, which meant she was constantly visiting him in St James's Hospital, or 'The Union' as it was known. Like many who went into it, he died up there, and never knew how much I would reap the benefit of his early influence on my football career. So I was determined, if and when I became a professional footballer, to look after my mother as best I could and, in fact, the only regret I have about not getting paid the vast Premiership salaries of today is that I could have looked after her better if I had been a lot richer.

Admittedly, I was considered by my sisters Anna, Kay, and Pauline, and probably my younger brother Christy, to be the pet, though they never held this against me, and we've always been on the best of terms. They might well have been right too, but I wasn't aware of it. I know my sisters found our mother a bit cranky in later life, but I'd put it like this: I will always appreciate what my father did for me in my football life, but it was my mother that I loved.

She never went on a holiday, unless you count the time that my Uncle Jem was doing some work on the football pitch at Seafield Road in Clontarf, and we were able to stay in the pavilion while the work was going on. It wasn't exactly Paris but, as they said, it got her out of the Square for a while. Any other journey she went on was in the company of Frank Sinatra.

Yet she still had that ability to judge a person's character – something my father never had, even though, like many men of that time, he saw a bit more of life. It was regarded as normal for married men to continue to live like bachelors, in the sense that they spent a lot of time out of the house drinking socially, partly because there was nothing in the house for them to do, or at least nothing that they considered worth doing. There was nothing for them to fix, it was mostly four walls and a lot of noisy children.

I don't remember my father being at home at night. He would be off at the races or the dogs, or at a game of cards up at the distillery on a Sunday morning after the match on Saturday, slipping my mother a fiver a week whether that was enough or not.

He was 'a great drinker' as they used to say, one of those men who could drink an awful lot of Jameson Ten without showing any obvious signs of being drunk – except to close family.

Occasionally he'd come home early, maybe with a few jars on him, and he'd see me doing my homework. He expected me to be as good at sums as I was at kicking a ball, so he'd be looking over my shoulder and getting cranky when he saw me struggling with the work. Then my mother would get cranky with him for getting cranky with me, and there would be a row.

He thought he knew how the world worked – and he really did know how football worked – but he was gullible. My grandfather, who was a practical joker, set up an April Fool's joke that shows this side of him. Early in the morning, I climbed out the back window, over the wall, and came back to our front door. I knocked at the door, which was answered by my mother, according to plan.

'Jock McCosh is at the door,' Kate called to my father.

Jock McCosh sounds like a Scottish comic-strip character but he was actually a real person who was the manager of Drumcondra at the time and, to my father, Jock McCosh was God. Everything was Jock McCosh – Jock McCosh said this, Jock McCosh did that. It was only about eight in the morning so there was great panic as my father tried to absorb the news that Jack McCosh had actually called to our house, looking for him.

'Jock McCosh is round at the pub for you,' he was told, as he got himself ready for what could only be something very important.

His mood, when he returned, was not good.

He couldn't laugh at himself in this situation, all dressed up and nowhere to go.

'Fuck off, you fucking oul' eejit', was the best Dickie could do, as my grandfather savoured his April Fool triumph, ably assisted by the rest of us.

But Dickie had genuinely bright ideas, if only he had the

business acumen to see them through. He had somehow acquired the recipe for making a high-quality pine disinfectant. And as he knew so many people in working-class Dublin, particularly in the pubs, he had plenty of customers. This also gave him a really good excuse to go to the pubs at any time of day or night to have his few drinks, and still show a profit.

He had a variety of jobs. He was a coffee taster and a tea taster for a while, but he lost that job, maybe due to the effects of alcohol on his taste buds. He used to drive around the schools delivering sandwiches. He built the low wall that still stands around the pitch at Tolka Park. I think he worked for a while as a clerk.

Perhaps his most brilliant scheme was a thing called Football Promotions, which involved junior and schoolboy clubs selling coupons, for which they would receive sets of gear, nets and footballs, depending on the number of coupons they sold. There would also be prize money, of course, which could be as much as £60. So on Monday mornings in our house, all the coupons that hadn't been sold would be thrown on the bed, and he would start opening them up. There was high drama in this, because if the number came up, it would mean that he wouldn't have to pay out the £60 for that week.

There would be a great shout of delight if he got the right result, but if he went through every coupon without finding the magic number, 'Oh fuck!'

Dickie had little luck in business. But in football, I think he could sense that our number was about to come up.

When a working-class family realised that they had a gifted child, the parents tended to feel that they 'owned' the child, that he was their ticket to a better life.

I think my father 'owned' me in that way, but, back then, I didn't mind in the slightest. When he realised that I had a serious chance of making it as professional footballer, he put all his best efforts into me. He would even start his own schoolboy football team called The Leprechauns, and I believe he did this to spend more time and have more influence with me. And to make sure that others didn't influence me the wrong way.

But long before it got to such an organised level, and all the time he was providing me with a football education of the best type – the type you don't realise you're getting.

St Columbus had folded after that one season of glorious defeats, because our manager Joe O'Brien had other commitments. Soon afterwards, a notice appeared in the evening papers that Dublin City were holding trials in the Phoenix Park, and even though the youngest category of schoolboy football at the time was still under-14, and I was still only nine years old, my father sent me up there along with all the other lads from the Square.

Dublin City – later called Munster Victoria – was run by an elderly gent called Tom Tunney, a well-known and highly respected football man. He bought the gear, picked the team and sent the kids out to play. Mr Tunney was pale, grey-haired, wore glasses and walked with a limp, but even if he'd been a lot younger and fitter, it just wasn't in his nature to be carrying on like some of the coaches of junior teams today, shouting and roaring at the kids, pressuring them to win the game – mostly for the glory of the coach himself. Whether the team won or lost, Mr Tunney would be quiet.

He realised that young players, then, as now, had a natural desire to win. So his approach was ideal, especially for the more creative kids, who need to be encouraged and cultivated. They would be willing to try things with the ball that non-creative players would never try and, as a result, they'd be more inclined to make mistakes and to lose possession. Mr Tunney understood this, which meant he never criticised us, but encouraged the creative players to persevere.

Mr Tunney looked at me and said, 'You're too small. Come back in two or three years.'

Devastated, I managed to mutter that my father had sent me.
'And who is your father?' Tunney asked.
'Dickie Giles,' I said.
'OK then, we'll have a look at you.'

Dickie would watch me frequently playing for Dublin City and
having assessed what he had seen, would give me various exer-
cises that were designed to improve aspects of my game, such as
heading, ball control and shooting. He was also able to involve
me in the game at the top level in Ireland, at least in a peripheral
way. Because he had become manager of Drumcondra – yes, he
had succeeded the great Jock McCosh.

Like most of my pals at the time, I was Drums mad. I would
go to Tolka Park to watch the likes of Dessie Glynn, Kit Lawlor,
Benny Henderson and my cousin Christy Giles. There was very
little going on in the 1950s in Dublin to compete with the League
of Ireland and this meant that Tolka Park would be filled with
about 10,000 people for a game between Drums and Shamrock
Rovers. So there was tremendous excitement when my father
became the manager, and an extra treat when he started to take
me to away games.

I remember clearly that my first time on the bus with the
team was to Dundalk, a relatively short distance up the east coast
compared to later expeditions west to Sligo and south to Cork.
It was such a thrill to be able to mix with these players who were
my local heroes, that I hardly said a word to any of them. But
I would sit and listen to their talk, their views on the game, and
it sparked further my ambition to belong to that world, to be a
professional.

Not that the lifestyle of the Drums players would be recommended by the sports scientists of today. After a match in Tolka,
for example, the players – and, of course, the manager – would
all pile into Fagan's pub to drink and to talk football. I'd be
there drinking minerals, maybe eating bags of crisps and wanting

to get home. I'd be getting increasingly sick of the minerals and crisps as the pints kept coming for my father, despite his promises that this would be the last one . . . and *this* would be the last one . . . and this would be the *last one* . . . but you couldn't drag him away from the drink and the football talk. He loved it too much.

In these situations, I had to learn the virtue of patience. After an away match in Cork for example, most of the players and management went off to socialise with the opposition. No matter how much they had kicked one another during the match, there was a sense that they all belonged to the football community, to this sect which had to look after itself in the Ireland of that time, a fraternity linked by a love of the game and a love of drinking and talking about it. So I would be left in the hotel or wherever was most convenient, with Dessie Glynn and Jack Kelly, the two players who didn't drink. The others would eventually return, usually with crates of beer to keep them going on the long journey home, and to fuel the singing – Kit Lawlor was not just a brilliant footballer, he was also a fine impersonator of Al Jolson.

Cigarettes would be freely smoked, the atmosphere was intoxicating in every way.

At some stage on the road back to Dublin, it would all get too much for me, and I would usually fall asleep. I don't think Dickie was bringing me on these trips just to keep me entertained, I think he was introducing me to the culture of football and of football men in a very deliberate way.

There were trips too with Dublin City. I was cutting out pictures for my scrapbook one night, when I saw a story about a secondary school team in Bury called Holy Trinity, which had not been beaten for two years. My father sent the cutting to Tom Tunney, with the result that Munster Victoria, as we were now called, challenged the Trinity team to a match at Gigg Lane, Bury's ground. It was the first proper pitch I played on in England. We won 6–1, and I scored four goals.

The teacher in charge of the Holy Trinity team was Gordon Hill, who would become one of the leading league referees of the 1970s. I would play in a lot of matches which he refereed and, apart from the fact that he was generally very good, I remember him as one of the few referees of the time who would swear as much as the players.

But the best of the trips was the annual visit to Liverpool. Tom Tunney would arrange a number of matches against teams in Liverpool for the different age-groups, and about thirty of us would get the boat from the North Wall, an eight-hour journey on the *Munster* or the *Leinster*. We would stay with local families for the few days, and we might even get to see an actual First Division match on the Saturday afternoon. On a particularly memorable visit, Mr Tunney booked us all into Goodison Park for the game between Everton and Blackpool. I stood there with the lads from Dublin City, watching some of my heroes in the flesh. Stanley Matthews, Stan Mortensen and Harry Johnston were all playing for Blackpool, while Everton at the time had the three Irish stars, Jimmy O'Neill, Peter Farrell and Tommy Eglington.

I would eventually play many games at Goodison Park myself and at the other great grounds of England, in the same big-match atmosphere. However, some of those games have faded from my memory, and I'd have to think hard before I could tell you whether we won or lost, but I will never forget that day, or that feeling, watching Everton and Blackpool playing a 2–2 draw, standing in the boy's enclosure with Matthews and Mortensen out there, and Eglington and Farrell, wanting so badly to be a part of all that.

Of course, Matthews didn't really know the game – according to my father.

Once I came across a photo of Dickie with Matthews and I was hugely impressed that he was in the same picture as the great man.

'What's he like?' I asked.

'He's a lovely man, but his knowledge of the game isn't great,' he said.

He had the highest regard for Matthews' talent and for his achievements in the game, but he was able to draw a distinction between a player's football ability and his football knowledge. Many years later, I met Matthews when we were both in Dublin for Liam Brady's testimonial dinner. Ten of the Leeds lads were over, and Stan was there with Jackie Mudie, a former Scottish international who had been a team-mate of Stan's at Blackpool and Stoke. We were delighted to join Stan and Jackie in the hotel lounge, the atmosphere was great, and Stan was in good form, really enjoying the company of the players – we in turn were delighted to be in their company. He was indeed, as my father said, a lovely man, a most unassuming fellow, given the scale of his reputation. But when Stan started talking about football, a consensus grew among the Leeds players that even though they loved him . . . his knowledge of the game wasn't great.

I sat there talking to Stan, but thinking of my father – right again.

All this knowledge and experience he was pumping into me was adding greatly to my store of ammunition – and in football you can't have too much ammunition. I gained a bit more when I was playing for The Leprechauns, the team he had founded with me specifically in mind. We had George Lamon, a big, goal-scoring, centre-forward, and Paddy Freaney, a tough midfielder, both of whom used to come to the Square. I was still only eleven, playing for the Under-14s and Under-15s, when I went into a game feeling a pain in my right leg which got worse when I was taking a penalty kick. I had burst a blood vessel in my groin. At the time, it seemed like a disaster, with the doctor ordering me to keep off my right leg for several weeks and not to attempt any serious football for about four months. But I found it impossible to stay away from the ball. Clearly, I couldn't play in any organised matches, but still I had the bouncer and I had Ormond Square. While I couldn't use my right foot, I still had the left – and the more I used it, the better I got.

Even when I was fit to play again in competitive matches, I was careful to protect my injured leg. And by the time I trusted my right foot again, I was as comfortable and confident with my left. It was a crisis that turned into an opportunity for which I would be grateful throughout my career. Dickie was also introducing me to the more specialist aspects of the game, such as positional sense. By that I mean taking up the correct position to receive the ball from one of your team-mates. It is one of the more important things in football and even today in the professional game, it is given far too little attention by coaches.

In general terms, it is called 'reading the game'. In reality, it is receiving the ball in space. Understanding time and space are essential in mastering the game of football. You might have the ability to pass brilliantly, but you won't be able to execute it if you don't have the time.

Perhaps it is a tribute to Dickie's teaching, but about this time I was starting to form opinions which didn't necessarily coincide with his.

There was a trial for the international under-15 side which was memorable in itself for the fact that I was thirteen and still in short trousers, so my mother had to buy a special pair of 'longers' for the day to avoid embarrassment. I played reasonably well, but had been struck by the obnoxious behaviour of one of the other lads. Throughout the game, he was loud, boastful and critical of others. On the way home, my father said I should be more like him. He believed that trial games were one-offs and that you had to make sure you were noticed. Which went against all my instincts at the time, and still does. It reminded me just how different we really were.

And, anyway, my attitude on the pitch seemed to be working, because at some point along the way, I had been noticed. In fact I had been noticed in a big way.

I had been noticed by Manchester United.

2

'JOHN, THIS IS DUNCAN EDWARDS'

'I HAVE something to tell you,' my father said.

We were in the pantry in 7A, a tiny room, and I had no idea what he was going to say.

'Manchester United want you to go over . . .'

Until that moment, I wasn't aware that United had any interest in me, of any kind, let alone that they might want me to go over. As I listened to him telling me that United – my team – wanted me to join them for two weeks in the summer, during their pre-season, I felt a burst of elation beyond anything I had ever felt in my life. In that moment, the dream stopped being just a beautiful thought in my head and in my heart. It was going to happen.

'Manchester United . . . want you . . . to go over . . .'

I was going to train with the Busby Babes in the summer.

I was fourteen.

Billy Behan was United's chief scout in Ireland and, apparently, he had been watching me for some time. My father and Billy went back many years, and my father knew that Billy was thinking of recommending me to United. The connection had been made.

But he never let me know about it. He got that right too.

Billy Behan was a tall, easy-going man, who had played for United as a goalkeeper. Over the years, he had famously sent over players from Ireland such as Jackie Carey, Liam Whelan, Joe Carolan and, later on, Tony Dunne and Kevin Moran.

He had a kind of a sixth sense for identifying the players who would make it, a bit like the way that, say, Vincent O'Brien could look at a yearling and in his mind's eye, see a Derby winner. At United, they valued their Irish links, not least because of the calibre of player that Billy Behan had found for them. Matt Busby and the assistant manager Jimmy Murphy would come over to Dublin to meet him, and he would be in regular communication with the club's chief scout Joe Armstrong.

Billy would be mosey-ing around the junior football matches of Dublin, either standing on the sidelines or refereeing matches, a football man to the core. And he was not just a talent-spotter, he was an amiable man who was good at fostering relationships with a young player's family – he was a non-drinker, which perhaps also helped to steady the nerves of worried parents. But even Billy, with all his powers, couldn't quite convince my mother that it would all turn out fine. As I prepared to leave for Manchester, she was fretting so much, she took the extreme precaution of sticking a safety pin through a pound note – which was a lot of money at the time, certainly in Ormond Square – and fastening it to the lining of my jacket, to be used in an emergency. She blamed Billy Behan for disturbing the peace at 7A.

Yet, especially by today's standards, her concerns were probably justifiable. After all, I was not flying over to Manchester on a first-class ticket with Aer Lingus, accompanied by my parents and my agent, and perhaps even my media advisor, as the promising fourteen-year-old footballer of today might.

It was 1955, and I went over on the boat, on my own. I arrived in Liverpool early in the morning, and then I got the train from Liverpool to Manchester, on my own. Joe Armstrong was waiting for me at Manchester Central station. So amid all the excitement, I had worries too, about getting lost, or getting on the wrong train in Liverpool, or otherwise seeing my dream getting away from me through some mad misfortune.

My mother couldn't bring herself to see me off at the North Wall. She would probably get too emotional, thinking that this might be our last goodbye. It was my father who took me down to the boat for the night crossing. If he was worried in any way, he didn't let it show.

He knew I'd get there.

On the train from Lime Street to Manchester I saw Old Trafford for the first time.

It looked much bigger than I had ever imagined it, like some gigantic beast perched over the city. It was a sight that I found both awe-inspiring and thrilling.

I didn't know what Joe Armstrong looked like, and he didn't know what I looked like, but he spotted me easily enough, his eyes well trained after many years of watching young footballers getting off the train and arriving in wonderland. I stayed with Joe at his home in Stockport over the weekend, before settling into the digs on Monday. But first we got the bus to the ground. Nearly everyone at United got the bus in those days, when the maximum wage was £20 a week and £18 a week during the close season. Even Duncan Edwards got the bus.

As we got near the ground, I saw Duncan Edwards for the first time. He was sitting on top of a post box on the Stretford Road, eating an apple while he waited for the bus.

He was already famous, a full England international at eighteen, and widely regarded as the greatest young player anyone had seen for a long time. And since he was basically still a big kid, his potential was frightening. Joe introduced me to him.

'John, this is Duncan Edwards,' he said.

Duncan Edwards, sitting there on top of the post box, acknowledged me, and then went on eating his apple.

*   *   *

I reported to Fallowfield on Monday morning. In his fatherly way, Joe Armstrong had treated me as if I was a member of his own family, helping me greatly to adjust to my new world. In those days, everyone at the club trained together in pre-season, which meant that I was training alongside Duncan Edwards, David Pegg, Tommy Taylor, Liam Whelan and the rest of the Busby Babes. I was the youngest player out there. I was in heaven.

It was the last year they used Fallowfield for pre-season training, and it was a beautiful place, in an area better known for the cycling track next door. There were two football pitches which were also used for cricket and we changed in the cricket pavilion rather than a football dressing room.

Everywhere I looked, I saw these great players doing their stuff, getting ready for the new season. I saw Jimmy Murphy giving the instructions and I met Matt Busby for the first time. The impression I formed of him after that brief meeting was that he was a very pleasant, modest, charming man. I would eventually learn that my first impression was just about right.

It was the club's aim under Busby and Murphy to go out and find the best schoolboy international players in England, Ireland, Scotland and Wales, an enlightened policy which was already paying off – this team would win the league in the coming season of 1955–1956 and it was a privilege to be so close to them as they were making the breakthrough.

They were very kind to me for the few weeks I was there, especially the Irish lads such as Tommy Hamilton. I can't speak highly enough of Tommy's generosity and his patience. And though I was probably a total nuisance in the circumstances, I was given a great welcome by the late Jackie Scott, and by Liam Whelan, a Cabra kid who had established himself at inside-right in the first team the previous season.

Liam was known in England as Billy, the way that Jackie Carey became Johnny in England. Farther up the line, my own name would change to Johnny too, whether I liked it or not, but I was still John at Fallowfield in 1955. My own family and everyone I had ever known back home had always called me John and, later on, if someone called me Johnny, my mother would shake her head and say, 'Ah, he doesn't know you.'

Likewise, Billy Whelan was always Liam to me, a big brother.

Freddie Goodwin, the centre-half who I would later play with at Leeds United, was also very friendly. He also had the distinction of being one of the two United players at the time who owned a car, the other was the team captain Roger Byrne who also played for England. They were not big cars, they might even have been second-hand cars. It was not uncommon at the time for footballers to play county cricket during the close season, and Freddie who played for Lancashire was one of these dual stars. Presumably, the extra money he made from the cricket enabled him to splash out on the motor.

I remember watching the first and second teams playing each other, and it was a measure of the talent at the club that Bobby Charlton, then seventeen, couldn't get a starting place in the reserve team. But I saw him coming on as a sub in practice matches a few times, and I thought he was special. I now believe that Bobby is the greatest player I have ever played with or against, but with the Busby Babes in training that summer, he was just a substitute. In fact he was a sub for the substitutes.

I knew him mainly as my bowling buddy. After staying with Joe Armstrong and his family over the weekend, I had moved into digs for the fortnight. And as there wasn't much to do there, I would go to a park nearby, where they played crown green bowls. I developed a liking for the game. Bobby Charlton didn't have much to do in his digs either, so he would also find his way to the park, where we would play bowls together. I've always liked Bobby as a person and revered him as a player.

He could be a bit quirky, but a really decent human being. A decent bowler too.

Just as I was about to leave Fallowfield after this glorious two weeks, I got an injury which, like the burst blood vessel in my groin, had a happy outcome. You could hardly even call it a football injury in the accepted sense.

Liam Whelan had the Giles family trait of playing practical jokes and one morning after training, he threw a bucket of cold water over me while I was in the shower. I grabbed a bottle of water and chased after him to return the compliment, but I slipped on the wet floor and fell on a bottle, which gashed my hand badly. After I had been to the hospital to be stitched, I looked at my wound – a pretty horrible sight – and imagined my mother's reaction. I felt that I couldn't let her see me in this condition, after all her dire warnings, so I asked Jimmy Murphy if I could stay on for another two weeks, and he agreed. He didn't want the club to be creating a bad impression with a nervous parent either.

After another two weeks in Manchester, the hand was healed and my mother never found out about it. But I had other trials to endure, back home.

I had to go back to school in September but I just wasn't interested in it and I couldn't wait to get out. If everything worked out perfectly, United would sign me and I would be going back to Manchester the following July, but there was still this ordeal ahead of me. School, for me, hadn't got any better since my grandfather used to drag me along to the nuns in George's Hill, in many ways it had got considerably worse. When I moved on to the primary school at Brunswick Street (Brunner), it wasn't just the sums and the Irish language and the homework that got me into trouble, it was also my love of soccer, or the 'English game' as it was regarded in schools run by the Christian Brothers.

I was selected for the Gaelic football team in primary school, but I decided that if a Gaelic match clashed with a soccer fixture,

I just wouldn't turn up to play for the school, even if it caused trouble. In fact, I never turned up to play Gaelic in primary school.

So at secondary school, my father had to sign a commitment that I would play for the Gaelic team if I was selected. As a result of that, I played Gaelic at Brunner, at right-half-forward, and actually enjoyed it. In my first game I didn't know where the right-half-forward played, so I just watched where the left-half-forward went and headed to the other wing. But had my father refused to sign me up for it, I would not have been admitted to the school. Which is some indication of the level of hostility at Brunner to the 'soccer men', otherwise known as 'the corner boys going up to Dalymount Park'.

I would hear this talk of 'corner boys' and I didn't actually know what they were talking about, let alone that I was supposed to be one of them. I would confuse the word 'corner' with 'cornet', thinking they were making some reference to ice-cream.

Soccer men would also have been condemned by the Archbishop of Dublin, John Charles McQuaid, when Ireland played Yugoslavia at Dalymount in 1955. McQuaid said that Catholics were being persecuted in Yugoslavia by the communist regime, but he didn't deter about 22,000 corner boys going up to Dalymount to see Ireland lose 4–1.

In fact, the idea of soccer as the foreign game was drilled into us to such an extent that, for a few years after I left school, I didn't feel Irish at all. Even though my mother's family had hidden Republicans from the British soldiers and the Black and Tans when they had lived in the tenements around Charles Street, in the inner city. When my mother had been a young girl, she had actually been inside Croke Park on Bloody Sunday in 1920, because my grandmother was a dealer, selling fruit and colours at the matches, and had brought along my mother as a helper. So she had witnessed the panic and the terror.

But it didn't matter where you came from, if you were one of the corner boys going up to Dalymount Park, you would get a hard time in Brunner. Not that anyone got an easy time under that regime. I remember this Canadian kid who had arrived over in Ireland and was sent to Brunner and I remember the look of total astonishment and terror on his face as he sat in this classroom with dusters flying past his head and all sorts of savagery being inflicted on the pupils by both the teachers and by other pupils. They must have had gentler methods over in Canada, because this poor kid looked like he had landed on another planet where everything was as bad as it could possibly be. It seemed that the authorities were allowed to do almost anything they liked to the pupils, short of murder, especially if they weren't academically minded, which I wasn't. I envied the lads who were bright in an academic way, not realising at the time that academic intelligence and actual intelligence can be totally different things.

I just knew that the lads who got higher marks than me got an easier time of it.

Even the better teachers were no softies. When I was about twelve, I was taught by Paddy Crosbie, who was about to become famous for his RTÉ radio programme *The School around the Corner*, in which he used to chat to schoolchildren and generally give the impression that school was a place where you'd have a load of laughs and lots of banter.

In fact, he had just started the show in the year that he taught me, and to get in a bit of practice, he used to experiment on us. We didn't realise at the time that that was what he was doing but, looking back, we were definitely the guinea pigs for his show.

To his credit, Mr Crosbie would occasionally take us out of the school to show us various places of historical interest, such as Christ Church Cathedral. Such a trip would be considered normal today, but at the time there was a great reluctance to let us out of the building at all, once they had got us there. So Mr Crosbie wasn't the worst of them, but he was still a lot crankier with us than he was with the boys on the programme.

That's showbusiness, I guess.

And there was one relatively nice Christian Brother too, who made some effort to understand what was going on in my life, with the 'soccer men' and all that, but who still couldn't quite get his head around it. He spoke to me one day about my plans for the future.

'Would you have any ambition of playing for Dublin in Croke Park?' he asked me.

'No,' I said.

I couldn't dress it up any better.

'So what do you want to do?' he asked, genuinely puzzled.

'I want to play for Manchester United,' I replied.

He seemed sad about that, but he just left it there. Did he understand what I was saying? I don't know. But at least he asked.

Impossible though it seems, on my return to Brunner from summer training at United, things were about to take a turn for the worse. News of my stay in Manchester had made its way into the local papers, but some of the teachers were not impressed. There was a lay teacher we called Boxer who seemed to have a view of education that was all about crushing the spirit of the pupil, rather than nurturing it. And Boxer was determined to make me pay for my association with the English game.

In a maths class one day, I made the terrible mistake of writing my answers in a copy-book meant for English. This, in Boxer's eyes, was a grave sin. He hauled me up in front of the class and publicly scorned my hopes of making it as a footballer. It so happened that Tommy Hamilton had just left United around that time. And Boxer used Tommy's return to Ireland to illustrate how foolish it was for any of us to contemplate a career as a professional footballer.

In fact, Tommy had left because he was about to be called up for national service in England and figured he would rather come back and play with Shamrock Rovers than spend two years in the army, by which time his already slim chances of making it at United would have disappeared altogether. But Boxer was blind to the finer points, in his urge to falsely present Tommy's story as one of miserable failure.

Bizarrely, after denouncing my work and my ambitions in front of the class, Boxer took me across the room to an adjoining class to repeat the humiliation. He was, as they say, pulling out all the stops.

'Hands up the lads who were in Croke Park yesterday,' he would say, exposing the 'corner boys' to further embarrassment.

And as I vowed to leave school at the first legal opportunity, I couldn't help recalling that it was the same Boxer who had once tried to make me feel better about my surroundings at Brunner. I was in a special class at the time for boys who weren't doing well, and Boxer delivered this inspiring message to us:

'You must remember this,' he said. 'When you get to the age of forty, I can assure you that you'll say, my schooldays were my happiest days.'

That I didn't just go ahead and commit suicide at the thought of that is a tribute to the power of football. Because no matter how low I felt, during those hellish years at Brunner, I knew that the football was always there for me as a consolation. At four o'clock every day, I could get the ball out and none of that other rubbish would matter any more.

And you would think that my father, a football man, would empathise with me in this, and agree with me wholeheartedly that I should leave school as soon as I possibly could, in order to devote myself to the game. But that wasn't how he saw it. When I told him that I wanted to leave school at Christmas, when I had turned fifteen, not only did he not agree with me, he was the main objector.

Because he was very intelligent himself, he saw no reason why I couldn't play professional football during the day, and win the Nobel Prize for physics in the evening.

In this, he differed from the usual image of the sports-mad parent as someone who wants the child to concentrate totally on the game, to the exclusion of all else. But then Dickie differed from most people, in most things.

It wasn't that he lacked belief in my ability to make it as a footballer, he just wanted – and expected – more from me. Unfortunately, he wasn't going to get it.

He finally conceded that I could leave school at Christmas and look for a job. At last, I was free. Almost immediately, I started at Hendron Brothers' engineers' suppliers shop up at Constitution Hill on Dublin's northside. It wasn't exactly a top job. I was on a five-and-a-half day week and just served in the shop, or fetched and carried. But, to me, it was a vast improvement on Brunner. The nightmare of homework had gone for ever, and I had some money in my pocket.

I felt that I had been suddenly released from a long jail sentence. I was paid a couple of quid a week and though I gave it all to my mother, she would give me back ten bob, which seemed like a fortune. So I was happy enough there for six months, but I was going to be a lot happier at the end of it.

Manchester United had confirmed that they would sign me in July.

It didn't bother me that I had no safety net. Back then, most families were delighted to see their son go to an English club, whether or not he had completed his secondary education. All the best players I knew were street footballers who came from working-class areas similar to mine, where the chance of making it as a professional footballer would be seized as a once-in-a-lifetime opportunity. In an odd way, the absence of a safety net only sharpened the desire of the young player to succeed. Certainly, that was the effect it had on me.

These days, I would probably have been signed up in my early teens, and promised professional forms as part of the deal. Back then, you didn't sign professional forms until you were seventeen, which kept you hungry for a lot longer than the talented kid of today, who might conceivably be assured of twenty grand a week when he's seventeen, even if it turns out in the meantime that he hasn't got what it takes.

I believe that there aren't as many talented young players coming into the game now because they have all these other distractions and opportunities, quite apart from the constant menace of a minority of self-serving coaches who desperately want to win the under-10 league for their own glorification, and who are prepared to sacrifice the more creative type of player in the process – anyone can teach a lad how to play the 'holding' role, it takes knowledge and patience to produce a Xavi or an Iniesta.

Parents too, have increasingly difficult choices to make. At one level, it is entirely sensible for a young lad to do his Leaving Cert and then pursue his football career at the age of eighteen with something to fall back on if he doesn't make it. But what is sensible in most areas of life is not necessarily sensible in football.

For me, those years between the ages of fifteen and eighteen would be about learning my trade as a footballer, something that was far more important to me than anything else in this world. It would be all or nothing.

In those months before I left for Manchester in August, I was enjoying life on the pitch more than ever. My father had stepped down from managing The Leprechauns, and I went from there to Stella Maris, along with two lads, Billy Bauer and Mick Millington, an outstanding young player from around Winetavern Street who would later play for Cork Celtic and Dundalk in the League of Ireland.

Stella was a terrific schoolboy club, and still is, and my father felt I had a better chance of being selected for the international schoolboy team if I played with them – schoolboy international

selections were very political back then, and it wasn't always the
best players who got picked.

It was a hugely enjoyable season at Stella and, by the end of
it, three of our team, John Keogh, Dave Malone and myself had
made it into the international side. We played against England
at Tolka Park and lost 1–0. They had some good players – David
Gaskell, Barry Bridges, who later played for Chelsea, and Willie
Carlin, who went to Derby County. John Osborne, later a
colleague and a good friend of mine who played in goal at West
Brom, actually played at left-back that day. Bridges was the
outstanding player on the field, his tremendous speed caused
problems in our defence and enabled him to score the winner.
Running on to a through pass, he outpaced our defenders and
coolly lobbed the ball over the keeper's head as he came out to
narrow the angle.

We couldn't quite win it for Ireland – thanks to Boxer and
friends, I was still finding it hard to see myself as Irish at all –
but at Stella we had become almost unbeatable. We won the 15A
League and the Evans Cup, a national knockout competition for
under-15 sides. In fact, there was a strange end to the Evans Cup
for me, because problems with the fixture-list meant that the final
was postponed until later in the year, around Christmas. I was
already in Manchester by then, and had to come back to Cork
to play in the final, against a Cork team. There had been a few
mentions of me in the local papers, this lad who was at Manchester
United who would be playing for Stella Maris at Turner's Cross
– in the pouring rain at Turner's Cross, as it happened. In fact,
it always seemed to be pouring rain in Cork – or maybe I'm just
haunted by the memory of that game, in which I was sent off
after about fifteen minutes.

The Cork lads were steaming into us from the start. One of
them had a go at me in a tackle, I had a go back at him, the
referee called me over.

'What's your name?'

'Giles.'

'Off.'

It may be worth mentioning that the referee was from Cork.

At Easter, my father had taken me back to Manchester for a visit, during which we saw Manchester United beating Chesterfield 8–0 in a reserve match at Old Trafford, with Bobby Charlton scoring five goals. I was despondent after watching that match, fearing that I could never be regarded as an equal by such brilliant players.

'I don't know if I'll ever be as good as those, Da,' I muttered.

My father turned on me.

'What?' he said, as if genuinely shocked. 'You're going to be better than them! Remember you're only fourteen now. These are all four or five years older than you.'

A lot of other fathers might have said 'maybe you're right', but not Dickie. He just felt I needed a bit of time to get there.

As for his own standing as a football man, he talked to Matt Busby and to Jimmy Murphy as equals – whether they regarded him as an equal is unknown, but they were bound to have appreciated his knowledge of the game, and Jimmy Murphy would happily have a drink with him. Murphy was a Welshman who managed his national team in his spare time, and was a big drinker anyway. Maybe it was during one of these sessions that my dad somehow persuaded Matt and Jimmy to play me in the A-team against Rochdale during our Easter visit.

The A-team was effectively the third team – but they were good players. And on the coach to Rochdale, I could feel the resentment towards me, this fifteen-year old who might well do something stupid and deprive these serious professionals of their match bonus. At the time, they were on £2 for a win and £1 for a draw, with some of them on overall wages of about £8. So the £2 for a win was an additional 25 per cent on their weekly pay.

I was put on the right-wing, from which I had a clear view of Dickie standing on the touchline alongside Matt and Jimmy. I could also hear him clearly – all too clearly – when we got a free kick outside the box, and he shouted to me, 'You take that!'

I was mortified to hear him shouting orders to me, on a Manchester United team, as if it was Stella Maris on a Sunday morning. I don't think I have ever been as mortified by anything before or since. But we won 1–0, so at least the lads got their bonus.

It was back at Stella around that time that I first encountered someone who would play a significant role in my life in the fullness of time. He was just a ten-year-old kid then and he lived directly across the road from Tolka Park. At Stella, we older lads regarded him as a bloody nuisance because he was always hanging around, running away with the table-tennis ball and generally annoying us. I have clear memories of irate table-tennis players dragging this poor little guy across the floor, shoving his face into the ground and demanding to know what he had done with the ball. He refused to be intimidated – in fact, we never got that ball back.

When he wasn't disturbing the peace at Stella, he was said to be an outstanding young footballer. His name was Eamon Dunphy.

For a while I had kept pigeons in a loft that had been built by my uncle in the back yard. I hadn't intended to get into the pigeons. But it so happened that on our way home from Brunner every day, myself and a pal Paddy Hayes had a ritual whereby we'd throw a stone at a row of pigeons, scattering them from the top of a wall at the Jameson warehouse – we weren't proud of it, especially on the day I caught one of the birds on the leg and, with a bad conscience, brought it home to try to save it. I couldn't tell my mother that I had actually done the damage. With the help of one of the few lads who had no interest in football, Sean Hegarty, or 'Hego', we looked after the injured bird and got it right again. And my career as a fancier took off from there. But my father disapproved of the pigeons, because he thought they were taking my mind off football. I had to give them up anyway, because everything started to change.

I was going away, to take my chance. In fact, the whole family was on the move from Ormond Square out to the Navan Road. It seemed that the first part of my life was over, and I was leaving it all behind, but, of course, I never have left it behind.

In my mind I can go back there any time I like, kicking the ball with my grandfather at the age of three, feeling the satisfaction of kicking it right, or trying on the miniature boots that my father bought me in Belfast, that fitted me so perfectly, or being on my own late in the evening, trying to hit the number 7 outside our door.

I can still hear Sinatra on the radio, and Flanagan and Allen, and Gracie Fields.

In 2006, a couple of days before the World Cup final, a plaque was unveiled in Ormond Square, with my name on it. Shay O'Brien, who got me into the gang all those years ago, came over from New York for the ceremony. Aodhan O'Riordan, who was organising the event for the council, had hurried things along because Shay had been ill for some time with cancer, and was awaiting the results of tests. Shay always went down to Ormond Square anyway, whenever he was back in Dublin, and he didn't want to miss this day, along with members of his family and my family and a few pals from the old days. The weather was good and it was a lovely day, with a celebration afterwards in the Clarion Hotel. I think I enjoyed it as much for Shay as for myself, because he was in great form, just concentrating on having a good time along with his sisters Dolores and Maura, his brothers Paschal and Eamon. Although we continued to keep in touch when he went back to New York, that was the last time I saw Shay. Sadly, he passed away the following year.

When I think of that plaque in the Square, it brings to mind that old woman who used to leave her door open in the hope that our bouncer would come to her, so that she could burst it. If she were to come back somehow and see the plaque, no doubt she would be disgusted.

She didn't see that one coming.

3

LEARNING MY TRADES

THERE WAS one cherished thing I brought with me to Manchester. I had first seen it when I was about eight years old. It was a picture in one of the English Sunday papers of a match at Old Trafford on a misty Saturday afternoon one November. The picture was being used for a Spot the Ball competition, but I was not interested in putting my X where I thought the ball should be. I was mesmerised by the picture itself, and the atmosphere it conjured up in my mind. It seemed so perfect, to be playing at a big ground in England with the stadium packed, on a misty Saturday afternoon in November. I wanted to put myself in that picture. I wanted to know what it felt like to be in that picture.

I searched for that feeling for a long time, but I could never quite get it. Until one day, it all happened for me.

The game was being played on an English afternoon on a different winter's day, a bit of dampness in the air. The ground was full, it was an important game. With about fifteen minutes to go, the ball came to me about twenty-five yards out, and I caught it perfectly with the outside of my right foot.

It was a beautiful goal. We won the game. My perfect vision came true for me.

It happened. But it didn't happen at Old Trafford, and I wasn't playing for Manchester United.

*　　*　　*

The way it worked at the time, United would recruit as many talented schoolboys as they could, and put them on the ground staff until they were seventeen. Then, the club would decide whether to release them or to sign them as professionals. But my father didn't agree with this system, at least not for me. He figured that instead of working on the ground staff, I should learn a trade. Which is how I found myself starting an apprenticeship as an electrical engineer with Switchgear and Cowen in Altrincham.

Again it showed how unusual Dickie was, that he was so obsessed with football, and with me becoming a footballer, and yet he wanted a bit more besides. Effectively, he wanted me to learn two trades. I suppose he knew the game so well that he recognised how many things could go wrong and that I needed a bit of insurance. But he probably also felt it would be no bother to me, to play for Manchester United and to be an electrical engineer in my spare time.

There were five levels at United: the first team, the reserves, the A team, the B team and the juniors. I was in the juniors, an under-19 side that played in the Altrincham Junior League. We trained two evenings a week, on Tuesdays at The Cliff and on Thursdays at Old Trafford, and the rest of my time was given over to Switchgear and Cowen.

The days were long. I rose every morning at six o'clock, and had a long bus journey for an eight o'clock start at work. There was another journey to be made to The Cliff every Tuesday, which was on the other side of Manchester from Switchgear.

The digs, to be honest, were poor. United painted a pretty picture when they were trying to sign young players, giving all sorts of assurances about the quality of the digs and how they'd ensure we had a healthy diet. But the reality was different. The reality was myself and Jack Hennessy, another young player from Dublin, sharing a little room in the attic of a three-storey house in Norwood Road in Stretford, about a twenty-five-minute walk from Old Trafford. Jack was on the ground staff at United, so at least he only had one trade to learn.

The food was actually quite good for about the first week or so, but it got steadily worse until we found that we couldn't survive on the various scraps of cold meat we were getting, without frequent visits to the chippie for fish'n'chips or steak'n'kidney pie. And the attic was so cold in the winter that we slept with our clothes on.

The landlady, Mrs Robb, was Irish. Which the club probably thought was another smart move on their part, telling Irish parents that their kids would be looked after by one of their own. There were actually two Irish mothers on the premises, as Mrs Robb, a widow with three sons, had her mother living with her. But like most landladies from any country, Mrs Robb was just a hard-pressed woman taking people in because she needed the money. United paid £3 a week for the digs, and sent another £3 home for me. I was earning another £3 a week at Switchgear.

When we went home for Christmas, we kept the system going ourselves by telling everyone we were living like kings   the club probably banked on that too. We didn't really want anyone to know that myself, Jack Hennessy, and maybe a couple of students who were also staying there would be down in the sitting room of the digs at about 10.30 at night, when a hand would come around the door and switch off the light. It looked like a ghostly hand, but it belonged to Mrs Robb's mother.

Nor did we want to tell everyone that we would sit there trying to entertain ourselves by listening to Billy Cotton on the Rediffusion radio, with the electric fire on – only the one bar.

But I don't want to give the impression that I was miserable all the time or that I hated being in Manchester. I didn't even have any hard feelings about Mrs Robb. Really, I didn't know the woman at all. I may have arrived there with my suitcase like so many other Irish kids in the 1950s, but I was luckier than most because, despite all the discomforts, I never felt strange

there – any place where I could get ahead in football was home
to me. I had a future – at least I thought I did. Which is all you
really need when you're fifteen. I was never one of those kids
who got homesick after they had gone to an English club.

And while my Irish lodgings might have left something to be
desired, I got along fine with the lads at Switchgear – Alan Cooke,
the brothers Alf and Denis Brown, and Trevor Humphreys – after
I could understand what they were saying. *Coronation Street*
hadn't started yet, so people from outside the region weren't as
familiar with the northern English accents as they are today.
Certainly when I started my apprenticeship there, I had almost no
idea what they were talking about and, to them, my thick Dublin
accent sounded like Chinese. But we got on with it anyway. I
remember having Sunday lunch in Trevor Humphreys' house and
staying overnight. Trevor was one of the younger lads, but I still
couldn't understand what he was saying.

About a hundred people worked in Switchgear's two-storey
premises which looked a lot bigger inside than you'd imagine
from the front, and most of them cycled there. The lads I knew
had their small work spaces in the corner of the building. And
while it was clear from the start that I was never going to be an
electrical engineer, there were a few things I could do, and generally Alan Cooke was delighted with me. I couldn't describe what
exactly it was that I did – something about machines that you
had to fit things into – but whatever it was, I had a bit of a knack
for it. Basically when he told me what to do, I could do it.

He even got me a new coat. I had this brown coat that I used
to wear to work, and Alan brought me in a better coat which
he thought would fit me. We were all working-class lads who
understood each other despite the 'language' barrier.

Above all we understood football. They were mad United
fans, in those days before United became the global giant it is
today – in fact before the war, City was the big club in Manchester.
So tickets prices at 1/6 or two shillings on the terraces were

affordable to most people, and crowds of up to 60,000 would pile into Old Trafford.

I would soon be able to get them 'comps' for the reserved area, which wasn't quite seated but wasn't quite the terraces either. They, in turn, took me out to a Snooker Exhibition featuring Joe Davis the world champion, and his brother Fred.

They would talk a lot about their holidays. Now this was strange to me, this talk about holidays. In Ireland, people like us never went on a holiday. But in Altrincham, they would always be talking about going to Blackpool for a week or two. Not Spain – there was no such thing as Spain back then, for these lads – but the holiday in Blackpool was the big deal.

Like most Irish people back then, I was happy enough to see sunny places in the movies, without actually going there. And it is no exaggeration to say that I must have seen every movie that was made between the years 1956 and 1960, at the Essoldo in Stretford or later on at the cinemas in the centre of Manchester to which United players had a pass. Rock'n'roll was also starting, but it didn't mean much to me. I never liked the screaming of Little Richard. I liked Perry Como.

The Altrincham Junior League, in which the United juniors played, was an under-19 league, so I was still playing against older lads. Which was nothing new and didn't bother me, but which probably held me back for a while in the juniors. I got the feeling from the club that they thought I was too small to move up to the B team.

Jimmy Murphy told me not to worry about it. He was happy with my progress and was prepared to wait for me to develop physically. And Jimmy knew the game, but I disagreed with him anyway. I was short, but I never considered myself too small. I believe that football is a game of wit, imagination and creativity. No matter what size you are, you can get into a position where you can receive the ball and avoid a clash. And when there is contact, you can develop the ability and the strength to protect the ball. These are things you learn on the street, and they are as true today as they were in 1957. In this present era of the footballer as athlete, the 'box-to-box player', the more creative type of midfielder is becoming virtually extinct. Paul Scholes is the only such player England has produced in a generation.

And yet Spain won the World Cup with a team featuring players such as Xavi and Iniesta, and the most successful club side is Barcelona where those two 'little guys' are the most influential players, along with Lionel Messi.

That is the beauty of the game – Xavi, Iniesta and Messi are physically on the small side, in a general sense, but no one is saying that they're too small. For the most obvious reasons – league and cup victories, Champions League and European Championship and World Cup victories – their size isn't an issue.

However, even when such players were more common, back in 1957, I had to wait while bigger lads moved up to the B team. Maybe it's all about scoring goals, not making them, I thought, as a lad called Leo Thornton scored five goals playing up front for the juniors and got into the B team the following week. So I scored six goals in the next match, but it didn't work for me.

The juniors may have been the lowest team in the United set-up, but the home games were played on a superb surface at Wilbraham Road, from which I definitely derived some benefit. And what really kept me going for that season was being selected to represent Cheshire Youths. Cheshire was one of the smaller counties, so it was considered a major achievement when we went all the way to the final of the English County Championship. In the final, we were up against Hampshire, who had Terry Paine, later of Southampton and the England World Cup winning squad of 1966, playing on the wing. We won the away leg 1–0 in Basingstoke – I think some of their best players missed that match – and we lost the home leg 2–0 at Gresty Road, Crewe Alexandra's ground.

But that run with Cheshire Youths was a hugely enjoyable experience, and no doubt it helped to persuade United that my future might not lie in electrical engineering. Jimmy Murphy suggested I should give up my apprenticeship at Switchgear to concentrate on my football and, to my surprise and delight, my father agreed. I couldn't sign professional terms until I was seventeen, but now at least I could train with the squad.

There's an old pal of mine who works at a Premier League club who told me a story about modern training methods. He was supervising training one day with the manager, who told him he was increasingly sceptical about the way things were going. Everything was becoming 'scientific', with players being wired up to machines to test their fitness, and systems such as Pro-Zone which allegedly measure performance levels, and all sorts of professional advisors, nutritionists, analysts and psychologists. Then there are the regular stoppages to drink water.

Lowering his voice so that none of his staff could hear, the manager turned to my pal. 'Do we really need all these guys?' he asked.

'Nah,' my pal said.

And deep down the manager probably agreed with him, but felt powerless to buck the trends. After all, Bill Shankly wouldn't have had a psychologist around the place, because there was already a psychologist there, one B. Shankly.

I asked my pal if the pre-season training is much different now – is it easier than it was when I was playing?

'Nah it's still hard graft, it's probably about the same,' he said. 'Except for one thing.'

'And what's that?'

'There's a lot more water.'

When I started to train with the United squad, we didn't drink any water. You might get a drink when it was finished, but you wouldn't be taking water on board every few minutes to rehydrate your-self. And while some may scoff at these modern notions, my early experiences at United mean that I am not exactly misty-eyed about the old ways either.

It wasn't that we lacked these scientific training methods – more that there were hardly any training methods at all.

First, we would run around the track, unsupervised. Then Tom Curry, the old trainer, would arrive with a couple of balls and two teams would be picked, after which we would play a game at the back of the stand. Senior pros and junior pros like myself would all play together, so that a typical game might be fifteen-a-side. It wasn't a whole lot different to an average day in Ormond Square, except instead of Paddy McManus and Tony Guy and Shay O'Brien and Tony Byrne, I would be knocking it around with Duncan Edwards and Liam Whelan and Dennis Viollet and David Pegg.

The Busby Babes were preparing for first division games in front of huge crowds in a way that was roughly similar to how St Columbus used to prepare for a game in the Sodality League. Not that most of the teams they'd be playing against on the Saturday would be doing much different. This is how it was done at the time. No doubt some of today's methods are bunkum, but the way they were doing it at United and at a lot of other clubs back in 1957 wasn't any better. Certainly it wasn't much good for me.

In these games at the back of the stand, I was too inexperi-enced and too shy to impose myself. The level of talent was incredible, and I was over-awed. I wanted to train, but I didn't have any guidance and didn't know what to do.

Tuesday was ball morning, Friday was spike morning. The latter involved putting on our spikes and doing our sprints. The spikes were pretty horrible things, and quite dangerous. You could easily injure yourself or others during one of those sessions.

Even running around the track doing laps was a bit complicated for me, because I'd be afraid to run past the senior players. I didn't want to draw attention to myself in that way.

In fact I had no idea how to assert myself in such illustrious company. I was constantly aware of how good these guys were, that it was the law of the jungle and that I mightn't be strong enough to survive.

I ran into Bill Foulkes one day, in the silliest way. To smarten things up, a rugby union trainer called Eric Evans had been brought in to take a session maybe once a month. These sessions were better than the usual ones, being actual squad sessions, properly organised. Except I didn't understand some of the lingo. 'When I clap my hands, you sprint ten yards on the spot,' Evans said. But I didn't quite get the 'on the spot' part. So I sprinted forward and ran straight into the back of Bill Foulkes' legs.

Now of all the fellows there, Bill Foulkes was probably the one into the back of whose legs you would least want to run. He was the hardest, the crankiest. His verdict was harsh.

'Stupid little Irish twat,' he growled.

This had not been in the dream.

Ball morning up at The Cliff was the one time of the week specifically given over to working with the ball. Which again seems incredible, though they had a funny way of explaining it at the time – the less of the ball you saw during the week, the hungrier you'd be for it on Saturday. And, again, I am slow to knock the luxuries of the modern game when I think of the gear and equipment that the Busby Babes regarded as normal. You would have shorts and a jersey, maybe a tracksuit top, hanging up in the dressing room. But what really struck me were the socks. There'd be a big pile of socks on the table, and it would be first come, first served. Some of the socks would have holes in them, and the socks system in general seemed to be designed to ensure that any foot diseases or infections that were going around would be spread to as many players as possible.

This had definitely not been in the dream.

Whatever Manchester United were spending their money on, it wasn't on training gear.

And there was a lot of money there. It was said that they could run the club on the Central League gates, because they'd be getting crowds of about 20,000 to see the Reserves, and maybe even more for Youth Cup matches – the Youth Cup had started in the early 1950s and it was a big deal, with United winning it for the first five years.

Yet it was quite a job at Old Trafford to get a new pair of boots. I remember having to show the trainer Jack Crompton my old boots, to prove that they were really past it. When he was satisfied that you weren't making it up, he'd give you a chit to get a new pair of boots. You'd take the chit into town to a sports shop with which the club presumably had some arrangement.

It seemed that nothing had changed since the time that Matt Busby and Jimmy Murphy themselves were players back in the 1930s, down to the ball morning on Tuesday and the spike morning on Friday. Football in general was making very slow progress in these areas of basic training. It wasn't just the fact that the best training sessions were run by a rugby man, there was a little gym under the main stand which was a perfectly fine little gym, except that it was laid out as a boxing gym, meant for boxing and nothing but boxing. It wasn't a relic of ancient history, it was part of the new stand that was built after the old one was bombed during the war. Yet the football men had failed to adapt it to their own needs, to imagine ways in which it could be better used. So it had a punch bag and a speed bag and a medicine ball and all the stuff that boxers use, but which are of limited use to footballers. It was the strangest thing, that gym.

Creature comforts in general were sparse. There was no canteen, in fact no food of any kind was available on the premises. After training there was a pot of tea, and another teapot which actually contained Horlicks.

I need hardly add that there was no bottled water, still or sparkling.

On match days, I was floundering in the B team, and I couldn't see any clear way ahead.

For the first time in my life, I seriously doubted myself. I signed pro officially on my seventeenth birthday in November 1957, but it made little difference to my situation.

There was no lavish signing ceremony. I was just called up to Matt Busby's office to sign the forms. There was no negotiating, the amount was the same for everyone according to age, whether it was me or Duncan Edwards. The procedure was as plain as Matt's office itself, a ten-minute job at most, after which he wished me all the best. I knew I'd only be in there again if I was in trouble or if I was leaving.

There might have been a line in the paper about it, but it wouldn't be world news. In fact, there must have been a line in the paper about it, or word must have got around somehow, because, a couple of days after signing, I was approached by Mark Jones, centre-half with the first team, while I was running around the track. He wished me the best of luck.

Mark wouldn't have known me at all – I was just one of the many – but he took the trouble to wish me well anyway, and that meant a lot to me. Harry Gregg, too, was always very friendly and helpful. Matt had signed him from Doncaster Rovers after he'd had a blinder for Northern Ireland against England. The fee was about £25,000, which made Harry the most expensive goalkeeper in the world at the time.

I was now officially a full-time professional footballer just like Harry Gregg and Mark Jones, but there was just a slight catch. I would be earning less money when I signed as a professional than I had been getting as an amateur. When I was an amateur working in Altrincham, United paid the £3 for my digs, and sent another £3 home for me, that, along with the £3 a week I earned in

Switchgear, brought my weekly total to £9, which wasn't bad. When I signed as a pro, the rate went by age. So, at seventeen, I would get £8 a week in the winter and £7 a week in the summer, but there was £1 deducted in tax. By the time I'd pay £3 for the digs and send £3 home, I only had £1 for myself, to do the week.

My father asked the club to pay for my digs but he said they refused. I found out afterwards they did pay rent for some of the other lads, which I suspected at the time.

Even though money went a long way in 1957, I had those other expenses such as fish'n'chips and steak'n'kidney pie to supplement the food at the digs. So I'd usually be skint on Thursday. Which wouldn't be much different to most lads of my age at the time, except I was supposed to be living in the land of dreams.

Jack Hennessy decided to go home. Jack's birthday fell around the same time as mine, and the club took the view that it would postpone a decision about him signing pro until the following summer. This upset Jack and he returned to Dublin to play for Shelbourne, which meant that I was left on my own in the digs.

I wasn't playing well. I wasn't training well. I was lost.

I could probably go on a bit more about all the relatively small things that were getting me down at United at that time. What I didn't properly appreciate is that it all faded into insignificance beside the much bigger things that Matt Busby and Jimmy Murphy were doing. Yes, there were probably other clubs who were starting to become more progressive than United, in their training and equipment – by 1957, some of them might have a gym suitable for footballers rather than boxers and might even be moving beyond the teapot with the Horlicks in it. But the one thing they didn't have, that United had in such abundance, was the great players. Murphy was responsible for the reserve and the youth teams. With the help of Bert Whalley, he would identify the ones who were ready for the first team. And then Busby would put them into the first team.

But he wouldn't put just one of them in, or maybe two, alongside the more experienced players, for fear that too much youth would unbalance the side, or that they just couldn't cope with it. If they were ready he would put them in, and that was that.

This was Matt Busby's genius. It wasn't just that he recruited the best young players from England, Scotland, Ireland and Wales. He would then believe in them enough to give them their chance and to let them play, to let them become these great players who had already won two league titles, who had an average age of about twenty-two and who'd been playing in the first team for years.

Their success led to qualification for the European Cup, into which they were entered by Matt Busby in defiance of the insular mentality of the Football League, which had been opposed to English teams playing in the competition – Chelsea hadn't taken their place in 1955. It was Matt's courage and vision that made it all happen, when lesser men would have been ducking out of the challenge, taking the short-term view.

He might have had to bring in some rugby man to improve the levels of physical fitness, but he knew that, ultimately, anyone could do that. But to bring in the most gifted young players of their time and to know when they're ready and to have the moral courage to back them all the way – few men could do that. Matt Busby would put them into the first team, and he would put them all in. That is what made the difference.

That is why he was great, and why they were great.

4

MUNICH

I WAS in the home-team dressing room at Old Trafford when I was told about the Munich disaster. I had just finished training for a Youth Cup match. We had showered and were almost ready to go at about 4 o'clock, when old Bill Inglis, the reserve team trainer, came into the dressing room. He looked terrible. Bill was usually good-humoured and a joker so, by the look of him, we had a fair idea that something was seriously wrong.

'Terrible news,' he said. 'The plane has crashed in Germany.'

There was just a moment of confusion at the mention of Germany – United had been playing in Yugoslavia, not Germany, in the quarter-final of the European Cup. And then we stood around in silence, trying to absorb the shock, but not really understanding the true nature or scale of the thing. At that stage it didn't occur to me that anyone might have died. Bill Inglis didn't say anything about that.

'You'd better all go home and wait until you hear from us,' he said.

I walked to my digs in Norwood Road, still shocked by what I had heard, but still thinking that no one had died. I had in mind some sort of a crash on the runway, but nothing that couldn't be put right. I got back to the digs and went to the sitting room to listen to the Rediffusion radio. With Jack Hennessy gone back to Dublin, I was on my own there.

By about 6 o'clock, the enormity of it was starting to sink in.

The plane, which had been carrying players, officials and journalists, had crashed in Munich during the third attempt at take-off. Conditions were terrible. It had been snowing.

Then the radio was telling us what old Bill Inglis hadn't been told – or what no one had had the heart to tell him – many had died.

And then the names of the players – Roger Byrne, Mark Jones, Eddie Colman, Geoff Bent, David Pegg, Tommy Taylor, and my friend Liam Whelan were all dead.

So were Tom Curry and Bert Whalley of the training staff, and club secretary Walter Crickmer. And eight journalists, Alf Clarke, Donny Davies, George Follows, Tom Jackson, Archie Ledbrooke, Henry Rose, Eric Thompson, and Frank Swift, former goalkeeper with Manchester City and England. About half of the forty-four who were on that plane would not be coming back.

Matt Busby was gravely ill. And so was Duncan Edwards.

Images of the players flew through my head – Roger Byrne, the only player apart from Freddie Goodwin who owned a car; Mark Jones, who had been kind enough to come over and wish me well when I turned pro; Duncan Edwards, sitting on top of a post box on the Stretford Road, eating an apple and waiting for the bus; and Liam, who had made me feel at home when I first came to the club at the age of fourteen, Liam from Cabra who was young enough to be a friend and old enough to be a hero.

It seemed only a few minutes ago that I was chasing Liam Whelan around the showers at Fallowfield with a bottle of water, cutting my hand on the broken bottle and getting to stay at United for another two weeks. How could he not be coming back?

My own shock and grief was reflected in the reaction of millions, struggling to understand this terrible thing that had happened, how these young men who had been so lucky, so gifted, had also been destined for such a cruel end.

I went into the club the next morning. I have seen articles which say that the flags were at half-mast but I don't remember any flags. Nobody really knew what to do. In the days that followed, the club effectively closed down and we were told to stay away until further notice. They said they would tell us if they wanted us to go to any funerals.

Over in Munich, Matt Busby was still fighting for his life. Twice, he would be given the Last Rites. After fifteen days, Duncan Edwards would lose his battle.

It emerged that after the second attempt at take-off had failed, and the passengers had disembarked, Duncan had taken the opportunity to send a telegram to his landlady in Manchester saying that the flight had been cancelled and he'd be flying back tomorrow. Which underlines the madness of it all, the foolishness of getting onto that plane for a third time after two failed attempts. With the snow coming down at the airport in Munich, the flight could have been cancelled – but it wasn't, even though a lot of them were scared stiff at that stage, and rightly so.

Instead, there were bodies coming home and we were going to funerals. I remember going to a couple of the funerals in Manchester, that of Tom Curry, the trainer who used to arrive with the footballs to start the games at the back of the stand; and Eddie Colman, regarded as a lovely lad, but one of those senior players who hardly knew I was there at all because I was so in awe of him. In fact, I was afraid to go into the same dressing room as Eddie Colman or David Pegg or Duncan Edwards. So I was almost embarrassed to be representing the club at funerals, because I felt as if I didn't really know them and because I was such a young and unknown player.

Liam Whelan I knew.

For the Irish lads at the club – Jackie Mooney, Joe Carolan, Jimmy Sheils and myself – there was a flight back to Dublin for Liam's funeral. I went up to his home in Cabra the night before with my father. So did Joe Carolan, who was also from Cabra.

The house was open to everyone on the night, and it was crowded. I saw Liam's mother for a moment, but the poor woman didn't know where she was. Everyone was shell-shocked. I spoke to Liam's older brother Christy, who'd been over in Manchester a few times. I know Christy to this day, a gentleman.

Liam was buried in Glasnevin and there were thousands at the funeral. Dublin, like Manchester, was under a pall of gloom. It couldn't be any other way in a city with such a football tradition, a city full of kids like me, dreaming of playing for Manchester United. These days, if a disaster of this magnitude were to happen, there would be all sorts of help available for those affected in any way, but back then, you just went to the funerals and carried on as best you could.

In fact, in all the time I was at United, I don't ever remember any talk about Munich in the dressing room. Not a word, for years. Maybe it was too raw and painful, especially for the likes of Bobby Charlton, Bill Foulkes and Kenny Morgans who survived it, and who came back from it to resume their careers.

The world is still mourning the Busby Babes, still talking about it. Inside the dressing room, there was total silence.

And we should still be talking about it, but in a different way. To my mind, it has always been seen as a football tragedy, rather than a human tragedy. So when United won the European Cup ten years later, all the headlines were about justice being done, about Matt Busby triumphing over adversity, as if winning the cup had made it all worthwhile.

I just wonder how the relatives of the dead were feeling when they saw all that. There was little or nothing about them, about Roger Byrne's widow who was raising a family, or Duncan Edwards' mother who wasn't faring too well.

There had been no insurance scheme for the players, no foundation which might easily have been started at the time and provided some comfort for the relatives.

To put it bluntly, they got nothing.

It was the 1990s before anything was done for them, and what was done, was not by the club itself, but by the ex-players association, which arranged a testimonial match at Old Trafford.

The story of Munich will always have a terrible power – the Busby Babes added greatly to the legend of Manchester United. They had experienced so many of the best things in life and, then, the worst of all things. Few of us will ever know such extremes.

The club seemed to appreciate that, but only in football terms. There was a human side that they didn't see at all, or didn't want to see, and when the story moved on, the bereaved were left to fend for themselves. United would rebuild after Munich and, in time, they would come back gloriously with more great players and more great teams, but it was the club's darkest hour in more ways than one.

Of course Munich was a football tragedy too, a story of a team which had just reached the semi-final of the European Cup for the second year in succession by holding Red Star Belgrade to a 3–3 draw in Yugoslavia, winning 5–4 on aggregate. A team with an average age of twenty when it won the Championship in 1955–1956, which won the league again the following year, and which narrowly missed out on the double when they were beaten 2–1 by Aston Villa in the FA Cup final.

I may have stayed out of their way around Old Trafford, but I was able to see the outstanding qualities they possessed as individuals. Captain and left-back Roger Byrne was fast, used the ball well and was an inspiring leader. And on the other flank Bill Foulkes was a hard, rugged competitor, the sort of player every side needs.

At right-half Eddie Colman could beat any defender. They called him 'Snake Hips' because of his bewildering dummies and body swerves which would often leave opponents on their backsides. Left-half Duncan Edwards was perhaps the greatest player of all at United. He had speed, stamina, good ball control and passing ability, he had everything. Mark Jones was one of the best centre-halves in England. He was great in the air, strong in the tackle and a fine reader of the game. Inside-right Whelan and inside-left Dennis Viollet are entitled to special mention as neither of them ever really got the credit they deserved. Whelan had any amount of natural ability and he always wanted the ball. He scored an amazing twenty-eight goals in the season before Munich. He was a bit slow, but it was rarely noticed because he used the ball so well.

As for Viollet, I would go on to play with him many times and I believe he was one of the best forwards I have ever played with. I am convinced that if Sir Alf Ramsey had been in charge of the England team when Viollet was at his peak, that slim, graceful player would have won a lot more than two international caps. Basically a striker, Viollet always got into excellent positions to receive a pass, could hold the ball and lay it off exactly at the right moment. I would rate him in the same class as Denis Law as a goalscorer. He did not have such quick reflexes as Law, but he could beat opponents more easily. Before Munich, he played as a striking inside-forward and after it, he could play as target man. I enjoyed playing with Dennis Viollet enormously.

In Johnny Berry and David Pegg, United had two wingers with different styles. Berry was faster and more direct, while Pegg although not as exciting to watch, had the ability to jink past opponents on either side, and rarely lost possession. Then there was Tommy Taylor, a centre-forward who would be worth about £30 million in the transfer market of today. Brilliant in the air and with better ball control than he was given credit for, Taylor was certainly more polished than most orthodox centre-forwards.

And then there was Bobby Charlton.

He had become a first-choice player just a few games before Munich, having previously deputised for Liam Whelan or Dennis Viollet – again it was a measure of the talent in that side that

Bobby wasn't in it automatically. After Munich, Bobby was forced to take on more responsibilities, and he matured very quickly as a player. In fact, Bobby, Bill Foulkes, Dennis Viollet and Harry Gregg, the goalkeeper who had been as brave at Munich as he was on the pitch, all recovered from their injuries to play a part in United's FA Cup challenge that year. And Charlton was absolutely brilliant in those games.

I don't think Bobby has ever got all the credit he deserves at Old Trafford, perhaps because he was a model professional, and never engaged in controversy. He was gifted with pace and balance, and had a tremendous shot with either foot. When I first came to Old Trafford, I was told that when a team-mate was in a good position, you should give him the ball simply and quickly. As a midfielder, I needed players to pass to, as a way of getting nearer the other side's goal. But Bobby didn't. He could do it himself, often ignoring better-placed colleagues, stopping between defenders and shooting for goal.

And he never seemed bothered by the physics of the game. For example, when the opposition was preparing to take a goal kick, I believed we should balance where our players were on the pitch. Bobby would wander over towards me and I would say, 'Push up, Bob, push over.' I recall once saying this three or four times and Bobby replied, 'Fuck off and leave me alone.' What was wrong for other people was right for Bobby. He's been a hero of mine from the first time I saw him play.

But he was still injured for the club's first match after Munich, a fifth-round cup tie against Sheffield Wednesday just thirteen days after the crash.

We had been back at training at the White City greyhound stadium, just down the road from Old Trafford. We trained as best we could, but it was totally surreal, knowing that so many friends and fellow-pros were no longer with us. Jimmy Murphy was now in charge. He hadn't been on the trip to Yugoslavia, as he had been managing Wales in Cardiff. It was a quirk of fate which meant that there was some sort of continuity, a sense of life going on.

Murphy and Busby had originally met in Italy during the war when, according to legend, Busby apparently overheard Murphy talking knowledgeably about football, liked very much what he heard and struck up a friendship. With Busby still drifting between life and death in the hospital in Germany, and Murphy needing to rally the troops in this terrible situation, the war had probably been the best preparation they could have had for the task that confronted them.

Murphy had to assemble some sort of a competitive team for the Sheffield Wednesday game. For the first time, a club was allowed to sign players who were cup-tied. So Ernie Taylor was bought from Blackpool and Stan Crowther from Aston Villa, and both of them would play against Wednesday. Incredibly, two players who survived the crash, Harry Gregg and Bill Foulkes also played. Others at the club who hadn't made the trip, Ian Greaves, Freddie Goodwin, Ronnie Cope, Colin Webster, Mark Pearson, Alex Dawson and Shay Brennan made up the team.

Shay, who would become the first man to play for the Republic under the parentage rule, had been friendly towards me from the minute I walked into Old Trafford, and would become a great pal of mine until the day he died in 2000. I miss him still.

Before that first international, Shay was staying at the Four Courts Hotel in Dublin, and I was staying with my parents at home. I rang the hotel to see how he was doing, and when he came on the phone I disguised my voice and pretended to be Noel Dunne of the *Irish Independent*. Now I knew Shay, like most English-born lads, wanted to play for England. But when he resigned himself to the fact that he wasn't going to make the England team, he took advantage of the new parentage rule, which led to 'Noel Dunne' asking him what it meant to him, to play for Ireland.

'It was always my life-long ambition to play for Ireland,' Shay said.

He said it was a proud moment for him and that his Uncle Pat was coming up from Carlow for the match and his parents and family were all delighted.

After he had poured his heart out, I laughed down the phone at him, 'What a fucking spoofer'.

Then he recognised my voice and pleaded, 'Don't tell anyone about this, will you?'

I promised him I wouldn't tell anyone – not even his Uncle Pat from Carlow.

Back in the spring of 1958, when it was still Shay's lifelong ambition to play for England, he was the real surprise choice by Murphy for the cup tie against Wednesday. He had been playing inside-forward on the A and B teams but, like myself, had not been playing very well. Despite his poor form, Shay was a really good footballer, a fact recognised by Jimmy Murphy, who picked him at outside-left on this night, the most emotionally charged in the history of Manchester United, perhaps in the entire history of the game. In the match programme, the United line-up had no names, just blank spaces representing the players who died. I have never experienced an atmosphere like it, such an over-whelming desire for a team to win. And that was just on my way to the ground.

If the result of this game could have been determined by sheer force of will, United would have won it about 14–0. Whenever a United player touched the ball, 60,000 people went delirious. I found a place to watch, sitting on top of the wall of one of those old open-air toilets. From there, with my legs dangling over the side, I was able to see Shay Brennan becoming a star.

Much later, I would be talking to Shay and making a confession, 'When we were playing in the A and B teams, I didn't think you were going to make it,' I said.

Shay thought about it, and made his own confession, 'I didn't think you were going to make it either.' But he was making it on this night, of all nights, against Sheffield Wednesday. He scored two goals in a 3–0 win. The first was scored direct from a corner kick that somehow drifted into the net, and could be regarded as a fluke – or divine intervention, as was seriously suggested by many of the crowd. But the second was all Shay's doing. He took it well, going through the middle and placing it past the keeper.

The massive crowd, the world's press, everyone was looking for a hero that night, and it turned out to be my pal Shay, who was gracious enough to be totally embarrassed by it all. Bragging wasn't Shay's game.

As they did the year before, United would go on to reach the 1958 FA Cup final, beating West Brom and Fulham along the way but, despite the magnificent contributions of Charlton and Viollet, they were beaten 2–0 by Bolton Wanderers at Wembley. They would also beat AC Milan 2–1 in the home leg of the European Cup semi-final, before losing 4–0 in the San Siro. That they were still competing at that level at all, given the trauma which they had suffered, is a miracle in itself.

For my part, I would also be disappointed in another big cup competition. I was a member of the team which was beaten in the semi-final of the FA Youth Cup that season, but, overall, I felt that I was starting to make some progress. We had also got to the semi-final stage the previous season, only to be beaten by Wolves, and this time we were knocked out by a Blackburn Rovers side which included Keith Newton, later of Everton and England, Mike England, later of Tottenham and Wales, and Fred Pickering, later a centre-forward with Blackpool – though I recall on that day Pickering was playing left-back. And Blackburn also had the late Paddy Mulvey, an outstanding Dublin schoolboy.

It was hard to take, because I really felt we were good enough to win it this time. But Munich changed everything, and led to the promotion of a number of our best players to the first team, among them Alex Dawson and Mark 'Pancho' Pearson, our star forwards.

In fact Dawson, who was built like a tank, had a remarkable game for the first team in the cup semi-final against Fulham. After a 2–2 draw at Villa Park, United won 5–3 in the replay at Highbury, with Dawson getting a hat-trick. Neither Dawson nor Pearson had the impact on the game in later years that I thought they would, but they were brilliant as eighteen-year-olds. With my own form starting to improve, I took the fact that some of my junior team-mates were doing so well as another positive sign.

Soon I was promoted too. I wasn't becoming an international hero like Shay Brennan but, towards the end of that season, I suddenly found myself playing in the Central League, on many of the great grounds I had read about as a boy. Villa Park, Bramall Lane and The Hawthorns were no longer just places in my imagination, I was actually playing there in front of the large crowds who used to watch the reserve games back then.

I wasn't even playing particularly well, but I was playing. Above all, I was playing at Old Trafford, the holy ground itself. I was hanging on to my dream.

But this awful period of disaster and mourning had not quite finished. I had left my digs with Mrs Robb and moved in to digs with Joe Carolan, not for any of the normal reasons, but for a truly tragic reason. Mrs Robb had three sons, one married, two unmarried. All three of them were killed in a car crash about a mile away from the house in Norwood Road. For reasons that can only be imagined, Mrs Robb left Manchester and went to live in Australia.

It seemed that death was everywhere.

5

THE CHANGE

THAT SUMMER of 1958, I felt the benefit of being back home in Dublin. We had moved out from the inner city to a three-bedroomed, semi-detached house on the Navan Road. The surroundings had changed but my mother's cooking was still the same, still great. It's just that I was now starting to appreciate it properly. Where once I had refused to eat, I now devoured everything she put in front of me, and I could feel myself getting stronger.

My body was maturing anyway. But that summer, after all the traumas of the season, I could feel almost every meal of steak or chicken or coddle building me up, and doing me good.

My father felt that I could be using my new-found strength to go out and enjoy myself the way a Manchester United player should – the way he would certainly have done had he been in my position. In the years to come, when I would start to become well known, I would be sitting at home during these summer breaks, just relaxing and doing what I wanted to do – which was very little really – and I would catch him looking at me with an expression of total bafflement, as if he had no idea how I could possibly be related to him. He just couldn't understand how a professional footballer with one of the top sides in England could be sitting there doing nothing, rather than being out there enjoying himself – or at least doing the things that Dickie would have been doing out there to enjoy himself.

From the start, even in these early days, I think he felt that my career was wasted on me, that I had no idea how to make the most of it – unlike him. In fact, I genuinely believe that my father probably got more enjoyment out of my career than I did myself. He loved it.

He would go out to the pubs on my behalf and talk the talk for me, and have the good time that I didn't want, or know how, to have.

I am now convinced that for all his knowledge, Dickie could never have made it as a player. All the things I detested – the fame, the celebrity – he would have embraced. At the first sight of the bright lights, he would have been gone. That would be Dickie, the showman. But I wouldn't begrudge him the fun he got out of the playing career that I somehow carved out for myself with my dull approach. In his own eccentric way, and at a deeper level, he had earned it.

Having a good time out on the Navan Road was a bit different to what we knew in Ormond Square. Instead of football, football and more football, there was now the slightly more exotic game of tennis, which you could play at a popular venue called the Ashdale Tennis Club, which meant that instead of kicking a tennis ball around Ormond Square when we couldn't afford a bouncer, we were now using racquets.

I had already started to play a bit of tennis over in Manchester, having been introduced to it by a chap in the digs called Stan Rosenthal. So it seemed that they were right in Brunner after all, and that I wasn't a real Irishman, with my fondness for the English games. And this was before I took up the golf.

So I found myself playing a lot of tennis in the Ashdale with Louis Kilcoyne, who had been a year behind me in Brunner, and who would later, among other things, become the President of Shamrock Rovers and of the FAI. There were also dances at the club featuring a young singer from Cabra called Dickie Rock.

And I met someone else in the tennis club that summer of 1958, the best of them all as it turned out. I was introduced by my sister Kay to Anne Dolan. I knew that Anne had a brother, Paul, a very good athlete who had represented Ireland in the Olympics. What I didn't know at the time was that Anne Dolan would become my wife. Though deep down, maybe I knew it from the first time we met, at the Ashdale Club.

Looking back, those couple of months in Dublin and the period that followed when I returned to Manchester was a very important time for me, a lucky time. I would meet and be influenced by people who would change my life, and all for the better – Anne, of course, in Dublin, and Jack Crompton and Jimmy Sheils in Manchester.

Returning to Old Trafford feeling so much better, I saw changes that would transform my career and finally banish the unhappiness and helplessness I had felt before Munich. The first involved Jack Crompton. He had been United's goalkeeper for years and had played in the 1948 FA Cup-winning team. He had left Manchester shortly before Munich to become the trainer at Luton Town but, after the crash, he returned to Old Trafford in the same capacity. Instead of the disorganised and unsupervised sessions that had left me wandering like a lost soul, Jack introduced squad sessions which he oversaw, and I now knew what to do and how much to do.

He also organised circuit training in the gym with weights. I was delighted with that.

There was a new togetherness around the place, and I felt a sense of belonging at last, a sense that there was a place for me at this great club. I will be eternally grateful to Jack for the impact he had on my career.

The second change was more personal – and just as important. It involved Jimmy Sheils, a full-back from Derry. When I left Mrs Robb's and I moved in with Joe Carolan at his digs, I was replacing Jackie Mooney, who had been released by United

and returned to Shamrock Rovers. Jimmy Sheils had palled
around with Joe and Jackie, but Joe was now going steady with
his future wife Maureen. Which left Jimmy and I at a loose end,
so we palled up.

Jimmy was much more outgoing than I was. With his reddish
hair and Northern Irish accent, he seemed to have a stronger
personality all round. And clearly I was open to his influence at
a very formative time because I learned a lot from being around
him. I guess this sort of thing happens during your teenage years.
When your pal is much better at getting on with people than
you are, and you see how well it works, you just want to be more
like him.

Just from being in Jimmy's company, seeing how people
warmed to him, I started to become less shy and introverted,
and more confident in my relationships with the rest of the
players at United. I realised that I had been too quiet, and that
maybe it had been holding me back where it mattered to me
most, on the pitch. Now I recall my father's advice after that
schoolboy international, that I needed to get myself noticed. He
wasn't right about how – I didn't need to be loud and obnoxious – but I did need to become more open and outgoing. It
took Jack Crompton, with his training methods, and Jimmy
Sheils, with his charisma, to really bring me out of myself at
United.

I can't emphasise enough the influence Jimmy had on me, just
in the way he would take the piss out of everyone, wisecracking
with the likes of Duncan Edwards, Tommy Taylor and Roger
Byrne, without making any enemies. He had arrived the same year
as me but was three years older, so he would have been with the
first-team squad in Germany for pre-season training. He was able
to have a laugh with these guys that I had found so intimidating.

Jimmy's world was a place I wanted to be, and needed to be.
But, as footballers, we know that our world can end in an instant.
In a training match, Jimmy, who played full-back, was running

back towards the keeper Gordon Clayton, who dived over the ball and caught Jimmy's knee, giving him a cartilage problem that wasn't diagnosed properly, and that wasted a year. When that happened, you were a cert for a free transfer and Jimmy duly went off to Southend for a year. By the early 1960s, Jimmy was out of the game but starting to do very well in the fast food business. We are still friends, and it is a joke between us that he curses the name of Gordon Clayton to this day.

Jimmy might have had a football career, if it wasn't for Gordon.

I mightn't have a football career, if it wasn't for Jimmy.

As it happened, for my debut with the first team, I went along as the odd-job man.

I was playing regularly for the reserves, and playing well. But there was still stiff competition for places. Inevitably, this meant that some players in the reserves would be left out for a game, which is what happened to me one Saturday when the club had arranged to play a friendly against Swansea at Vetch Field.

It was a 'free' day, as both teams had been knocked out of the FA Cup in the third round.

It was decided that I would travel with the team even though I wasn't down to play. As there were no subs in those days, my duties were menial – to collect the kit and generally do all the running that needed to be done, off the pitch. But this being a friendly, both sides relaxed the rule on substitutions, agreeing to have one sub apiece. So I was told to get changed. For the first time, I was on the bench.

It was a hectic game. There were four goals in the first fifteen minutes and then United's centre-half Ronnie Cope had to come off injured. So they called for the odd-job man.

Amazingly, I was on. My dream was alive – in a friendly at the Vetch Field on a slow Saturday, but alive nonetheless. I was

out there playing alongside the likes of Bobby Charlton and
Dennis Viollet. And the ground was packed. More pleasingly, I
didn't feel that I was out of my depth. We won 7–5 and I felt
I'd given a good account of myself in front of Matt and Jimmy.
The elation I felt on that journey back from Swansea can be
compared only to the feeling I would have when I played my
first international.

And then it was straight back to the reserves.

But I was happy now. In this season of 1958–1959, I felt I was
getting there. I was improving all the time and my confidence
was growing. Matt Busby was back at work at Old Trafford, planning another generation of Busby Babes with Jimmy Murphy.
They bought Albert Quixall from Sheffield Wednesday for what
was then a British record of £45,000, and the club did better
than anyone could have imagined, finishing runners-up in the
league behind Wolves.

I would also attain my first honour with United that season,
in the reserves, helping them to win the Central League
Championship. I came under the influence of Jimmy Murphy at
this time, always cajoling from the sidelines when Busby would
be a calmer presence.

Jimmy had been a good player at West Brom, an action-man-
type player. He didn't have the charm of Matt – he was a bit
gruff and wouldn't be as at ease socially. Though I can recall him
getting on well with Shay Brennan, over a few drinks, but then
everybody got on well with Shay.

Jimmy could give you a roasting too, if you made a silly mistake
or ignored his instructions. I missed a penalty in the last minute
against Huddersfield Town reserves at Leeds Road during the
Christmas period. I pulled it wide with the inside of my right
foot. We would have won if I'd scored. Murphy didn't take the
line you hear a lot these days, that anyone can miss a penalty,
that at least I showed bottle by standing up and taking it. In

fact, he was so angry, he reduced me to tears in the dressing room afterwards.

'What the fuck were you thinking about, missing a fucking penalty,' he raged. 'And in the fucking last minute.'

Murphy loved to win, even against Huddersfield Reserves. Even if you were in tears, he wouldn't hold back. But I never lost respect for him, nor did other players – Bobby Charlton in particular – on whom he had such a huge influence. Anyway, as was the custom at Christmas, we played Huddersfield Reserves again in our next match and I scored the winner. After the match, Murphy came over to me and said, 'Tell your Dad I'm very pleased with your progress.'

From Jimmy Murphy, this was huge praise. And it was his way of saying sorry.

There was another member of that reserve team who hadn't quite made it to the first team on a regular basis, but who would become a World Cup winner in 1966, one of the great characters of the game, and a close friend of mine to the present day.

Nobby Stiles joined United a year later than me, in 1957, and we hit it off immediately. He may have had a ferocious presence on the pitch but off duty he looked more like a professor than a warrior, with his thick glasses. In fact, in his street clothes, most people found it hard to believe that this was the same Nobby Stiles of the explosive temperament, unless they were to see him on the golf course – then his competitive juices would start to flow again.

He is also my brother-in-law, a process that started in that summer of 1958 when he spent some time with us in Dublin. I introduced him to my sister Kay. Nobby says he loved her the first time he saw her, but she was going out with someone else at the time, so he would have to wait. He was only sixteen.

Nobby came over for several summers, during which time he settled in and became part of our family. Those summers would also be notable for the fact that at some point, probably in 1960, Anne and I brought Eamon Dunphy to his first dance. He was a bit younger than us, and I think he was a bit lost. Certainly, he never asked to come out with us again. We were probably too dull for him.

At the time, I mainly knew Eamon as a youth player with United, actually a very good player. Over in Manchester, I would bump into him in Longford Park, which was near the area where so many of us were in digs. Jimmy Sheils and I would see him when everyone would come out on a Sunday to have a coffee or an ice-cream, to play tennis or to use the putting green. Of course, I remembered him from Stella too – how could I forget him and the struggle for all those table-tennis balls?

To him, we were friendly faces from home. He was on the ground staff at United and we kept an eye out for him. He was friendly with Barry Fry, who would later become manager of Birmingham City among other clubs, and a bit of a character, but who was regarded back then as possibly the most brilliant schoolboy player in England. Unfortunately, he peaked at seventeen.

Back in Dublin, for that first dance, Anne and I took Eamon to this venue near the Gresham, where a man called Tommy Nolan, who used to do Sinatra stuff, was singing. He would later become better known as the father of the Nolan Sisters. And Eamon would become better known too, for many things.

But the main memories I have of that time are of days spent playing golf – a big discovery for me – with Nobby and a couple of friends called Richie Gernon and Tom Morris. My mother would pack a picnic lunch for us early in the morning, and we would be off for the day to play thirty-six holes at Donabate. In those days, when golf was mainly the preserve of the professional classes and the odd professional footballer, we would have the course virtually to ourselves. I always remember the cardboard sign outside the clubhouse at Donabate: Members Required.

But desperate as they were, I don't think they required the likes of us, with our juvenile carry-on, the endless lengths to which we would go to annoy one another, to wind up the hot-tempered Nobby or Richie, insisting that they tee up a few inches back, just as they were about to drive, always trying to gain some ridiculous or petty advantage.

The tennis club closed down, but golf had grabbed me, and it has kept me entertained and challenged for most of my adult life. If football was the dream, I see golf as the impossible dream, this desire to strike the golf ball the way I want to strike it, the way I can kick a football, all the time knowing that I'll never quite get there. But loving the pursuit anyway and being grateful for all the times it took my mind away from football.

I don't think it was quite as relaxing for Nobby, who, in his time, has left a fair few golf bags abandoned in the bushes.

But at football, Nobby was making himself a player. He knew the two most important things in the game – to have the confidence to do what he could do and, just as importantly, to have the intelligence to know what he couldn't do. After he had won the ball, Nobby would have no problem just giving it to Bobby Charlton, which was exactly the right thing to do. These were qualities he had from the start. He had been Man United mad, like his father before him, and now he had replaced Jack Hennessy in the youth team. And he helped me greatly to settle down in Manchester – he and his mother, a lovely woman who was as good a cook as my mother and whose Sunday lunches we still speak of with awe.

Incidentally, if I'm giving the impression that we young players were totally obsessed with food, that's because we were. There is nothing quite like living in digs to concentrate your mind on food, especially when you're trying to build up your energy all the time, to train and to play. On a Sunday, Jimmy Sheils and I would get the bus from outside Old Trafford to the Stiles household in Collyhurst, a big Irish-Catholic area of Manchester, and

then the feasting would start. Mrs Stiles was a brilliant cook, who
would bring us dinners of roast lamb, or roast beef, and we would
eat so much, and enjoy it so much, we'd think that we'd never
be able to eat again.

Then we'd sit around in the little front room of the terraced
house, playing LPs for the afternoon. Jimmy and I would play
Nat King Cole and Johnny Mathis, Nobby was more of an Andy
Williams man. Sometimes, the music would have to compete with
the sound of the trains that ran just behind the back yard. And
then, at about six, Mrs Stiles would announce that we could have
a tea of bacon and eggs, if we liked. Somehow, we would get ourselves back to the table again, for the finest English tea. Sometimes,
perhaps fearing that we wouldn't be able to move for the rest of
the night, Mr Stiles would give Jimmy and me a lift home. Tired
but happy.

Even the way I took up golf in Manchester was connected to
food.

On Mondays a bunch of us United players would go from
the ground to Davyhulme golf club, where there was an arrangement that we could have lunch. We'd sign in and have a nice
lunch, organised by a lady called Doris. And then, at tea-time,
we'd enjoy another meal – or maybe more than one, if Jimmy
could persuade Doris to part with another gammon, egg and
chips, with his persuasive manner, or by flashing a few bob, something he did as a last resort. At that, Doris would always come
up trumps.

There was almost nothing you wouldn't do for food when you
were in digs.

At some point during all this eating at Davyhulme, we would
get a few clubs from the pro, and scamper around the course.
And that's how the golf started for me. In fact, I really have to
pay tribute to our old friend Boxer and all the gang back in
Brunner, for seeing through me, and realising that I had this love
of English ways. Apart from playing golf and tennis, and bearing

An early picture of myself, second from right, with the blond ringlets, with my sisters Anna and Kay (to my left and right), and cousins Joan and Jimmy (far left and front).

Mammy in Ormond Square where I grew up and first learned to kick a ball, or 'bouncer', as it was then.

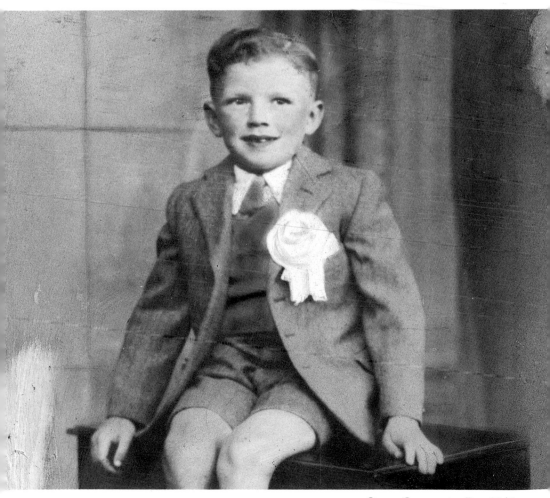

On my Communion Day, 1947.

Stella Maris, 1956, Evans Cup winners at Turner's Cross, Cork. We beat Southend
Cork 4–1 in the final. I was sent off early in the game. I'm front right.

November 1959, Ireland versus Sweden. Unusually, President Eamon de Valera made an appearance at a
soccer international, which was my first for Ireland. Here he is shaking my hand in the line up. From right:
Joe Haverty, Joe Carolan, Charlie Hurley, myself, Fionan 'Paddy' Fagan, Capt Noel Cantwell (partially
obscured) and Mick McGrath.

Goal! My first one for Ireland hits the back of the Dalymount net, an unforgettable moment. We beat Sweden 3–2. I was 18 years old.

The morning after.

Outside Old Trafford, c 1960.

Man United first team squad, 1962, with Matt Busby, far left. Nobby Stiles is middle row, second from right; Bobby Charlton is front row, far right; Noel Cantwell is back row, far right; Denis Law is front row, second from right; and I'm front row, far left.

Assistant Manager Jimmy Murphy, above, had a great knowledge of the game and was my mentor in the early days at Old Trafford. Jimmy probably contributed as much to the Busby Babes and to the success of Manchester United as Matt Busby himself.

Training in the early days at Man Utd.

Celebrating after beating Leicester City 3–1 in the FA Cup final at Wembley, 1963. Left to right: Bobby Charlton, Noel Cantwell, Paddy Crerand, Albert Quixall, David Herd and myself.

FA Charity Shield match, 1963, versus Everton at Goodison Park.
It was to be my last game for Man Utd.

29 August, 1963 – signing for Leeds United, watched by Don Revie (left), Jimmy Murphy and Matt Busby. Are these men smiling because I'm leaving?

Leaving Old Trafford with Don Revie. I was glad to go and, thankfully, I was going to the right place.

With my mother, my father 'Dickie' and Anne at the 'do' in the Savoy after the '63 FA Cup win, soon before myself and Anne got married. Dickie had a huge influence on my football life, and he probably enjoyed my career as much as I did.

With a dashing young Eamon Dunphy and Jimmy Sheils at Nobby Stiles's wedding to my sister Kay in 1963.

in mind all the games of crown green bowls I had with Bobby Charlton, I was also getting very partial to the great game of cricket.

Although if truth be told, we actually used to play a form of cricket back in Ormond Square, with a lamp-post as a wicket, a wooden bat and a tennis ball. And there was a real cricket ground up around the Navan Road. But in Manchester, I really got to know the game. The United players had passes to the Old Trafford cricket ground, which was very near to my digs. So I'd spend half the day there, watching a very good Lancashire side at the time, featuring Brian Statham, a great fast bowler.

And yet, the influence of Brunner wasn't entirely lost on me. When England played Australia, I'd be cheering for the Aussies.

While it might seem that I was an all-round sporting enthusiast, I hasten to add that I would have had nothing to do with any of these other sports if they affected my football in any way.

It was really starting to come together for me now. I'd had another good summer in Dublin, during which I'd picked it up again with Anne. We were now officially a couple. I'd had another good rest, plenty of golf, and – I need hardly add – a lot of good food. You had more time to recuperate back then between the seasons. The clubs didn't insist that players should maintain a level of fitness during the close season, but I was always aware that the pre-season training would be even harder if I came back overweight. So I went into the 1959–1960 campaign feeling stronger than ever, still in the reserves, but sensing that I was about to make the breakthrough.

In one midweek match against Leeds, I scored a hat-trick for the reserves in an 8–4 win. Something that no doubt helped my cause the following Saturday when Albert Quixall was injured, and I was picked for the first team to play Spurs at Old Trafford – not Swansea at the Vetch Field in a friendly, but Spurs on the cusp of greatness with Dave Mackay just after coming down from

Scotland and terrific players such as Cliff Jones the left winger, Tommy Harmer 'The Charmer' and Danny Blanchflower. They would nearly win the league that season – they blew it at Easter – but, the following year, Spurs would become the first side in the twentieth century to win the double.

It was against these guys that I made my first-team debut at the age of eighteen. It was September 1959. This, at last, was the real thing. Spurs beat us 5–1.

We got a hiding that afternoon, but I still managed to enjoy

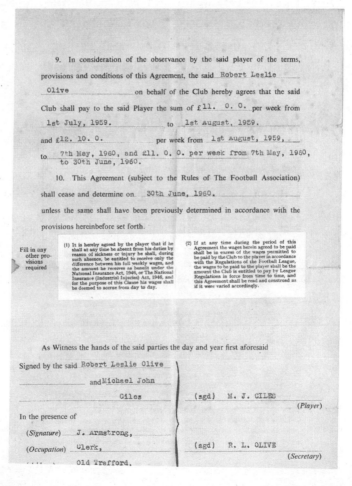

A page from my 1959 contract with Manchester United. I earned £11 per week.

the day, a glamour game, a full house and a big occasion which I realised on the day wasn't too big for me. I could cope with it, and maybe more.

I shook hands with Danny Blanchflower as we were coming off the pitch, the same Blanchflower who was already a legend to me after leading Northern Ireland to the quarter-final of the World Cup in 1958. He said to me, 'I didn't play like that in my first match.' I decided to take that as a compliment.

I was back in the reserves for the next game. But soon afterwards Quixall got injured again and I played against Wolves at Molineux. Managed by the great Stan Cullis, they would go on to win the FA Cup that season, narrowly missing out on the double. They had Peter Broadbent, a terrific player who never gets the credit he deserves when people talk today about former players. Wolves also had the England half-back line of Flowers, Slater and Clamp. Bill Slater was a schoolteacher who played as an amateur for England and for Blackpool in an FA Cup final. He then turned professional, captained Wolves and played for the full England team. A real gentleman, I can vividly remember him giving me a right telling off for swearing on the pitch. These guys were another formidable proposition, and they went three up, before we pulled it back to 3–2.

I had been involved in games against two of the top teams in England and I had played well.

Now I really felt that I could perform at this level. I felt that I was going to make it.

6

THE DALYMOUNT ROAR

JOE CAROLAN was reading the *Daily Mirror* one morning when something caught his eye.

He read it a few times, to take it in and to make sure there was no mistake, then he turned to me and said, 'We're playing for Ireland.'

We were in a hotel room in Blackpool with the United squad on a training break. Joe, who was my room-mate, had just established himself in the United first team. But this would be his first cap for Ireland too. Noel Dwyer the West Ham goalkeeper would also be making his debut. The match was against Sweden at Dalymount, just a few days before my nineteenth birthday. I felt a rush of excitement at the news, and also a twinge of worry. It doesn't seem possible to combine these two emotions, and yet the FAI had somehow managed it.

At one level, I had this ecstatic vision of running out at Dalymount Park, getting my first international cap, with my father up in the stand watching me, bursting with pride.

And at another level I couldn't stop wondering what would have happened if Joe hadn't gone out and bought the *Daily Mirror* that day. We had received no other notification.

The FAI gave the information to the papers, and the papers gave it to the players – or at least to those players who had bought the paper that day – and everyone just hoped for the best.

I was shocked to learn that this is how they did things at

Merrion Square. Little did I know that this would be just the first of many shocks that the FAI would have in store for me in the years ahead. I would later learn that the selection committee, the notorious Big Five, was itself selected from the ranks of the Council of the FAI which contained a representative from every League of Ireland club. So if a man who ran a butcher's shop put a couple of grand into his local club, and became that club's chairman and its representative on the council, pretty soon he could find himself in the Big Five, picking the Ireland team. And yet the Big Five had somehow picked me to play for the Republic while I was still a teenager, after just two first team appearances for United. Something that obviously redeemed them somewhat in my eyes.

By a happy coincidence, United's youth team had a friendly against Home Farm in Dublin on the Wednesday before the Sweden match. But Jimmy Murphy wanted me to return to Manchester between the games. He thought it would be best for me to keep clear of well-wishers if I wanted to prepare properly. His plan was thwarted by fog which delayed the flight back to Manchester, and so I was given permission to stay on in Dublin and to train in Tolka Park on my own. Tolka had so many memories for me, from the days when we'd all come from Ormond Square to see Drums playing, to when my father became manager and started to bring me into the world of football men. Not to mention the wall that he had built around the pitch.

Tolka was a spiritual home for me, and I savoured those days before the big match. The Prole family who now ran Drums did everything to facilitate me, as I went through my routine of warm-ups and sprints, trying to stay calm about the match, but feeling the thrill of it all. And Murphy needn't have worried about me keeping clear of well-wishers. After every session at Tolka, I would get the bus on Drumcondra Bridge back into the city centre, and then another bus home to the Navan Road, where

I would sit quietly, and rest, while my father went out there to deal with the well-wishers.

He loved it.

By preparing in Dublin during the build-up, I was also missing out on the usual pre-match delights which players selected to play for the Republic enjoyed at the time. These would involve playing for your club in England on the Saturday, and then making your way immediately after the match to the plane – or more likely the boat – to reach Ireland hopefully in time to play a full international match the following day.

No one questioned this at the time, it was just the way it was done, and anyway it was an honour to be representing your country.

We faced a strong Sweden side that, the previous year, had finished runners-up to Brazil in the 1958 World Cup which they had hosted. They went 1–0 up in the final before they were eventually destroyed 5–2 by a Brazil side that featured a seventeen-year-old Pelé, who scored two goals. It was actually Garrincha, the 'Little Bird', who did more damage than anyone else for Brazil in that tournament, but Pelé was so young he got most of the attention. I recall watching parts of the final on a television with hazy reception, and even through all the snow you could see his class.

So this Sweden side had been up there at the highest level. They had beaten England 3–2 at Wembley on the Wednesday before our game on the Sunday. We had our own way of doing things, our own match-day instructions. We were to meet at the Gresham Hotel at about 11.30 a.m., having made our own way there from our various starting points. So I left the Navan Road with my boots in a brown paper bag and took the bus to O'Connell Street.

It was the sweetest feeling, being on that bus with this day ahead of me. I had dreamed of it, and yet it had come quicker than I ever thought it would. I timed it so that I could go to mass in the church on Arran Quay. I knew it couldn't do me any harm, that I could only benefit from the calm atmosphere, the mood of reflection – and maybe a few prayers. I knew my mother would be praying enough for both of us, but I needed all the help I could get.

I knew I couldn't just turn up today, enjoy the sights and sounds and contribute nothing of any consequence. I had to perform. My cousin Christy had also played for Ireland a few years previously and he told me he got so wrapped up in the occasion that he could hardly remember anything about it. That's what nerves do to you. I was determined that I wasn't going to let that happen to me.

But it's still one of the best feelings I've ever had in my life, that lovely wave of excitement I felt as I walked from O'Connell Bridge down to the Gresham.

I had never been in the Gresham before. It was a really glamorous venue. I was meeting some of the Irish players, such as Noel Cantwell, Pat Saward and Charlie Hurley, for the first time and I was feeling nervous about it – after all I had watched and admired them from the terraces at Dalymount. I knew only two of the players that day, Joe Carolan and Joe Haverty, but as I arrived into the lounge area of the Gresham, I was greeted warmly by everyone. Having introduced ourselves to one another as best we could, we moved in to the restaurant for the pre-match meal. We had steak.

Then it was off to the room which had been booked for the team meeting. Jackie Carey, the manager, gave us the team talk. This in itself was an awe-inspiring moment for me, because Carey was an idol of mine, captain of the United team which won the FA Cup in 1948, and the league in 1952, captain of the Rest of Europe against Great Britain in 1950, and Footballer of the Year in 1949. Jackie Carey was The Man.

Carey's instruction was to 'fizz it about'. That was his big thing, 'fizzing it about', basically sound advice aimed at getting a bit of urgency into our game. It was just about all that any manager could do in the circumstances, addressing a bunch of players, some of whom had never met one another before, coming together only on the morning of the match.

His aura was enough to inspire me, and no doubt the other lads felt the same.

At about 1.15 p.m., we boarded a CIÉ bus – not a luxury coach just an ordinary bus – for the short journey up to Dalymount, passing St Peter's Church on the way. I could see myself back there as a schoolboy, waiting for my father to arrive to take me to see Ireland playing, with my heart pounding because he was always late.

The bus pulled up outside the lane leading into Dalymount. We made for the dressing room, through the crowd which was already starting to build. There was nothing like the Dalymount atmosphere to get the adrenaline pumping. The green jersey with my number on it was hanging up in the dressing room below the stand, waiting for me, number 8. All the shorts were the same size, just about right for Noel Cantwell or Charlie Hurley, far too big for me. They came down over my knees so I had to roll them up a bit.

We could hear the crowd rumbling above us in the stand, and the sound of the brass band marching around the pitch. Noel Cantwell the captain did everything right, coming over to each of us with a few words of encouragement . . . 'settle down' . . . 'enjoy it' . . . 'get on the ball'. It wasn't the words he said that mattered, it was the fact that Noel Cantwell was talking to me. That was enough.

In fact, all day I had to stifle the urge to address men like Cantwell and Carey as Mister.

Then Cantwell led us out alongside the Swedes, to line up and to shake hands with President Eamon de Valera. The great and the good of Ireland were far more likely to be found at Croke Park, watching Gaelic games, than mingling with the 'soccer men', but the elderly Dev – whose favourite sport was rugby – had become President of Ireland in June of that year, so perhaps he felt that his new role permitted him to make this official appearance at Dalymount. And it was said that he had another reason to be there on this particular day, because we were playing Sweden, which, like Ireland, had been neutral during the Second World War, which meant that we would have more in common with them than we'd have with certain other soccer men.

Through the national anthem, and all these other preliminaries, I just kept telling myself that this was all terrific – I was loving every minute of it – but I had to play. De Valera was there to do his business and I was there to do mine. The fact that I was making my debut at the age of eighteen was a point of special interest, but when you get out onto the pitch, everyone's equal. There would be no allowances made out there just because you're a young lad.

We made a dreadful start. Sweden went two up early on.

Then came the moment that changed everything. Fifty years later, it is still perfectly clear in my mind. Fionan Fagan took the ball down the right and crossed it into the box. Dermot Curtis challenged their goalkeeper who was forced to punch the ball out. The ball came in my direction, bounced once, and I caught it on the volley, thirty yards out.

I caught it in the middle of the instep, the sweet spot, a contact that felt so perfect I could hardly feel it at all.

It felt very similar to what I had felt the first time I ever kicked a ball, when I was three years old, playing with my grandfather. I had that same sense of complete satisfaction at the contact I had made. Except this time the consequences were so much greater.

I could see the keeper sprawling across his goal at the Schoolboy End, as the ball screamed high into the net. And even now, I can hear the noise. The Dalymount Roar.

THE FOOTBALL ASSOCIATION OF IRELAND
cumann peile na hÉireann
INTERNATIONAL MATCH
IRELAND v SWEDEN
SUNDAY, 1st NOVEMBER, 1959

DALYMOUNT PARK DUBLIN
OFFICIAL PROGRAMME   SIXPENCE
Published by the Shelbourne Football Supporters' Club under the authority of the Council

Match programme
When I played my first international match for Ireland, I was one of the youngest players ever to have been capped for the team.

That goal changed the game, and Dermot Curtis scored twice to make it a famous 3–2 win. The Schoolboy End held about 4,000 people, but I have estimated that at least 25,000 people over the years have told me that they were behind the goal on that day. They may not have been there in person, but they were there in some sense.

My mother wasn't there in person either. But she knew I'd scored, because she was listening to the match on the radio at home. And when the ball screamed high into the net, and the

Dalymount Roar went up, the noise travelled all the way to the Navan Road.

She heard it.

I spent the £30 fee for my first international on a television set for her, the first she had ever had. She also wanted a small cabinet in which to store my football medals and caps.

But the mood at United was not quite as euphoric. My performance had apparently made little impression on anyone there, and I found myself straight back in the reserves. It was reassuring to know that I had now played for the United first team and for Ireland, and I hadn't been out of my depth, but this would have to sustain me as I dealt with the frustration of contending for a regular first-team place.

Probably as a reaction to all the madness of Dalymount, I didn't play well for a few games, but I picked it up again around Christmas. In my head, I felt that I was ready to go forward. So I was getting a bit impatient. I felt that I was good enough to play in a first team, ideally the United one, but, if that didn't happen, I couldn't see myself in the reserves indefinitely. Even at Manchester United, you don't want to play in the reserves too long.

But the reality of the first team was that Albert Quixall, for whom Matt Busby had paid so much money, was playing at inside-right, Dennis Viollet was playing at centre-forward and Bobby Charlton was at inside-left. I could see no way of breaking into the team in these positions.

In retrospect, I should have asked Matt to give me a run on the right-wing. But I was worried that that would seem a bit pushy. Even the best efforts of Jimmy Sheils hadn't blown away all that reticence. So in reserve games, I had begun to drift out to the right, figuring that this was probably my only route into the first team. Kenny Morgans, the Welsh international, had played brilliantly in that position before Munich, but he never seemed to recover his form after that, with the result that Alex

Dawson, who was really a centre-forward, ended up playing quite a few games out of position on that side. The right wing wasn't my natural position either, but I would rather play there for the first team, than at inside-forward for the reserves.

Matt saw fewer reserve matches, because they clashed with the first-team games on a Saturday. But he did attend a practice match up at The Cliff on a day I switched to the right for a while. He must have seen something he liked, because I was picked to play in that position for the first team the following week.

It was just another friendly match, this time against Manchester City. Both teams had a free Saturday after being knocked out of the FA Cup. But I played well. And it probably did me no harm either that the team was having a poor season, hence the free Saturday, and this game which resulted in a major positional change, with Bobby Charlton now on the left-wing, Mark Pearson at inside-left, and me on the right-wing.

In one sense, I wasn't playing where I wanted to play but in a far more important sense, I was playing exactly where I wanted to play – in the first team. I was playing well, in a team that was playing well. I stayed in the first team for the rest of the season. I wasn't yet twenty, but I felt that I had established myself.

There would even be an extra reward at the end of the season. Or at least that was the idea – an idea which, at every turn, went horribly wrong. The 'bonus' for getting into the first team, was that I was in the travelling party when the club went on a tour of America. I was really looking forward to this, because having seen all the movies, my head was full of magical images of America, of New York in which everything was luxurious, with even Bud Abbott and Lou Costello sleeping on silk sheets. I was savouring my new-found status as a regular first-team player with Manchester United and the scorer of spectacular goals for my country. And now I was off to the United States on the cruise liner the *Queen Elizabeth*, an official member of the most glamorous club in the world, to have a swell time. I was feeling pretty good about myself, and about life in general. But the way this dream trip turned out, I now wonder if the gods had decided that I had done too much too soon, that I was losing the run of myself, and that they would teach me some horrible lesson in humility. It happens in football, all the time.

First, I was sick from the jabs we were given before the trip. I was up at Nobby's with Jimmy and, on the way back, even after one of Mrs Stiles' monumental dinners, I felt weak. Back at the digs in which we were now staying, run by Mrs Gladwin, another Irishwoman, I went to bed but I was sweating profusely and my arm was sore. I was told that some people just get this reaction for no apparent reason, which was some consolation, but it set the tone for what was to come.

We left in fine style, on the *Queen Elizabeth*. But on the first day out from Southampton, I became ill. I was sea-sick, and we had an awful lot of sea to go.

Although I had never been sea-sick on the crossing from the North Wall to Liverpool, on the *Queen Elizabeth*, crossing the Atlantic, I was forced up on deck straight away, desperately taking in mouthfuls of fresh sea air to hold back the waves of nausea. I'm not sure how long it was before I could go down below safely, except to say that it was far too long.

In New York, the mood of the travelling party started to deteriorate when we realised the true meaning of the crazy itinerary that had been prepared for us. We'd all seen the movies, but we really had no idea of the vast distances you had to travel in America to get from the east coast to the west coast, as we did. Four matches had been arranged against Hearts, who had just won the League in Scotland. We would play them in Toronto, New York, Vancouver and Los Angeles. Again it would seem that the gods, or at least the promoters, were playing tricks on us. Overall we played ten matches, all the while going backwards and forwards across the vastness of the United States. So that by the time we were cruising home to Southampton on the *Queen Mary*, we were all completely browned off and exhausted at a time of the year when we were supposed to be getting a good long rest.

But this would be a comic opera compared to what was coming down the line.

It was November 1960 and I had just turned twenty. After America, at the start of the new season, I had continued in the first team, now playing more games in the inside-right position at the hub of the action, while Quixall moved to the wing. We were playing Birmingham City at St Andrew's on a day of incessant rain. In fact, there was some surprise that the game was not postponed but it went ahead anyway, on a bad pitch on a bad day.

And there were a few bad tackles out there too. Birmingham City had the reputation of being a bit of a rough crowd, and their right-half Johnny Watts was known as a hard guy even among that crowd. I received the ball facing my own goal, and shaped to lay it off to Mark Pearson, positioned about twelve yards in front of me to my left. It was not a place to be, at St Andrew's, facing your own goal. You don't see things you need to see. I would learn that later on, but now it was a mark of my inexperience that I found myself in this position, leaving myself open to a tackle from behind by Johnny Watts.

It was a two-footed tackle, the worst type, which wraps around you, so that your legs are trapped. It's as if your legs are in a vice, you can feel yourself going over but you can do nothing to stop it until you feel this horrible pain. I could feel it straight away, shooting up my left ankle and up through my knee and thigh. I knew I was done.

The ankle was so sore and swollen that Jack Crompton called for a stretcher and I was taken straight away to the nearest hospital.

My ankle was X-rayed, looking for broken bones, though none were found which, at first, was a relief. But the doctors really should have done better than that. I came home on the coach with the lads, who helped me into the digs. Jimmy Sheils was there, and he would watch everything get worse over the next twenty-four hours. The ankle, which was still bandaged, started to swell, which was unbelievably painful. I could feel bones moving higher up my leg, but they were the smaller bones, so it was not such a big deal, relatively speaking. The big deal was my ankle. Mercifully, I didn't try to put any weight on it, because after I was brought to the club somehow on the Monday, and taken off to another hospital, the real diagnosis started to emerge.

The X-rays now showed that there had been a broken bone, just below my left knee, but, much more seriously, the ankle ligaments had been so badly damaged that the bones had spread. It was going to be much more complicated to fix than had been expected, as the whole structure of my leg had been put out of place. There would have to be an operation to mend the ligaments and to tighten up the bones.

Even then, I don't think I grasped how serious it was. I was just too young to get a true sense of the enormity of it, to contemplate what I might do if this ended my career. Maybe it was better that way. Footballers don't talk about injuries, in much the same way that soldiers in a war don't talk about getting shot. You know it happens, but you hope it won't happen to you. When it does, obviously you have the sympathies of the others, in a general way, but they don't want to know about it really. I didn't realise it was all so harsh until I was lying there in a hospital bed, looking out at some nondescript area of Manchester, realising that the other players were just getting on with it, that, basically, I was on my own.

It was a lesson I had to learn – now it was just me and my surgeon, a Mr Cregan. He seemed to me like something of a toff and he made no effort to engage me in small talk. He was austere, he didn't want me to be his life-long pal, and that was fine by me. But Mr Cregan had the extraordinary skills needed to carry out the operation on my ankle which, he later informed

me in his understated way, was only the second such operation
he had ever performed. It was such a delicate affair that he thought
I only had a 50/50 chance of ever playing again.

Ted Dalton, the United physio, said I was the luckiest bloke
alive. He was sure that the ankle would finish me.

With the Johnny Wattses of this world trying to destroy my career
in their way, I now indulged in a little bit of self-destruction in
my own way. Not just me, but also Jimmy Sheils, Wilf McGuinness
and Shay Brennan. We became the notorious Water Pistol Gang.

It all started when Jimmy told us about all the fun he had
with a water pistol in Derry the previous summer. A group of
lads in a car would ask someone for directions. Just as the person
would start to answer, the lads would squirt them with water
and drive off.

On the face of it, we wouldn't be able to repeat these exploits
in Manchester – we had no car. Then I got the injury at
Birmingham and Wilf McGuinness was recovering from a broken
leg. So Shay Brennan, who did have a car, a black Morris Minor,
took pity on us. He'd drive us wherever we wanted, to the golf
club or into the city. And that gave Jimmy the chance to get his
water pistol out again.

They say that four men in a car are usually up to no good,
and in this case they'd be right. The four of us would go off on
a drive and then Jimmy would say, 'There's a cranky-looking
fellow over there at the bus-stop. Pull over.'

Shay would stop the car. Jimmy would ask for directions. He'd
make sure to lower his voice in mid-sentence so the person had
to lean into the car to hear what he was saying.

As soon as he did, Jimmy would let him have it, and we'd
drive away laughing our heads off. We would see some of the
victims taking note of the number of the Morris Minor, but we
were sure they were only pretending to write it down to scare
us. We assumed they would all see the funny side of it, until

one day we read in the *Manchester Evening News* that the police were on the trail of a 'mystery water-pistol gang'. Apparently, about forty of the victims did not have the required sense of humour.

At first, only Shay got a summons. Jimmy and I hoped we'd escape. Even when two letters arrived at our digs one morning, it didn't twig with us. But it was a summons for both of us, and Wilf got one too. So we had to go to court.

There was huge publicity surrounding the case, as can be imagined – Shay, a Manchester United first-team regular, Wilf and I who played in the first team when fit, and Jimmy, from the reserve team, were in trouble with the law. Happy days.

I felt particularly sorry for Shay, who was the only one of us in the first team, playing for United every week in front of crowds asking him if he'd brought along his water-pistol. We were charged under some hundred-year-old Act or other, fined something small, and bound over to the peace for twelve months. And the magistrate took the opportunity to give us a right telling off, holding forth about footballers being a bunch of layabouts who don't know how lucky they are, going around annoying decent people.

It is remarkable to think that the image of footballers then was not much different to the way it is today – guys with too much money and too much time on their hands – except we didn't actually have the money. Around that time, I was out of the first team and on £12 10 shillings a week. I would go up to Stretford with Jimmy to gaze longingly into the window of a shop that sold record-players, figuring that we might just about be able to afford the cheapest model, which cost about a tenner, on which you could play just one record at a time – we had enough money to buy our Nat King Cole and our Johnny Mathis LPs, but we hadn't enough to buy a player.

We had once seriously discussed the possibility of getting part-time work in the afternoons. Yet we were being viewed in roughly the same light as the lads today with their wags and their fleets of Ferraris, us with our water-pistols and the new suit that we bought once a year before we went back home, so we'd look all right for the folks.

But the magistrate let us have it anyway, and Matt Busby didn't see the funny side either. Wilf and Shay, the two senior lads, were called out to his house. Matt was having a right go at them until his wife Jean intervened, 'Ah for goodness sake, Matt. You were young once yourself.' He went easier on them, after that.

Unfortunately for me, the headlines made their way back to Dublin. My mother would still come to the Daisy Market from the Navan Road, and the dealers were now giving her a hard time. 'I see John's got into trouble in England,' they would jeer. Of course she would tell them it was all just nonsense, but she was raging.

I put my water-pistol away after that episode, and I haven't used one since.

After five weeks with my leg in plaster, immensely grateful that I still had a career, I worked harder than ever to recover my strength and fitness. I was back on the pitch by Easter, and I played the last five games of the season. It had been my first serious setback, and I had come through it. But it had been a close-run thing.

7

'A ROW OVER A FIVER'

Early the following season, I saw something that changed the way I thought about the game and had an enormous influence on my career. In fact, it was so impressive, I could hardly believe what I was seeing. It was a revelation.

It was a midweek game at Maine Road between Manchester City and Fulham, and the extraordinary thing unfolding in front of me was the performance of Johnny Haynes.

He was a great midfield player with Fulham and England, with wonderful technique and passing ability, playing in a mediocre Fulham team. It was probably the fact that he was their star man that gave him the authority to play the way he did that night. Because he played in a way I had never seen an inside-forward play before.

At that time, inside-forwards, left and right, had dual roles in attack and defence. But they were basically restricted to their own sides of the pitch and, invariably, players used to stick to their positions. Haynes cast aside these restrictions, and freed himself to go wherever he could get possession. Ordinarily, you had to wait for the ball to come to you. Now, Haynes was making the ball come to him and getting into a better position than anyone else to receive the ball. He was dictating the play.

It made perfect sense when I thought about it, but Johnny Haynes had thought about it before anyone else, and was doing it in front of me. To do it successfully, you needed knowledge, positional sense and top-class distribution. Haynes had those qualities.

But I wasn't the only one who was deeply impressed by Haynes on that night. Apparently, Jimmy Murphy was also at Maine Road, because at the United training ground the next morning, I overheard him saying that Haynes' performance was one of the best he had ever seen from an inside-forward.

I had great respect for Jimmy's judgement, and it confirmed my opinion. Haynes was unique in what he was doing. And what he was doing was right.

Tommy Trinder, the comedian, who was also chairman of Fulham, had declared that he would have paid Johnny Haynes £100 a week if he could, but sadly he couldn't, because of the maximum wage rule. It probably never crossed Trinder's mind, as he made his bold statement, that he would get the opportunity to pay Johnny Haynes all that money – and a lot sooner than he thought.

Another Fulham player, Jimmy Hill, was becoming the figure-head for the Players' Union which, at the start of the 1960s, was pushing for change. It was happening everywhere else in society, maybe it could happen for footballers too. Around this time – let's call it Water Pistol Time – I attended meetings of the Players' Union, something that I had never done before, something that hardly anyone had ever done before. But now the meetings were packed.

In Manchester, we would go to Belle Vue, where on a happier night I would get to see Frankie Laine in concert, singing 'I Believe' and 'Cool Water'. It had been the custom that the maximum wage would go up every so often, entirely at the discretion of the Football League. It had gone from £12, to £15, to the present £20 which you would automatically get if you were a first-team regular (and which would go down to £12. 10 shillings if Johnny Watts put you out of the picture for a while). Now, there was much talk that it was about to rise to £30, which would have been very decent money at that time.

But the top brass of the Football League met and decided to put a stop to this dangerous talk. It was announced that not only would the maximum wage not be going up to £30, it wouldn't be going up at all. This finally stirred the players, including myself, to start going to the meetings, and even to talk seriously of going on strike. Clearly the bosses were starting to get worried about this, but there was another thing that they were even more worried about, and that was the George Eastham case which was also going on at that time.

The case involved something even more fundamental than the players' wages. It was about freedom of contract. George, then at Newcastle United, was the guinea pig for the union's effort to challenge what was called the Retain and Transfer system – basically it meant that when you signed for a club at seventeen, you signed for life, with the club entitled to 'retain' or 'transfer' you whenever they liked. It was totally immoral, and, as it turned out, illegal, because the judge in the Eastham case crucified the FA, speaking of slave labour and the like.

But in a clever manoeuvre on their part, Newcastle sold Eastham to Arsenal before the judgment was given, deflecting attention from the idea that players should have this freedom of contract, this thing that the FA feared more than the maximum wage. The Eastham judgment, combined with the threat of a strike, meant that the maximum wage was abolished. Tommy Trinder was given what he claimed was his dearest wish – he could now pay Johnny Haynes £100 a week.

The players, on learning this, thought they were in heaven. And you didn't hear much about freedom of contract after that. The thing that the FA feared the most, never happened. The slave labour which had been condemned by the judge as an affront to humanity still existed, but in a better paid form. Not that I want to be critical of the players. No matter how much haggling

goes on over money, then as now, no matter how much we find
ourselves talking about how many pounds a week we were getting
in 1958 or whatever, there is still a sort of innocence about footballers. Most of these guys were just like me, trying to make their
dreams come true. And trying – not very successfully at times –
not to get swallowed up by the reality while they were at it.

You only had to look at the shocking treatment of some of
the great players of earlier times – Wilf Mannion, Raich Carter,
Joe Mercer – to realise that their unworldliness was ruthlessly
exploited by horrible people. Even today, I don't begrudge the
players anything they're getting, partly because I can't think who
is supposed to be more deserving of all these rewards – the
chairmen and chief executives? And because, basically, I like footballers. I like that quality of innocence, which enables them to
give expression to their talent, but which also leaves them vulnerable to the bad lads who will always be knocking around.

I have known players who can look back and feel satisfied
that they got the most out of it, in every sense, but I have also
known players who lacked that awareness, who, in many ways,
had no idea what had happened to them. They played instinct-
ively, without really understanding how they did it, so they
couldn't pass on that knowledge. Nor did they realise how
cynically the clubs regarded them, how their dreams left them
open to exploitation. So you had to try to stand up for yourself, or you might be left with nothing but your dreams, or the
bitter memory of them.

Matt Busby had slipped up a bit too. It wasn't just Tommy
Trinder who used to make rash statements about the maximum
wage. Matt used to say the same, 'It's ridiculous, you lads should
be on £100 a week.' A man can promise whatever he wants,
when he knows he can't do it. But now, with the maximum wage
abolished, Matt could do it.

Unfortunately, something must have happened in the meantime to lower his valuation of the players, because Matt's first

offer was a basic £25 a week, and an extra fiver for appearance money. Such was his reputation that, when we first received that offer, we believed it must be all right if Matt said it was. But really we weren't happy with it, so some senior players complained to him and it was increased to £30 a week, with £10 appearance money. We heard that Liverpool players had been given the same paltry increase, and it was only later that it became known that Busby and Shankly had colluded to keep the wages down.

Both men had come from a poor mining area in Scotland where football was an escape from a harsh environment. Maybe they thought that to escape was enough, without wanting money as well. They saw how horribly the greatest players of their gener-ation had been treated, and yet as managers – and great managers too – they were as exploitative as those who had exploited them. The Liverpool players of that time are now well aware that Shankly and Matt got together to pay us and them as little as they possibly could – like Matt, Shankly would always favour the men who paid him, over the men who played for him. But like the old United lads, the Liverpool players never mention this when they're reminiscing about what a character Shanks was.

Back then, we didn't know what the going rate was, but we would be sent our contract, so we could compare it with the contracts of players we knew at other clubs, on a you-show-me-yours-and-I'll show-you-mine basis. Eventually, I showed Charlie Hurley mine, and Charlie showed me his, which is how I learned that Charlie had been offered £60 a week, and he thought that was unsatisfac-tory. And Charlie, though a very good player and the captain of his side, was playing for Sunderland in the Second Division.

I would later have a meeting with Matt to get an increase, but it was more of a protest than a genuine effort. Matt started by saying that he felt the club was being generous in giving us a £5 increase on the previous year's basic wage, which was now £35. I didn't think it was generous at all. I told him that most of my colleagues on the Irish team were on far more.

'You will find that they are the exception at their clubs,' he said.

'But this is Manchester United,' I replied. 'We should all be considered exceptional players.'

Matt had exceptional powers of self-control and he seldom lost his temper, but you could always tell when he was annoyed. His bright blue eyes used to shine even brighter – and now they were shining like diamonds. I left his office without signing a contract. All of which may have led to the claim that I left Old Trafford because of a row with Matt Busby over a fiver. I have read other accounts over the years, but the one about Matt Busby and the fiver has been the most popular. There was an awful lot more to it than that.

I could trace it back to a flu bug that I picked up in January 1962, shortly before the third round of the FA Cup. With Jimmy Sheils gone to Southend, I had actually moved in with the Stiles family in Collyhurst. Even in the early 1960s it did not seem strange for two Manchester United players to be sleeping in the same little room in a council house with an outside toilet. In fact, given the warmth of the Stiles family and the greatness of Mrs Stiles' cooking, I considered myself to be blessed with my new arrangements. And I still do.

But even breakfast, dinner and tea cooked by Mrs Stiles were not enough to protect me from the flu virus. They called a doctor who came to the house, and said I should certainly not play in the cup match against Bolton at Old Trafford the following day. But even though the club was informed, I was still told to report at the usual time.

Nobody on the staff asked me how I felt, and I had been picked to play. I didn't play very well even though we won 1–0. And I continued to play regularly, all the time feeling that I'd never had the chance to recover fully from the effects of that virus.

Our league form was modest, but we reached the semi-final of the FA Cup against Spurs at Hillsborough, and I believe that this is where the real damage was done. A game against Spurs had marked the beginning of my first-team career, and now another would mark the beginning of the end. It was that great Spurs team and they best us 3–1. I had a nightmare. I hardly put a foot right all afternoon. I believe that Matt Busby and his staff formed a view of me that day, and I was stuck with it. They thought that I couldn't handle the big occasion.

The only thing I can say in my defence is that I was twenty-one, playing against experienced players like Mackay and Blanchflower in the middle and, in retrospect, I expected too much of myself. There was no communication with me at all after the game. I had been at the club for five years, had come through the youth team and the reserves, and I believe what I needed most at the time was help and advice. But all I got were sarcastic remarks from Wilf McGuinness. Because of injury, he had retired early from football as well as from water-pistol shooting, and was now on the coaching staff. He told me, in front of a full dressing room, that I was being moved back to the right-wing and that after my performance in the semi-final, I was lucky to be in the side at all.

I tried to put it behind me during the summer, another of those breaks in Dublin which did so much to revive me in body and spirit, with Anne and me now going out together seriously, and all the usual carry-on at the golf in Donabate, along with the healing powers of my mother's meals.

But when I got back, the situation was getting darker for me. United had signed Denis Law that summer from Torino, for a new British record of £115,000. As a spectator, I had seen him for the first time years before playing for Huddersfield Town's youth team against Manchester United, and he was outstanding, a force of nature. Although he started out as a midfielder, he

tion shall be cancelled by this Association where necessary. Agreements between Clubs and Players shall contain a clause showing the provision made for dealing with such disputes and for the cancelling of the Agreements and Registrations by this Association. Clubs not belonging to any League or Combination before referred to may, upon obtaining the approval of this Association, make similar regulations. Such regulations to provide for a right of appeal by either party to the County Association, or to this Association.

13.   In the event of the Club failing to fulfil the terms and conditions of this Agreement the Player may, on giving fourteen days notice to the Club, terminate this Agreement such notice to be in writing. The Player must forward a copy of the notice to The Football Association and the Club shall have the right of appeal within seven days to The Football Association, which may either dismiss such appeal, or allow the same, and, if so, on such terms and conditions as it may think fit.

14.   The following special provisions laid down by the Competitions in which the Player will compete are accepted by and will be observed by the Player :—

(1) It is hereby agreed by the player that if he shall at any time be absent from his duties by reason of sickness or injury be shall, during such absence, be entitled to receive only the difference between his full weekly wages, and the amount he receives as benefit under the National Insurance Act, 1946, or The National Insurance (Industrial Injuries) Act, 1946, and for the purpose of this Clause his wages shall be deemed to accrue from day to day.

(2) If at any time during the period of this Agreement the wages herein agreed to be paid shall be in excess of the wages permitted to be paid by the Club to the player in accordance with the Regulations of the Football League, the wages to be paid to the player shall be the amount the Club is entitled to pay by League Regulations in force from time to time, and this Agreement shall be read and construed as if it were varied accordingly.

(3) The player agrees that he will not without the written permission of the Club grant interviews to nor write articles for or disseminate any information (acquired in the course of his employment by the Club) to newspapers or other publications nor take part in television or radio programmes.

15.   Basic Wages.
      £30.0.0 per week from 1st July, 1962 to 30th June, 1963.

      £   per week from   to
      £   per week from   to
      £   per week from   to
      £   per week from   to
      £   per week from   to
      £   per week from   to

16.   Other financial provisions :—
      (Fill in as required.)
1.   When playing in the First Team the player to receive:-
     (a) Appearance Money of £10.0.0. per match.
     (b) Additional wages of £1.0.0. for every 1,000 spectators between
         34,000 and 40,000 and £2.0.0. for every 1,000 spectators above
         40,000 for all home matches.
     (c) Additional wages of 4/- per 1,000 spectators over 30,000 for
         all away matches.
2.   A regular First Team player unable to play through injury will receive
     his wages, Appearance Money and half of any attendance bonus paid to
     members of the team under the above scheme.
3.   When playing in the Central League Team the player to receive:-
     (a) Additional wages of 10/- for every 1,000 spectators between 4,000

In 1961, the Football League abolished the maximum wage. Prior to this, a player's potential earnings were fairly paltry, no more than £20 a week, and the maximum contract length was one year. By 1962, contracts were becoming fairer and players could begin to earn a decent living – I negotiated that contract for almost three times more than what I'd been on in 1959.

became one of the great strikers. He had a mixture of explosiveness, speed and coolness under pressure, and an ability to get to 'impossible' balls in the penalty area. He had quicker reflexes than anyone I have ever seen, which meant that he could react before anyone else when a ball was driven across the box, or rebounded off the posts, or when the goalkeeper made mistakes. And if there was a simple pass available, Denis played it.

So it was getting a bit crowded at United, and I was now pushed permanently out to the wing. Clearly the arrival of outstanding players increases the competition for places, but it was also having an effect on team spirit. The culture of the club as I had known it was based on the idea that the players were almost like brothers, having grown up together in the youth and reserve teams. But in the years after Munich, the team became, of necessity, more 'cosmopolitan', with big-money signings such as Law, Quixall, Herd, Cantwell, Crerand and Setters. The side which started the season was an excellent side on paper, full of flair and experience. There was Dave Gaskell in goal, in place of the injured Harry Gregg; Shay Brennan, Tony Dunne, and captain Noel Cantwell at full-back; Nobby Stiles, Bill Foulkes and Maurice Setters forming a strong half-back line; and a forward line of myself, Quixall, Herd, Law and Charlton.

What could possibly go wrong?

But we'd got off to a disappointing start in the league that resulted in the players losing confidence – and directing their frustrations at each other. I could best describe it as a lack of togetherness. All teams have personality clashes of some kind, but if the spirit is right, they're able to put that aside when it matters. I probably only fully realised the lack of togetherness at Man United when I eventually went to Leeds United, but, even at the time, I knew that we were struggling to achieve a real sense of unity.

I thought I had started the 1962–1963 season pretty well, but as far as Matt was concerned everything I did was wrong. If I went inside the full-back, I should have gone outside; if I went outside, I should have gone inside. There still wasn't much communication with Matt, but such as it was, it tended towards the criticism that I was playing too many short balls on the right side of the field. In other words, he felt I wasn't opening up the game enough.

There was a bit of diversion from my troubles during the Big

Freeze, which brought the league and cup programmes to a halt in January and February. For match practice, United arranged to play a couple of games in Ireland. At a frosty Milltown in Dublin, we played Coventry City, managed by Jimmy Hill, who would get promotion from the Third Division that season – the match was a draw. And at a waterlogged Flower Lodge in Cork we beat Bolton Wanderers 2–0. I scored a good goal, going through the middle and chipping the keeper, with the large Irish crowd celebrating my continued success, one of their own doing so well for himself at United – if only they knew.

Matt seemed set in his belief that everything I did was wrong.

This and the increasingly sarcastic remarks from Wilf – 'see you had another stinker on Saturday!' – was about all the help I was getting.

I had come to hate Wilf McGuinness by this time. I hadn't always hated him – in fact, I liked him for a long time before that, and I got to like him again in later life – but during these years, I hated him, and I really should have gone to him and given him a punch on the fucking nose. He would say that he thought he was doing what needed to be done, letting me know where I stood with Matt, carrying the message down from above. And I realise now that I should have gone to Matt to sort things out, but I didn't and things got worse, contributing to an overall sense that I had fallen out of favour, and nothing would change that.

Around Easter, we were playing Leicester City at Old Trafford. I'd had a knock in training and went to Ted Dalton on the morning of the game. I was passed fit by the physio, but when I got to the ground I wasn't in the team – again, no communication.

The next day, we were playing Leicester again, as happened in the Easter programme in those days. At the ground before the trip to Filbert Street, Jack Crompton asked me if I was fit.

'I'm as fit today as I was yesterday,' I said.

This was reported to Matt and I heard he was angry. I was selected to travel to Leicester but I didn't play. We were having very poor results in the league, but mainly thanks to the brilliance of Denis Law, and Paddy Crerand, we had reached the semi-final of the FA Cup. Paddy had joined us in February, and would give outstanding service to Manchester United over the years. He was the sort of guy you'd want beside you in the trenches, as they say. Paddy had many qualities, but the one I admired the most was that he would never hide. Even if he was having a bad day, he would accept the ball and take responsibility. It is a quality that is not as common as people think it is.

By this stage, Nobby had come into the side at inside right, and Quixall (or 'Quicky') was playing on the right. So I was in and out of the team. I was originally left out of the cup semi-final against Southampton at Villa Park, but 'Quicky' pulled out with an injury on the Friday before the game, and I was recalled. A 1–0 win, with Law scoring again, took us to Wembley, but I still sensed that I would be left out for the next game four days later against Sheffield Wednesday. I was right.

Matt had his own way of dropping a player. He would call him to one side and ask him how he thought he was playing. And the player, trying to be modest, would usually say that he could probably do a bit better. Then Matt would say, 'I agree, so I'm giving you a rest for this match.'

On the morning of the Wednesday match, he called me to one side. I knew then he was going to leave me out, but I decided to beat him to the punchline. Before he could start the conversation, I asked him how he thought I had played against Southampton. 'I thought you played reasonably well,' he said.

'If I played reasonably well and we won the semi-final of the FA Cup, then I think I should be playing tonight,' I said.

He said it was a straight choice between myself and Quixall.

'I don't agree,' I said. 'Albert didn't play, and I think I should be playing tonight.'

Matt said nothing. He turned his back on me and walked away. I didn't play that night.

But I did play in the cup final.

I played because Nobby Stiles couldn't play, due to a hamstring injury he picked up during a match with Nottingham Forest the Monday before Wembley. Or rather he aggravated a hamstring injury he had been struggling with for a while. His own instinct was that the injury needed another few days' rest, but, at that time, when no substitutes were allowed, Matt felt it was essential for Nobby to prove his fitness on the Monday.

The injury flared up again, and Nobby was out. I knew if Nobby had been fit, he would have played instead of me, but, now, I would almost certainly be taking his place.

Not only was I staying with the Stiles family at the time, in the same room as Nobby, soon we would literally be one happy family, as Nobby was about to be married to my sister Kay. I had noted the stream of letters from Ireland coming to the house, addressed to him. Eventually, he sheepishly confessed that they were coming from Kay. They would be married in June of that year. Anne and I would be married in July, with both weddings taking place in the church on the Navan Road.

But in the run-up to the cup final, one of us was going to be disappointed.

I was about to play at Wembley against Leicester, because he couldn't.

The FA Cup final may have faded into virtual insignificance by 2010, but, in 1963, it was still a vast national occasion – a global occasion – and Nobby was devastated to miss it. Yet he knew that I wasn't picking the team, and there was no awkwardness whatsoever between us. He genuinely wished me well.

There would be another Irishman in the team too, at full-back, but it wouldn't be my pal Shay Brennan. It was Tony Dunne, who would become one of the best full-backs in the old First

Division over a ten-year period. In a team of extraordinary talents, the full-backs didn't get much of the credit, so Tony's contribution to the team's success is generally underestimated. But he was very hard to get past, very quick. And he was in the team for Wembley. But I was sad for Shay.

It was part of the elaborate ritual that we would spend three days before the final at a hotel in Weybridge in Surrey, playing golf and generally relaxing. On the Friday night, all the players congregated in the television lounge to see Noel Cantwell being interviewed on *Sportsview*. Cantwell was asked if there'd be any changes in the side against Leicester, to which he replied, 'Only one . . . Giles is outside-right and Quixall inside-right.'

This was the first I heard of it.

I asked Noel, 'Am I definitely playing outside-right?'

'Yes, didn't you know that?' he asked.

I didn't know that. I had assumed I'd be playing inside-right, as I had done in a few recent games. But then I wasn't getting much information about anything any more, from Matt Busby or Jimmy Murphy. Still, I would probably have expected to be told what position I was playing in the FA Cup final, before the presenter of *Sportsview* was told about it.

Traditionally, all the parents were invited to London for cup final weekend. So my father and mother came over. Dickie had been there for the finals of 1957 and 1958, but Kate had been out of Ireland only once before – they had spent their honeymoon in Blackpool.

It would become a tradition for me that whenever I got to play in the cup final, my father would get whatever tickets I had been allocated and distribute them to his pals. And then he'd say, 'If you have any spare ones, I could do with them'. It didn't seem to occur to him that you couldn't get 'spare ones' for a cup final unless you were prepared to do something very unusual or illegal.

My mother didn't go to Wembley. She went to see *The Sound*

of Music in the West End on the Friday night, and loved the whole thing, but she couldn't face Wembley. She had always been very nervous about watching me play, but she was particularly worried about Wembley, which had a history of bad injuries on the big days. Roy Dwight, now better known as Elton John's uncle, had broken his leg in the 1959 final, playing for Nottingham Forest against Luton Town. The following year Dave Whelan, who now owns the JJB chain and Wigan Athletic, broke his leg playing for Blackburn against Wolves. Bolton's Eric Bell was a passenger for much of the game with a torn hamstring in the famous Stanley Matthews final of 1953 and Bert Trautmann broke his neck playing for Manchester City against Birmingham City. Terrified by the 'Curse of Wembley', my mother gave me a Sacred Heart badge, which I put into the tie-ups for my socks.

I was trying to take a more rational approach. Despite all the unhappiness of the season, I was determined to enjoy this occasion, and to do well. Regardless of my diminishing status at the club, this was still every kid's dream, and my head was still full of images of Jackie Carey holding up the cup when United won it in 1948.

I might as well go out there and fizz it about, like Jackie. I might as well go out and play. I still had a lot of respect for Matt Busby, but I had taken his criticisms to heart, and I had been left confused and demoralised. I had had enough and, in an odd way, it liberated me from the tension of the occasion. I would just take the game on its merits, and do what I thought was right. So I was quite relaxed, considering it was Wembley with all the preliminaries and all the madness of an FA Cup final.

And I played really well – in fact, the whole team played well. We won 3–1, even though Leicester had been favourites. They had finished fourth in the league, and had good players like Frank McLintock, Mike Stringfellow, Davy Gibson and Gordon Banks. They had taken three points out of four from their last two games against us. But on the day, they favoured a cat-and-mouse approach which only gave our big players – Law, Crerand and Charlton – room to assert their natural superiority.

I was involved in two of the goals. For our second goal, I opened it up for Bobby to have a shot. Gordon Banks palmed it out and David Herd knocked it in.

Herd scored again after I sent in a high cross from the right, and Banks dropped it.

As we climbed the steps to receive the cup, I thought I had proved Matt wrong when he had seen me having a nightmare against Spurs and had felt that I couldn't handle the big occasion.

He didn't acknowledge that, or anything else about my performance, and I wasn't surprised. In fact, the only reaction I got was a very strange one a couple of weeks later, before a game against Roma when we were on tour. I went to the shower area, and I was surprised to see Matt and Jimmy Murphy there. When they saw me, Matt turned to Jimmy and said, 'And what about this fella in the cup final?'

I didn't take that as a compliment. I just turned away and walked out.

I didn't care.

On the way to the banquet in the Savoy Hotel with the cup, I was sitting next to Nobby, a bit embarrassed because, despite the win, I knew how disappointed he must have been. I remember hiding my medal so he couldn't see it, but he saw straight through me.

'Come on,' he said. 'Let's have a look at that piece of gold you've got in your pocket.'

I gave the medal to Nobby and he held it for a while. Then he smiled. 'I can't think of anyone I would rather see get it than you,' he said.

It remains my most cherished moment of the day.

There's a slightly less cherished moment from that weekend that remains with me. It was the Sunday morning, and we were relaxing in the park near the hotel, myself and Anne, my father and mother. My father was reading the papers, studying the match reports, all of which were full of Denis Law and Paddy Crerand, but hardly a mention of me.

He started brooding, in particular about this chance I'd missed early on. 'If you'd scored that goal . . . they would have had to mention you . . . imagine all the publicity you'd have got?'

I didn't give a damn. But he did.

I also have a very distinct memory of getting to the hotel after the match, seeing my mother, going over to her and giving her a hug. This was most unusual for me, and for her. Even when I'd be leaving home to go to Manchester, I'd say, 'See you, Ma', and that would be it. Neither of us was the hugging type, though she would later tell my sisters that she would like to have been more demonstrative in this way. It bothered her. It doesn't bother me.

'Have you been drinking?' she said, as I hugged her there in the foyer of the Savoy Hotel.

'No,' I said.

I didn't drink at the time, so I wasn't too sure myself where this hug was coming from.

Nor did I tell her what had happened to the Sacred Heart badge. During the game, as often happened at Wembley, I had got cramp, and had let my socks down. Later, I realised I had lost the badge, but she never found out about it. I let her presume that it was the Sacred Heart that had kept me out of harm's way.

We all went into the banquet to celebrate the winning of the cup and to enjoy the music of the Beverley Sisters. Not for the first time in my life, I knew that everything was about to change.

8

MATT BUSBY AND ME

RECENTLY, I spoke to Bill Foulkes about my departure from Old Trafford. He told me that the players were upset when I left.

'Kind of you to say so, Bill,' I said. 'But I don't really believe it.'

I believe that the only person at the club who expressed the belief that Matt was making a mistake at the time was Jack Crompton. As for the rest of the team, I was never that influential, never part of the inner circle of players like Noel Cantwell and Maurice Setters.

'The little boy with the man's head', is what one of them called me. Shay Brennan told me at the time that it was meant as a compliment, but I didn't take it that way.

Over the years, in different dressing rooms, I have seen how the manager's attitude to a player is reflected in the way that other players regard him. And Matt Busby's attitude to me, towards the end, certainly wasn't respectful. Which is why I replied to Bill Foulkes the way I did.

The club was never quite the same after Munich. The magic of the Busby Babes, with so many young players being brought up together in the club, had created its own special atmosphere. It felt fundamentally different to me in 1963. And yet, even in this new post-Munich world, Matt Busby would go on to create another great team.

He was – and let nobody be in any doubt about this – a great manager for the club. He just wasn't such a great manager for many of the individuals who played for him. He wasn't a great manager for me.

The end, when it came, was almost a formality.

At the start of the 1963–1964 season, I played in the side that was beaten 4–0 by Everton in the Charity Shield at Goodison Park. And when I was left out for the first league match of the season, I asked to go on the transfer list.

In football, when you ask for a transfer and the manager wants you to stay, he will do his best to talk you out if it. When he wants you to go, he'll tell you he's going to put your request before the directors. When I asked Matt for a transfer, he said, without any hesitation, 'I will put it to the board.'

The general perception that Matt wanted to get rid of me was only half-right because I wanted to leave as much as he wanted me to go. My old buddy Wilf McGuinness approached me in the car park after I asked to be placed on the transfer list.

'Go back up and see the boss. He might change his mind,' he said.

'He might,' I said, 'but I won't change mine.'

I was watching *The Time of our Lives* on Sky Sports, in which Jeff Stelling asked three United players – Alex Stepney, Denis Law and David Sadler, about Matt's main attributes. They all replied, 'His man-management.'

I couldn't agree less. He may have been a great man-manager for them, but he certainly wasn't for me. In fact, in my case he must have had a man-management bypass.

I now realise that management has many complexities, which helps to explain why none of the successful ones were alike. Bill Shankly and Matt, though they had such similar backgrounds, certainly weren't alike as managers. In fact Matt was considerably more worldly than Shankly, who would ideally have wanted the players to play for nothing, to be glad of the privilege of being able to play for Liverpool Football Club. Matt didn't quite believe that we were all like privates in the army who should know our place. In that respect, he was different to Shankly, who, in turn, was different to Stan Cullis at Wolves. Nor could you say that Brian Clough and Don Revie were kindred spirits.

They had unique gifts, which is probably why their success is so hard to replicate.

In the case of Busby, there were times when I and other players wondered what he actually did. Jimmy Murphy seemed to do all the important things, with his excellent knowledge of the game and the time he spent developing the young players. It was Jimmy who would tell Matt when he thought a player was ready for the first team.

Getting the right players into a club, players with ability, character, and the will to win, is the main ingredient for success. But Matt knew how to use that talent.

He believed in his players. He gave them the freedom to play, and he was extremely patient and brave.

For example, if we were winning 1–0 and were going for a second goal, but ended up drawing 1–1, Matt would not condemn us for pushing on. He would still encourage it. Yes, it might appear that Matt was doing little – but that was his genius.

He knew that it is better to say too little than too much. After a defeat, for example, it is easy and common for managers to lose their heads and to criticise their players. But you cannot take back what you have said in the heat of the moment, so the manager who has berated his players is then confronted with the problem of trying to build up their confidence again. In my time at United, I never, ever saw Matt lose control.

I saw his eyes shining like diamonds when I complained about my contact but, even then, I didn't see him lose control.

It seems that many of the negative things I have to say about
Matt Busby are related to money. But it's not really about
money. The money was just a good indicator of this weakness
in his character, his inability in matters not directly related to
football to strike a fair balance between the individual and the
institution.

It seemed that he could never err on the side of generosity.
When we won the FA Cup in 1963, there was a £200 bonus
for each player, based on the size of the crowd at Wembley.
Usually, players who had won the cup would also get a separate
bonus, something in the region of £1,000 per man. We appealed
to Matt for that bonus, but Matt informed us that there were
no such bonus agreements in our contracts. Of course, had he
wanted to, he could have put the bonus payments into the
following year's contracts, a practice which was common at the
time. He could easily have found a way, if he had wanted to,
but he didn't. Instead, he told us that the club would make a
gesture. The club would pay for the printing of the Players'
Brochure, a little handbook that the players themselves traditionally would bring out between the semi-final and the final,
with the proceeds going to the players' pool. The cost of the
printing was about £150 – when split between fifteen players, it
wasn't much of a gesture.

My own complaints at this stage were not really about money.
They were more of a token protest, and they were actually quite
juvenile. I was making them because I knew I was the last person
he wanted to listen to at that time on such matters. I should
have just asked for a transfer straight after the cup final – at this
stage, I was just using the bonus issue to annoy him.

All the time I was there, I felt that he didn't have to be
generous, but he could have been fair. Even when one of his
most loyal players was leaving, there was no fairness – even Nobby
Stiles, in the end, received the most shabby treatment.

If there was one man who personified the spirit of United

throughout the 1960s, it was Nobby. I saw Bobby Charlton on television one night, talking about 1968, when United won the European Cup. I heard him recalling how he had felt like coming off at half-time in the Bernabéu in the semi-final second leg against Real Madrid, with Madrid leading 3–0 on the night and 3–1 on aggregate. Bobby said that as far as he was concerned, the game was over. 'But Nobby kept saying to me and the other lads in the dressing room that we could do it,' Bobby recalled. 'He was convinced we could turn it around.'

Bobby was transformed on that night, listening to a team-mate who refused to be intimidated by a rampant opposition playing in front of their jubilant supporters. In that moment – and in so many other moments like it – Nobby Stiles proved that he was the moral core of the side, the one who drove the others on when the battle raged at its fiercest. And Matt knew that.

Yet it was all apparently forgotten when Nobby was eventually transferred to Middlesbrough. A fee of £20,000 had been agreed between the clubs but, considering the service he had given, United could have let him go on a free transfer, or, at worst, a considerably reduced fee which would then have given Nobby some scope to negotiate better terms for himself. But United took the full fee, giving Nobby no room to get a better deal.

Again I don't doubt that Matt did what was best for Manchester United. I am not criticising him on that basis. I am criticising him for what he did, as a football man, to other football men.

The terms on which Shay Brennan left, bordered on the farcical. Shay had joined United when he was fifteen and had been a great servant for fifteen years. When he was leaving Old Trafford, the club decided to buy him a pension instead of giving him a lump sum or a testimonial match, in order to save him from himself – Shay was known to enjoy a few beers and the occasional bet, and it was felt that he would certainly squander any lump sum.

So it was quite a sound idea to buy him a pension. Unfortunately, it was only £14 a week. Anyone privileged to be in Shay's company for any length of time would confirm that £14 would not have lasted the week and, much of the time, it would not have lasted the afternoon.

Publicly, most of the players of that time express no resentment towards Matt. Privately, it's a different matter.

I also believe that in many ways Jimmy Murphy was treated shabbily in the end, given the depth of his knowledge and his nurturing of the players. Jimmy made a contribution to the success of Manchester United that was arguably as great as that of Matt Busby himself. Yet when he retired, the Murphy family was said to be very unhappy with the settlement he received from the club, and the way he was treated overall.

It was breathtaking that Matt would allow such a thing to happen on his watch. But then he himself was destined to lose out in a big way, in his dealings with the institution that he cherished. It all went back to the early days, when Matt's priority at United was to get control of team affairs. This was no easy thing at the time, and it probably hasn't changed much to this day. Back then, the manager was not a significant figure and the culture was that the secretary and the directors picked the team. So Matt, like most football men, knew that if he was to succeed, he had to be in charge of all team matters.

As he became more powerful within the club, he knew it was essential to have a good working relationship with the chairman.

I believe that Matt encouraged Louis Edwards to become the majority shareholder in the club with this in mind. In this instance, Matt was thinking as a football man, rather than a businessman. If he had been thinking as a businessman, he might have made an effort to buy the shares himself. Over time, Louis Edwards' son Martin inherited the shares and eventually sold them for about £80 million. Meanwhile, Matt's son Sandy had opened the club shop and was apparently promised a place on the board by Louis Edwards. He sold the rights of the shop back to the club for a relatively small sum, and a pay-off for Matt which amounted to no more than a couple of weeks wages for one of United's stars of today. And Matt's son never got to sit on the board of Manchester United.

Once again at United, the football man had come out on the wrong side of the deal – though Matt would hardly have savoured the irony.

It may seem contradictory, that at one level I am saying that Matt Busby was one of the great managers in the history of the game, and at another level I am pointing out how poorly he treated so many of us. But I think this distinction can be made.

A lot of players don't talk fondly of their managers in one sense, but talk about them very fondly in another. John McGovern, for example, said that there was nothing he wouldn't do on the pitch for Brian Clough. 'I'd swim an ocean for him,' he said, 'but I wouldn't be going out for a drink with him afterwards.'

It seems that players are able to make this distinction a lot more easily than commentators.

In the crudest terms, it was put like this by a former Wolves player in Stan Cullis' highly successful team. Describing Cullis to me, he tried to find the words that would adequately convey the mixed feelings he had about the man. 'He was the biggest cunt I have ever met in my life,' he said. And then he added, with genuine warmth, 'Great manager though.'

In slightly more subtle terms, it's a bit like that odd distinction that my father made between the Stanley Matthews who played the game so brilliantly and the Stanley Matthews whose knowledge of the game was so poor. Both of these things were true, and I believe they give a sense of the man that is broader than the one-dimensional view which usually prevails.

So when all those old players are talking about what a great man Matt Busby was, they are telling the truth – up to a point. But like many of the great managers, like many of the great men indeed, there were great complexities in him too.

I was just a tiny blip in the overall legend of Matt Busby.

About six years after I had left, he said that letting me go was his biggest mistake. But it was the sort of mistake that any manager could make, in fact, it is a mistake I have made myself. In simple terms, I think he just took a turn against me. During that cup semi-final against Spurs, I let him down, and I let myself down in some fundamental way that made it impossible for him to see me again in a positive light. It happens.

It is not uncommon in the game for a manager to be unable to see any good in a player, even a player who is highly rated by others in the club. But there was a slight difference in my case, because I'd been there so long, and I'd already done enough to convince Matt that I deserved to be in the first team.

I believe that there was another way open to him, which would have been more beneficial to everyone. He should have got a hold of me and said something like, 'You've been at this club since you were fourteen. You had a very bad day out there, but I know enough about your character to know that you're not a bottler. You're only twenty-one, you can learn from this and get over it.'

The man himself may have run that line in his head a few times over the years, but he would also have known the futility of dwelling on it. He took a turn against me. And that was that.

In the context of his career in which he had won the FA Cup in 1948 and the league in 1952, with Jackie Carey as captain, and the famous forward line of Delaney, Morris, Rowley, Pearson and Mitten, he could be forgiven; in the context of a career in which he embarked on the marvellous and unique adventure that was the Busby Babes, who won the league twice and who would have won everything else too, he was entitled to a bad day at the office. And he also managed to win the European Cup without me. When he started out, Manchester United weren't even the biggest team in Manchester.

We did have one thing in common – an appreciation of the great players. That's what remains with me most from my seven years at Old Trafford, the great players I saw training up at Fallowfield during that beautiful summer when I was fourteen, and the great players who were my team-mates. I even played a couple of games with George Best just before I left. We played together twice in the reserves, and he did no more than all right in both games. By that Christmas, he was in the first team. By the end of the season, he was a superstar.

I now consider him to be the most talented player I've ever seen, with phenomenal levels of skill, balance, control and strength. He was blessed in all that, and cursed to be arriving at the time he did, a kid of seventeen with no protection, no mature advisor.

Despite all his achievements in the game, I don't think George ever reached his peak. He finished up as a serious player by the time he was 26 – normally the great players are at their mature best at around twenty-eight. Farther on down the line, we would have a brief and pretty ludicrous encounter, when Leeds played Manchester United in an FA Cup semi-final replay. This was an important game for both clubs, but particularly for Wilf McGuinness, who had succeeded Matt as manager. When we reached the ground, we heard that George had just been caught with a girl in his hotel room.

Even though I was a Leeds player, and it was to our advantage that he had caused disruption for his own team, I found the incident totally disrespectful to the club and to the game itself. And a few minutes into the game, I told George that as a professional he was a disgrace.

Today, I would view my reaction as totally absurd. And George seemed to be bit bamboozled by it too. He just looked at me and made a gesture with his thumb and fingers to show me that however much of a disgrace I thought he was, he was a lot richer than I'd ever be. He was missing the point I was making, which annoyed me even more. It wasn't about his wealth, it was about his unprofessional behaviour. So shortly after that, I tackled him so hard I ripped his socks and left him on the ground. He wasn't injured. He was as brave as he was bold, and afterwards we never spoke about it again, this outbreak of pure eejitry.

After retiring as players, we bumped into each other from time to time, and although we were never close, you didn't have to be close to George to detect the note of sadness that betrayed his laughter. To me, it was clear that he hadn't just given up on the game, in the end, he had given up on himself.

Leeds won that semi-final, which put more pressure on Wilf McGuinness. I didn't hate Wilf any more, I was just happy that it had all turned out well for me. I really think he had been trying to help me that day when he had caught up with me in the car park and had pleaded with me to go back up to Matt, to ask him to take my name off the transfer list.

He had really meant it. Wilf would have believed that nobody leaves Old Trafford and does well. And in fairness to him, he had a fair body of evidence to support that belief. But I had come out of that meeting with Matt Busby, with no desire to crawl back and ask for anything, least of all another chance. I didn't want anything any more, except to leave.

Anne and I had just got married, and there we were, on the move. As far as I was concerned at the time, Matt Busby had destroyed my dream. But he had done something for me as well, something for which I ought to be for ever grateful. He had given me another dream, another ambition that was burning already as I walked away from Manchester United.

He had given me an almost overwhelming urge to prove myself, and to prove him wrong.

I said it to Anne.

'I am going to haunt him.'

9

THE HUNGER

I WENT on the transfer list at Manchester United on the Tuesday and I signed for Leeds United on the Thursday. Matt told me that Leeds had come in for me and that the clubs had agreed terms.

'Don Revie's on his way to see you,' he said.

I had admired Don Revie as a player with Manchester City, and I was also aware of what he was doing at Leeds. They were in the Second Division but, the previous season, they'd had a great run from Christmas, and had finished strongly in fifth. When you're in the game, you keep an eye on these things. I'd heard that Blackburn were interested too, but I made the calculation that Leeds were a Second Division team on the way up, whereas Blackburn were a First Division team going nowhere.

Leeds had a lot of young players, but they also had Bobby Collins, who had been a great player at Celtic and Everton, a hero of mine since childhood. It sent out a strong signal to me, that these people knew what they were doing. And they had come in quickly for me with a bid of £33,000. It was a modest enough fee but after the demoralising time I'd had at United, I felt that if somebody wants me, they obviously rate me. Which was what I was looking for more than anything else at the time.

Matt was his charming self as he introduced me to Don Revie and the Leeds chairman Harry Reynolds in his office at Old Trafford. There was no bitterness on Matt's part. He told them

I was a good lad and he was generally relaxed about it all. Don later told me that Matt had happily accepted the Leeds deal rather than rival offers from Blackburn and Manchester City, because he had a policy of selling a player to the lesser club – that way the player was less likely to embarrass him.

There was nothing extravagant about the meeting. I went with Don Revie into a side room where he told me what he was trying to do at Leeds, and where he offered me a weekly wage which turned out to be twice what I had been getting at Old Trafford. I would now be in the £60-a-week bracket. We didn't haggle.

I went off on my own to have a think about it, which didn't take very long.

Any transfer is going to be a calculated gamble, but there were many reasons for me to feel optimistic about the move, from the enthusiasm of the manager, down to the simple fact that I had happy memories of Elland Road. I liked the ground. It was a nice big pitch on which I had played twice, and won both times, first in the Youth Cup and then on the Wednesday before my first-team debut against Spurs, when I scored a hat-trick for the reserves.

Don was delighted, all parties were apparently delighted. I learned that Don could have made a profit by selling me the next day. But he was taking a somewhat longer view.

It was a fresh start for me in every sense. Anne and I had not been married long. After our reception at the Central Hotel in Dublin, we had hired a Mini and driven around Ireland for a couple of weeks, down to Killarney and up along the west coast. There was no *Hello!* magazine at the time to buy the rights to our wedding, so that was at least one decision we didn't have to make. When we had got back to Manchester, at this time of uncertainty, we'd moved into a 'club house' on the King's Road in Stretford. All clubs had these houses, which were usually near the ground, for players who couldn't afford to buy their own house and who paid a small rent. Soon, we would be trying to buy our own house in Yorkshire.

Anne was completely supportive of the move to Leeds. But I still had to discuss the move with a certain party back in Dublin, who would have strong views on these matters. Actually, in a sign that his influence on my career was waning, I had made all the decisions before I contacted Dickie, who received my call at a neighbour's house.

'Are you sure you're doing the right thing?' he asked, understandably enough. After all, I was moving from the club of my dreams to some Second Division outfit in a place where they preferred rugby league.

'No,' I said, 'but I'm going to do it anyway.'

He didn't try to talk me out if it. It was a big move for me, but of course it was a big move for him too. And he handled it quite well.

I was learning how to handle a new Austin 1100. I had just passed my driving test, another piece of good timing, as I was now driving for hours every day between Manchester and Leeds. Back then, you had to drive through places like Oldham and Huddersfield, to get across the Pennines. On days when the weather and the traffic were bad, I could be making an early start and then spending three to four hours altogether on the road. Which didn't help my football for a while. But I could live with it.

From the first day I arrived at Leeds, I could feel the camaraderie, the energy, the work ethic.

These guys were young, and they were bursting with ambition. Freddie Goodwin, the part-time cricketer whom I had first met at Fallowfield, was the only player I knew. Soon I would get to know the other players, people like Paul Reaney, Gary Sprake, Paul Madeley, Norman Hunter and Terry Cooper, who were too young to be known by anyone. But you only had to spend a few minutes with them to know that they were determined to change that.

After the lack of togetherness at United, I loved this atmosphere. I was only twenty-two, but as someone who had played in an FA Cup final and had come from such a big club, they tended to see me as a senior player. I liked that feeling too, the sense of responsibility it gave me. And we all saw Bobby Collins as a senior player, a professional of the very highest calibre as it turned out, a truly remarkable man.

We beat Bury in my first game at Elland Road. It was a strange experience for me, though, as the crowd was considerably smaller than what I was used to at Old Trafford, and the team played with a much more direct style than Matt Busby's side. At Manchester United, there was a very sophisticated style of play, in which I always got a good supply of ball to my feet. At Leeds, with less ball to feet, I wasn't making the sort of contribution I could. It would take me a while to get myself fully involved in games.

I realised I was in a new world when I went to my first Monday morning training session.

Over the years, the training facilities at Manchester United had improved greatly from the time that the socks were available in a big heap on a first-come-first-served basis, but even after all the modernisation at The Cliff, this Second Division outfit had a system that was just a bit better.

Don's attention to detail was extraordinary in any context, but by comparison to what I'd known, it was startling. I'd been accustomed for the previous seven years to a sort of a high-class law of the jungle in which some of the most talented players of their generation were put out there on the training ground and given their chance, and only the very best survived. At Leeds – and none of these players would object to me saying this – there just wasn't that level of talent. But there was this huge desire on the part of each player to get better, to work on his game. There was this fierce hunger in them.

And Don was always on the training ground, supervising, analysing, correcting whatever he felt was wrong on the Saturday. But everything he did was made so much easier by the presence of Bobby Collins. He set the standards for us in training, and on the pitch. Many times I would be in the dressing room with him when players were missing through injury or suspension, but regardless of the size of the challenge, Collins believed that we could and should win every match. He was the most inspiring captain, a true general. It is a cliché now that a midfield player is a 'general', but Collins really deserved the title.

During a match, his voice could be heard all over the pitch, shouting encouragement and advice, or cursing and cajoling anyone who wasn't performing.

He had been regarded as over-the-hill when Leeds bought him from Everton in 1962, as he was then thirty-one, and no longer able to command a regular first-team place at Goodison. Yet over the next three or four years, Collins was reborn, driving this Leeds team to the top of the game, being recalled by Scotland after a six-year absence and being voted Footballer of the Year.

Just in passing, it should also be noted that Collins was only five feet three inches tall, and weighed little more than ten stone. Like me, he had never considered himself 'too small', though he must have been tormented by that nonsense from an early age.

Also like me, I think he was lucky to arrive at Leeds at the time that he did. Leeds found something special in the resurgence of Bobby Collins but, by the same token, I think Bobby Collins found something special at Leeds. Instead of going into a decline at thirty-one, I think he was really stimulated by what Don Revie was trying to do, and he threw himself into it completely, recognising the commitment, the energy, the single-mindedness. In short, he rediscovered his love of the game.

I'm guessing that that's what happened for Bobby Collins.

I know that it happened for me.

*   *   *

Not that I didn't have a few low moments driving across the Yorkshire Moors through the fog and the snow in the winter of 1963, my nerves a-jangle by the time I parked the Austin 1100 outside the training ground. It would take about four months for us to find a house in Leeds, so it was a mistake in the first place not to stay in a hotel in the city during that time, rather than undertaking this horrible journey every day.

I wasn't just that I was tired by the time I reached Elland Road, it also meant that, in this early period, I was still a bit detached from the group. I wasn't in the thick of things. And, all things considered I wasn't playing well, which was a bit embarrassing.

I'd never believed in this 'settling-in' business, the idea that it might take you a while to play at your best when you moved to another club, but it seemed there was something to it after all. I've only had two moves in my career, to Leeds and later to West Brom and in both cases I needed this settling-in period.

Around Christmas, with Anne now pregnant, we eventually found a house in the Cookridge area of Leeds, a modest, detached, three-bedroomed house in a nice area that cost about £3,500 – an average amount to pay at the time. I was now a twenty-minute drive from the ground, which changed our lives greatly for the better. And we liked Leeds in general. It was more compact than Manchester. You could be out in the countryside in about fifteen minutes – though, in my case, a long walk in the fresh air is always more enjoyable if I can stop to hit a golf ball every so often.

While I was acclimatising, the team was getting on with it. They weren't going to adapt to me. They were top of the table after thirteen games with twenty points, followed by Sunderland, Swindon and Preston. Soon, the promotion race would develop into a three-way contest between Leeds, Sunderland and Preston – and that's the order in which the teams finished. Leeds only lost three matches all season and were promoted as champions.

Clearly, I had made a very sound decision after all, moving to rugby league country. There was a mixture of joy and relief, and there were high hopes. Now, I just needed to find my form, and make the contribution that I knew I could make. Don actually dropped me for a match late in the season, against Southampton at home. And I was quite relieved that he dropped me at the time. We both knew that I was struggling, but we also knew that I wasn't in the grip of some terminal decline.

I was back in the team for the next match, an important one away to Middlesbrough, which we won 3–1, and in which I scored. Otherwise, the young lads were doing it for Don. And probably the key man was a wonderfully talented kid from South Africa called Albert Johanesson, who scored fifteen goals in the campaign, a post-war club record for a winger. One of the first black players to play in England, he had amazing close control and he was exceptionally quick. He was also one of the most naturally fit players I have ever seen. During the cross-country runs in pre-season training, most of us would be gasping for breath and desperately longing for the finishing line to come. We would look ahead to see Albert 200 yards in front of us, running effortlessly and leaping to pull a leaf off an overhanging tree.

But I remember talking with him on the train journey back from Swansea the day we clinched promotion, when he asked me what it was like to play in the First Division on the big grounds. I told him how wonderful it was, and how much he'd enjoy it. But instead of looking forward to it, Albert seemed to be troubled by it all, terrified at the thought, a reaction that was entirely the opposite to what you might suppose. Albert stayed with the club for a few seasons after that, but he never touched those heights again, and gradually he drifted out of the game altogether.

He was also succumbing to alcoholism, which in turn led to a period of homelessness in Leeds and, ultimately, his sad death on the streets.

But no one could take away from Albert that one glorious year, when he played so brilliantly and did so much to send Leeds into the First Division, and when everything seemed possible. These young lads were all so full of promise, but there was an older lad who was also having a fine season.

Jack Charlton was twenty-seven, and had been at Leeds when Don Revie had arrived. Don's main task for the first couple of years was to weed out the players whom he felt he couldn't work with, and one of the first to be called into his office was Jack.

I would say that Don was the making of Jack, whose career had been going nowhere in a culture in which bad lads had become the dominant force. For example, players would be messing about in training in all the wrong ways. When weights would be put out for circuit training, a few of the lads would just dump them by the side of the pitch. Don had to sort them out.

The great managers create an environment in which good lads can flourish. Young players need role models, they need a Bobby Collins to show them how it's done. Guys like Norman Hunter, Terry Cooper and Gary Sprake were just nineteen, and Don wasn't going to have them picking up a lot of bad habits from a lot of bad lads.

Jack always had the potential to become the top player that he did, but it was Don who brought it out of him. At the age of twenty-seven, he was at the peak of his powers and when he had got a grip of himself, he started to make a big contribution.

Already, I could see that he was not like other men. Jack scored quite a few goals from corner kicks or set-pieces in general, probably more than most centre halves. But instead of running towards his team-mates to celebrate, or to the player who had sent over the perfectly flighted cross, Jack would just run straight back towards his own half, for all the world as if the goal was entirely his creation. You would think that he had crossed the ball to himself, and then somehow got on the end of the cross to head it in, that nobody else was involved in any part of it. Such independence of spirit would eventually see Jack becoming the proprietor of a sort of a hut at Elland Road that sold Leeds United hats and scarves and pennants and signed photographs and what we now call merchandise – he was still a player at the time, so the shop was run by his wife Pat, but Jack was able to see better than any of us the way that the commercial side of football was heading.

And yet despite that level of self-absorption, it was also clear, as you got to know him a bit better, that Jack was quick to forgive and forget, a really admirable quality. If I felt I was in the wrong after a row we'd had on the pitch, I'd apologise to him, and he'd look at me as if I had two heads, apparently unable to remember it.

Jack had a knee injury for a while that season, and was replaced at centre-half by Freddie Goodwin. In an accidental collision with John Charles at Cardiff, Freddie's leg was broken. The former Busby Babe and one of the friendliest faces at Fallowfield would not play at any serious level again.

His place, in turn, was taken by the nineteen-year-old Paul Madeley. At the time, I didn't think Paul was going to make it. He looked a bit cumbersome and he didn't dominate in the air as centre-halves were expected to do back then. But he worked harder than anyone I have seen in football, trimmed down and became a great athlete. In fact, his speed would become one of his more remarkable attributes. In time, we would discover that this bulky kid seemed to be blessed with an extra gear. When he was playing in midfield with myself and Billy Bremner, and we lost the ball, we would be running flat-out to get it back, and suddenly Paul would appear, go into overdrive and leave us in his slipstream. It would be hard for a newcomer to form a true opinion of Paul anyway, because he was so quiet and didn't show any emotion. We called him Mr Spock as he never seemed to get excited about anything. If he scored, there would be a small grin but no extravagant celebrations. He was another strong character with a mind of his own, in a side which was starting to feature a lot of players of that kind.

Indeed, when I eventually left Leeds, a lot of the lads who had been at the club when I'd started, were still there. In 1963, Madeley, Cooper, Reaney and Hunter had just come in to the first team, Eddie Gray and Peter Lorimer were a couple of years younger, as was Mick Bates. David Harvey was there all along. And so was Billy Bremner, who was twenty the year that I arrived, having made his debut at seventeen. Already I could see that Billy had great ability. He was a good distributor, had good close control, great drive and a fine shot on his right side. But like so many of these young players, he had something else too. He was an outstanding character, the most confident player I have ever played with. I never saw him show any nerves in the dressing room before a game. In fact, I'm certain be believed he was going to be the star of every game he played in.

And, many times, he was.

When I arrived, Terry Cooper was playing mostly on the left-wing. You could see he had a lot of ability but I thought he was just drifting along. He seemed to be content playing in the reserves and occasionally getting in to the first team. But I believe he came to a critical decision, a bit like Jack in his own way, to stop drifting and to dedicate himself to his profession. He became one of the outstanding players of his time.

Norman Hunter, on the other hand, had a tremendous attitude from the start – a truly great player.

In training sessions, he always showed enthusiasm. I was a good trainer myself and wouldn't stand any nonsense, but Norman was exemplary. He read the game exceptionally well, and was the best defender I ever played with. Faced by two, or even three attackers, he could frustrate them and buy time until team-mates could recover.

I shall address the Norman 'Bites Your Legs' issues, but, from the start, it was clear to me that he was much, much better than that. I knew if Norman was thirty or forty yards from me, with the ball on his left side, I would receive the ball straight to my feet. Don Revie adored him. When we'd have a golf day, Peter Lorimer and I would always play Don and Norman. In the dressing room on the day before the golf game, Don would say, 'Are we taking them on tomorrow, son?'

'Playing with your dad tomorrow, are we Norm?' we would mock when Don had left the room. Norman hated it.

I had never heard of Paul Reaney before I joined the club, but, in time, he would become an England player and a terrific full-back. He was one of the fittest, quickest and hardest players I've played with or against. Straight as a die, he would also become our money man. You could tell from way back that Reaney had that hunger, that he would get everything out of the game that he wanted. And that he would deserve everything he got.

Mick Bates became an understudy to myself and Billy, and is a good pal of mine to the present day. His career also provided a neat illustration of Don Revie's cleverness as a man-manager. A player like Mick was invaluable to the team and Don knew it. So he'd made sure that Mick never suffered financially from not being a fixture in the first eleven. He would be paid the same bonuses as those who played all the time. And even as an understudy, he would play about 200 games for the club.

Our push for promotion that year had also been greatly assisted by players such as Ian Lawson, Jim Storrie, Don Weston, Willie Bell and Alan Peacock, who scored many important goals in the campaign. There were others coming through, such as Jimmy Greenhoff, who went on to become an outstanding player for Man United, and Rod Belfitt, one of the young and enthusiastic players I'd met when I'd first arrived, a big strong brave lad who played more than 120 games for Leeds, before going to Ipswich and then Everton.

Among the ones who would eventually become household names for Leeds, Peter Lorimer and Eddie Gray were still too young to make their mark in that first year.

Gray had already suffered the injury which would torment him so much throughout his career. He injured a thigh muscle when he was fifteen, and then played when he shouldn't have, getting calcification in the muscle which then required an operation, which, in turn, led to further calcification problems. I don't think he ever fully recovered. But he probably loved the game more than any of us. And anyone who watched him play loved him, as he was highly intelligent and had immaculate control, seldom giving the ball away. His best position would probably have been midfield, but with Billy and myself already there, Eddie played on the left wing, where his brilliant control, skill, and balance would be seen to devastating effect at Wembley in the 1970 FA Cup final.

Peter Lorimer would ultimately play more than 520 games for the club, and score 250 goals. He appeared to have a more relaxed attitude than the others. Indeed, early in his career, some of us felt that he was a bit too philosophical after a defeat. Even before a match, his approach appeared casual. There was a rule that every player had to be in the dressing room an hour before kick-off. Peter would turn up on time, but would then disappear back to the players' lounge to watch the racing. About fifteen minutes before kick-off, he'd come back and slip into his gear before going out to perform.

But he would perform superbly. He got stuck with a cartoon image of being a one-dimensional hot-shot, but he was better than that. His distribution was brilliant. His crossing was as good as Beckham's and he got more goals. In time, I realised that his philosophical attitude – you play, you do your best and, win or lose, you get changed and life goes on – was the right attitude after all.

Terry Yorath was on the ground staff when I went to Leeds.

Like so many of these lads, he was a real worker, with good attitude. He told us later that he had been overawed and very nervous
when he came up to the first-team squad. I felt he had a very
good knowledge of the game, but couldn't always do what he
wanted on the pitch. But I rated him. In fact, many years later,
when I became a manager at Vancouver I would buy Terry from
Spurs, and make him captain. As his career at Leeds developed,
he deputised for Billy or myself, and was a major influence for
the good.

And there was Gary Sprake. Though still a teenager, Gary was
already established as the first-team goalkeeper when I arrived.
He was very talented and made a major contribution towards
getting us promoted. He played well for a few seasons after that,
but he was probably not as resilient a character as the others.
Famously, he would lose his nerve after making a few mistakes,
and he should have been left out of the team much earlier than
he was. His deputy David Harvey waited in the wings far too
long, becoming frustrated, and mystified that he wasn't getting
his chance.

Don would ultimately admit that he had a blind spot as far as
Sprakey was concerned, that he felt a sense of loyalty after all the
good things he'd done, and all we'd been through together. As
it turned out at various crucial moments, it was a misguided
loyalty. But then Don had cultivated these values of togetherness
at Leeds, and, for most of the time, it was a source of strength.
He had got these lads young, had taken control of them, and
made demands of them which would be to everyone's benefit.
In return for this extraordinary level of commitment on their
part, he would feel an extraordinary level of commitment to them.

And if you wanted to see the point of all this, you would need
to be with us when we played behind the Iron Curtain, somewhere in the wilds of East Germany, when we were on our own
out there. My God, the Leeds lads would stick together.

And on the toughest grounds in England, when the pressure

was at its most brutal, that spirit would never fail. As for my first impressions of Don Revie himself, one of the things which impressed me the most was how humble he was. He had been a top-class player himself, with the Manchester City team that had reached the FA Cup final in 1955 and won it the following year. He had played for England and been voted Footballer of the Year.

He had also brought something new to the game with the so-called Revie Plan, whereby he wore the number nine shirt but played in a more deep-lying role. At a time of very fixed positions, commentators were so struck by this change of plan, they named it after him.

I had admired him as a player for these reasons and for his good distribution of the ball, but Don Revie himself was extremely modest about his own playing career. There was also another Footballer of the Year on the staff, looking after the youths – and he would talk about himself even less than Don did.

Syd Owen had been a first-class player, an England international, captain of Luton Town's FA Cup final team and Footballer of the Year in 1959. He spoke only of football, but not about his own contribution to it.

In fact, he was a football fanatic in the pure sense, a man totally devoted to the game and a hard taskmaster with the young players. But he was hard on himself too. He saw no way to achieve things other than by utter dedication and work, work, work.

Les Cocker, who was more involved with the first team, was equally fanatical.

Les would take training, and work with injured players. He was very conscientious, painstaking, all these virtues that were the bedrock of what was to come. And Maurice Lindley, Don's assistant manager, worked mostly on the administrative side.

This wasn't Manchester United, where they had the pick of the young players from England, Ireland, Scotland and Wales.

This was a place where they had to go about it in a different way. This was a place where they started with a few hungry lads, and a lot of decent attitudes, and a set of values on which they would never compromise, and where they would create – I think it is fair to say – one of the best teams ever to play in the football league.

This was Leeds.

10

THE GOOD LADS AND THE BAD LADS

Bobby Charlton, Nobby Stiles and Shay Brennan came to watch Leeds's first home match in the First Division, an evening fixture against the reigning champions Liverpool. And they were very pleased with what they saw.

We beat this excellent Liverpool team, with players such as Ian St John, Roger Hunt, Ian Callaghan and Peter Thompson, 4–2. The United players regarded Liverpool as their main rivals for the title that season, so this was a good result for them. What they didn't realise was that Leeds would also beat Manchester United at Old Trafford, that Leeds and not Liverpool would become their main challengers that season – and that they would overcome the challenge of Leeds by winning the league on goal average.

I scored that night against Liverpool. I had reflected during the summer about how I had performed in the previous season and I concluded that it was no use getting into good positions on the wing if I wasn't getting the ball. So I thought I would move farther inside from the wing and become an extra midfield player. Already in the first game, away to Aston Villa, I was feeling more like the player Don had bought, than the one who had struggled in the previous campaign. We won that game too, 2–1, coming from a goal behind against a powerful Villa side.

I had also become a father that summer, when Anne gave birth to our first son, Michael.

I have been blessed in my marriage to Anne, who has always

been so understanding of the demands of professional football, on herself and the rest of the family. It can be a bizarre way of life, full of extremes which would not be encountered in most normal situations. I would be physically absent for days and nights, with the team staying at a hotel on the eve of matches. Even if the child was sick, I would have to get my sleep. And I would be absent in other ways for about twenty-four hours after a match, unable to sleep, my mind racing, still high on the adrenaline until about five o'clock the next day, when suddenly it would all drain away and I'd be on a downer.

I would have regarded myself as the most normal guy in the world. But Norman Hunter's wife Sue, who had a husband as obsessed with football as any man could be, said to me on a social occasion, 'You know what's wrong with you, John? You've got tunnel vision.' I was shocked and devastated, still thinking myself to be a fairly well-rounded individual.

So Anne's support and understanding has always been immensely important to me. In fact, the older I get, the more I realise just how lucky I was to marry Anne. Because I can still find myself being amazed that professional sportsmen don't automatically put their game first. I would look at Xabi Alonso missing an important Champions League match because his wife was giving birth and somewhere deep down I would find myself disapproving. I would see the cricketer Michael Vaughan leaving the field because his wife was giving birth, and I would think that this guy is in a very privileged position to be the captain of England, and you have to pay a price for that along the way. I suppose I'm old-fashioned. I still feel that if you want to achieve all you that you can in professional sport, you don't want to be too well rounded.

When Michael was born, one of the first bunches of flowers received by Anne was from a certain Don Revie. I was learning that he was very keen to create a homely atmosphere at the club – homely being a word I would never have associated with

Manchester United, but which was definitely the style at Leeds, and which I liked. Certainly, anything as important as a new baby would be greeted with flowers, and generally Don would take an interest in your family.

In fact, I think if he could have chosen your family for you, he would have done.

Because he had got hold of a lot of the players at an early age, when they would arrive at the club Christmas party with a new girlfriend, Don would feel free to make a judgement. He would be as subtle as you can be in that situation – 'she seems like a nice girl' – but the lads would be in no doubt that if Don's judgement was a positive one, they were now fully expected to settle down with this girl and to get married more or less immediately.

Most managers at the time, and probably to this day if the truth be told, would prefer their players to settle down and get married as soon as possible, hopefully to the right sort of girl. To have a young man with plenty of money and a certain amount of fame wandering around out there with no limits and no responsibilities, is something that causes much anxiety to managers. And for Don, who regarded some of these young men virtually as his own sons, the anxiety must have been almost unbearable.

So he wanted to cultivate a family atmosphere at the club, hence these Christmas parties, to which all the wives and girlfriends would be invited. It all might seem a bit corny now, but he did it. The directors would be invited too, and Don would be conscious of the need for us to behave ourselves in this environment. We would have a meeting at which Don would issue the final instructions to ensure that the evening would be a success: 'And don't forget . . . enjoy yourselves.'

In fact, it's hard to think of a member of your actual family who would give you the sort of attention that Don regarded as a routine part of his job. When I was away playing for Ireland, I would always receive a telegram from him, wishing me good luck, and reminding me of the words I should remember at all times in a game, 'Confidence and Concentration.'

When my father would come over from Dublin for a match, he would call around to the hotel we were staying in. Dickie would normally arrive early, and Don himself would be up early. So he'd see my father there and would immediately make him feel welcome, having a cup of tea with him until the rest of us arrived down. With the players he was literally 'hands-on', joining the other staff who would give us massages on a Thursday, when we would be recovering after a midweek match, easing our muscles and having hot baths. He would be available every minute of the day. There was nothing he would not do for you, for the good of the cause. He would personally go down to the Labour Exchange to get people to help him to put straw on the pitch, if the game on the following day was in jeopardy due to frost. He would be out there with the workers he had recruited, putting out the straw and then taking it up again. I suppose these days he would be called a control freak, but then he would probably say that it was his job to be a control freak, and that there was every indication that his approach was working very well.

It was only much later, when things had gone so badly wrong for him in the England job, that Don's style of management would be criticised, to the point of mockery. But at the time, as we became more successful, players in other clubs would be curious as to how we were doing it, as if there was some great mystery behind it. They would ask us what we had for our pre-match meals – was it steak or was it eggs – as if it made any bloody difference.

People would wonder if we had some secret formula. There would be articles about the carpet bowls and bingo we used to play in our hotel, as if there was some deeper meaning to it, other than the need to stop ourselves going mad with boredom in hotels.

In truth the pre-match meal, the carpet bowls or the bingo

in the hotel on the night before a match, were all completely irrelevant. They were just a way of passing the time and they meant nothing to us.

Hard work all week, good players, a good attitude, that is why we were winning games against Liverpool and Manchester United and Aston Villa, and challenging for the title in our first season in the First Division. There was really nothing more to it than that.

Hard work, good players, a good attitude – and a good manager. Make that a great manager.

We knocked Manchester United out of the FA Cup that year. And we knocked them out in the most painful way, in the semi-final replay, with a late, lucky goal. The first match at Hillsborough had been a bad-tempered goalless draw, one of those dreadful days in which you get every type of weather from hailstones to sunshine. The replay at the City Ground in Nottingham was a real cup match that was also scoreless until very late in the game.

Denis Law, most unusually for him, had missed a few chances, and we had hung in there. We were heading to extra-time until we were awarded a free kick near the halfway line. I took it, striking it deep into their penalty area. Billy Bremner, in attempting to get the ball back across the goal, misheaded it and somehow beat the goalkeeper Pat Dunne.

We probably didn't deserve it on the night, but it was sweet.

Nobby, the fiercest of competitors, was devastated to miss the cup final. And he wasn't happy either about the free kick from which we had scored. But he had some small consolation because of a pre-match agreement we had made – that the one who qualified for the final would give the other one his Wembley match bonus. We made the deal so that the loser on the night wouldn't be totally bereft and, if memory serves, I ended up giving him about £1,000. Not that this mattered a damn to him in the immediate aftermath of the defeat, and, in fact, his spirits weren't

greatly lifted either by a bit of very good news that had just
arrived. It was very good news too for Jack Charlton, because
both he and Nobby had been selected to play for England for
the first time. It seemed that Alf Ramsey knew his stuff, because
Jack was definitely the best centre-half in England at that time.
And for Nobby, that bleak, horrible night for him in Nottingham
started the process that would see him dancing in the sunshine
with the Jules Rimet Trophy.

I said that I would haunt Matt Busby. I hoped that that win
would be the first of many hauntings. I had already been back
at Old Trafford in the league, and had been made captain for
the day. Which wasn't actually Don's way of reminding Matt of
his error of judgement, it was more the custom of the time for
a player returning to his old club to be made honorary captain.
Apart from the strangeness of being back at Old Trafford in the
visitors' dressing room, I was very nervous about the day. With
a newly promoted club, there's always a danger that you'll over-
rate the opposition in the higher division. But after those early
wins against Villa and Liverpool, we felt that we belonged there,
and we were going very well by the time we went to Manchester
United. Still, this was a daunting proposition for me. There was
the elation of going back, but there was also the realisation that
we were in an untried situation, in a really big game against these
great players like Best, Charlton and Law.

We would find out something about ourselves against these
guys.

We were leading through a Bobby Collins goal when a thick
fog descended. With visibility close to zero, the referee took us
off the pitch. At Old Trafford, with the home team losing, we
were worried that the referee would give in to the pressure to call
it off and replay the match. But he stuck to his guns as the fog
started to lift and the match resumed. We hung on for a highly
significant 1–0 win. We would both finish the season on sixty-one

points, and Leeds would become the first team in the history of the league to get sixty or more points, without winning the title.

But we had a made a big statement.

There was another match in which both teams were taken off the pitch, a match between us and Everton at Goodison Park. And in the broader scheme of things, this would probably have a more lasting resonance. It was November 1964, and we had already gained a reputation as a tough squad, largely on the back of a report in the *FA News*, the association's official magazine, outlining the disciplinary records of all league clubs for the previous campaign. The headline-grabbing figures showed the number of times a club had had a player sent off, and it fingered Leeds as the biggest culprits.

There was only one problem with the report – it was totally misleading. It transpired that the report didn't just take in first-team matches, it also included the reserves and even the junior sides. Remarkably, for the club which had topped this table, we hadn't had one first-team player sent off the previous season, whereas Manchester United, for example, had had five players dismissed in the same period.

So the report was unfair and inaccurate, but the damage was done. The dog now had a bad name. I am not for a moment suggesting that we weren't well able to look after ourselves, as they say, but everywhere you went in that league, there were players who were well able to look after themselves. And to suggest that Leeds were somehow the exception, that we were uniquely aggressive, is not just obviously wrong as a matter of fact, in many cases it is bordering on the hilarious.

Yet Everton were clearly waiting for us on that day in November, to teach us a lesson.

They were an experienced side with a number of good, hard players, who were aware of our tough reputation and seemed determined to do unto us, what they thought we were going to do unto them.

And it would be no bother to them either, with the likes of Jimmy Gabriel, Sandy Brown, Denis Stevens and especially Johnny Morrissey in the side. But they underestimated our resolve. We would not be intimidated by anyone. From the kick-off, the crowd was hostile, as crowds were towards Leeds so many times, apparently feeling that we bad lads would be doing all these terrible things to their good lads.

But it was one of their good lads, Sandy Brown, who caused everything to erupt that day, when he tackled me from behind as I was dribbling towards goal. The two of us were on the ground with the referee in close attendance, when Sandy punched me. Even in those days when a lot of things were allowed, Sandy had to go.

I wasn't always innocent but, on this occasion, I was. The crowd didn't see it that way though. I was playing on the right-wing, close to the Everton supporters, and I received an education that day. They called me names I had never been called before, well beyond the regular 'pig' or 'bastard', and always with the word 'Irish' attached – and this in Liverpool, the most Irish of cities.

Their mood did not improve when we scored about ten minutes after the Brown incident. Then it boiled over just before half-time when Willie Bell and Derek Temple challenged for a ball in the air. There was a clash of heads and the two of them ended up on the ground. It was an accidental collision but the crowd saw Willie as the villain, again the bad lads from Leeds doing these terrible things to their good lads. It was the only time in my career I thought the supporters would invade the pitch. It was really scary. The referee obviously felt the fear too, and brought the teams off the field to allow the ugly mood of the crowd to subside. I believe it was the first time in the history of the English game at this level that a referee had taken this course of action. There was an appeal for calm over the tannoy and, after a ten-minute break, the crowd had calmed down enough for the match to resume, and, in fact, to be played without further goals or controversy.

If the Leeds dog had a bad name before coming to Goodison, it was now more or less established in the public mind that we were bad to the core, even though Sandy Brown had punched me, and in any fair-minded analysis he would be regarded as the aggressor.

Not that Sandy was the one we'd been worried about before the game.

Johnny Morrissey, a short, stocky lad, was not generally recognised as one of the 'hard men' of the game, but he was one of those players whom his fellow pros knew to avoid.

Big Jack in his autobiography recalled getting 'done' by Morrissey at Goodison. As Jack hobbled to the team coach afterwards, with his leg in plaster and using a walking stick, Morrissey was standing at the door smiling cynically and asking, 'How's the leg then, big fella?' Jack told him he would get him back if it took him ten years, and he did get him back, but then Johnny got him back for that, and so it went until they finished playing.

I knew what to expect from Tommy Smith at Liverpool. Tommy would threaten to 'break your fucking back'. He wouldn't actually break your back, but a tackle from Tommy could send you flying through the air. It was the type of tackle that was there for everyone to see and it looked a lot worse than it actually was. But because of their technique and expertise at close quarters, I'd be less wary about a Tommy Smith special than an encounter with Morrissey, or Bertie Auld of Celtic. They were both excellent players, who had top-class control of the ball.

Auld would actually top my list of players to be avoided, just ahead of Morrissey, though both were hugely influential players for their teams. Everton had signed Morrissey from Liverpool and, in his underrated way, he did much to help them win the league in 1970. But everywhere you looked at that time, there were hard men either of the recognised variety or the really dangerous ones who operated below the radar.

We had battles everywhere we played in those days. We were getting this bad reputation, and yet almost every team we played against had a few players who could really look after themselves.

The late George Heslop was the recognised hard man for Manchester City – but you always had to be on the lookout for a big centre-half. The players I would be even more keen to avoid were Mike Summerbee, Franny Lee and, perhaps more surprisingly, Tony Book. They were all terrific players, but, boy, could they look after themselves.

There was a saying about full-backs in those days that they 'could chip a good winger'. Usually in a contest between the full-back and the winger, the full-back would be aggressor, but the tables would often be turned in the case of Mike Summerbee, who could 'chip a good full-back'.

The same could be said of George Mulhall at Sunderland. George was another smashing player, a Scottish international who would always ensure that a trip to Roker Park would be a hard day's work. But I read an interview with him in *Backpass* magazine, in which he was talking about Leeds, saying that we had been a brilliant team and that we didn't have to do some of the things we did. I could only laugh and say, 'George, you didn't have to do some of the things you did either.' I could say the same to other Sunderland lads such as Johnny Crossan, Irishman Amby Fogarty, who would usually give you a tough time, and Len Ashurst, who, for some reason best known to himself, talked in a posh accent. After all these years, I can still hear him complaining to a referee after a free kick had been awarded against him, 'Referee, they are kicking me from pillar to fucking post.'

Sunderland, who had been promoted with us, had signed 'Slim Jim' Baxter from Rangers, which didn't do anything to lessen the bitterness of our rivalry. Jim was one of the most skilful players I have ever come up against, but, by time he got to Sunderland, he wasn't slim any more, and his expanding waistline was not exactly flattered by the Sunderland stripes. We descended into trading insults, and since Jim was a Scottish Protestant and I was an Irish Catholic, we didn't have to think too deeply to find a subject matter for our exchanges.

During one game, the ball broke loose between us, offering the perfect opportunity for me to catch the overweight Jim. I was confident and the odds favoured me. Jim buried me instead. 'Take that you little papist bastard,' he snarled, which taught me a painful lesson – never get too cocky.

Terry Paine of Southampton, my old adversary when he played for Hampshire Youths against Cheshire Youths, got too cocky one day at The Dell. Our trips to play Southampton were always interesting, with the intimidating prospect of facing tough, seasoned pros such as Denis Hollywood, John McGrath, Hughie Fisher and Jim Steele. But it was Terry Paine who attracted the most comment in the Leeds dressing room. He was a really skilful winger, small and compact, and the most frustrating of players because he was virtually impossible to catch. He would only go in to a tackle when he was hot favourite to come out on top. He frustrated Norman Hunter more than anyone else, until this match at The Dell when Terry was chasing the ball as it was going towards the touchline. Norman was tracking him and felt it was the ideal opportunity finally to catch him. But Terry was clever, and, instead of Norman catching him on the half-turn, Terry pushed the ball between Norman's legs. Terry was still sneering as he ran past him, but I was backing Norman up. Terry, in his moment of triumph, lost his natural wariness and didn't notice me, and I caught him with a heavy tackle. And as a delighted Norman passed him by, he ruffled Terry's head and said, 'That will teach you to nutmeg me, you little bastard.'

Terry had been caught at last. But be assured that Messrs Hollywood, McGrath, Fisher and Steele had noted the incident and were already planning some suitable retribution.

When Leeds visited Wolves, Bernard Shaw, the left-back, and Mike Bailey in midfield would let you know you were in a game. But the real threat was from the late Derek Dougan, or The Doug, the Northern Ireland international who had good control, was highly intelligent and could be very dangerous. I always thought that Dougan was one of the most underrated players who made the mistake of being a 'character' which distracted people from his exceptional abilities.

We'd always have a serious battle at Burnley, too. Andy Lochhead, the Scottish centre-forward, was big, rough and tough as granite. But the ones to whom I would pay special attention were Gordon Harris and Brian O'Neil; and the most dangerous of them all, John Connelly. They could really play, and they could dish it out.

Spurs at White Hart Lane was always a difficult game. Although they were regarded as glamorous, they had a few players in the 1960s who were, to put it mildly, aggressive.

The great Dave Mackay was there, and Cyril Knowles was a defender who really could chip a good winger. They also had Mike England, Jimmy Robertson and winger Cliff Jones, who was one of the great players of the era, and a major influence in Spurs' double-winning side – but no shrinking violet.

Steve Perryman as a young lad used to man-mark me in nearly every game we played together. I had a lot of respect for him. When he captained the Spurs cup-winning teams of 1981 and 1982, he had moved to right full-back, a position in which I think he should have been capped. He could give it and take it, but he never whinged. He never tried to get me booked or sent off, and he didn't feign injury.

Man-marking could be regarded as a compliment, but it was also a pain in the arse. And no one was more effective at it than Peter Storey of Arsenal. He was also a really good player, quick, could tackle and was as hard as nails. I think he would be a regular in the current England team in the 'holding' role which has now become fashionable. On the pitch, Peter didn't say a word, unlike Billy and myself who would conduct many verbal and psychological battles over the years. For example most players look for the respect of their opponents. Knowing this, Billy and I would go out of our way to be disrespectful. So when Bobby Gould, who himself wasn't shy or short of confidence, signed for Arsenal for £90,000, we would have a conversation within earshot of Bobby that went something like this.

'Hey wee man,' Billy would say. 'What about Arsenal paying ninety grand for this fucking clown?'

'I can't see it, Bill. Waste of fucking money.'

'Total waste,' Billy would agree.

Peter Storey was also a target. He had a sort of psychopathic stare, which came up in conversation after one of the papers reported that he and his wife had split up.

'Hey wee man, 'said Billy. 'What do you make of his missus leaving this mad fella?'

'Don't know, Bill. What do you think?'

'Just look at the mad eyes on that fucker. It's no wonder she fucking left him.'

Peter never said a word, but I knew as soon as he got half a chance, he would break Billy, or myself, in two. Peter and I lived by our own paradoxical code of conduct. We could kick each other but never feigned injury to have each other booked or sent off, and in fact it was part of the macho code of the time to pretend you hadn't been injured at all. You wouldn't give your opponent the satisfaction.

There's an almost absurd contrast here, with the present-day situation in which diving and feigning injury are presenting a genuine threat to the popularity of the game. A threat that may become even more apparent in the Premier League in the light of the general disillusionment among English football fans after another disappointment in the 2010 World Cup.

Clearly, the players have a responsibility here, with even an outstanding player like Steven Gerrard publicly suggesting that senior professionals at a Premier League team should have a word with one of their younger colleagues who dived to get a penalty. Shortly afterwards, playing for England, the same Steven Gerrard was awarded a penalty after an obvious dive.

Managers are also guilty. There was a perfect example when Robert Pirès was playing for Arsenal. He dribbled into the Portsmouth area at speed and knocked the ball past a defender who pulled out of his way. Pires threw his leg out sideways to make contact with his opponent and then fell to the ground. The referee gave a penalty. Arsène Wenger was asked about the incident and was non-committal, merely pointing out that the penalty was the referee's decision.

Shortly afterwards, Arsenal played Manchester United at Old Trafford, where Wayne Rooney got a disputed penalty after a tackle by Sol Campbell. This time, Wenger went crackers, accusing Rooney of diving. In passing, we should also mention another childish outburst at the same venue, when an Arsenal player was said to have thrown pizza at Ferguson. For all their rivalry, I can't imagine one of Matt Busby's players throwing his post-match meal at Bill Shankly and expecting to get away with it.

Wenger has been a great manager for Arsenal, but, like Ferguson, he appears to see only the diving of opponents, never that of his own players. Ferguson, one of the greatest managers of all time, even went so far as to try to convince us that Ronaldo wasn't a diver. Of all people, Ferguson is in a unique position to a show good example to younger managers and to the players. Instead, he plays 'mind games', trying to influence referees and making negative public comments about some of his fellow managers, behaviour which is thought by some to contribute to his success. No more than the diving culture, I don't believe his attitude does anything for him, or for the game.

Ferguson is a great manager because of his judgement of players, his creation of an environment in which good players can flourish, and his willingness to make brave decisions for the benefit of the club. Add to that his confidence, his enthusiasm, his drive and his man-management, and it seems to me that the famous mind-games are just an indulgence on his part, a waste of time.

Likewise José Mourinho was a brilliant coach for Chelsea, but he too just couldn't be kept away from this codology to which Ferguson and Wenger are seemingly addicted. Of all the divers and the feigners of injuries and the wavers of imaginary yellow and red cards, Didier Drogba would have to be one of the worst. Yet Mourinho never had a bad word to say about him, while wrongly accusing Stephen Hunt of intentionally injuring Petr Čech.

Mourinho didn't need to be doing any of that, but he did it anyway, caught up in this culture of mind-games which may even give a certain old-fashioned dignity to my struggles with Peter Storey in the 1970s. Whatever we were doing back then, we weren't faking it.

When the game was over, regardless of the result, we would shake hands and there would be no hard feelings. I hope that Peter had as much respect for me as I had for him.

I'm a lot older now, and hopefully a lot wiser. Looking back on those days, I realise I was a much different person, and that there were times when my behaviour left a lot to be desired.

But looking back too on that extraordinary collection of hard nuts and hatchet men, I would again insist that the idea that Leeds were somehow worse than all the rest, is not just amusing when the light catches it a certain way, it is laugh-out-loud funny.

And I haven't yet mentioned Chelsea, home of 'Chopper' Harris, John Dempsey and Eddie McCreadie. And, even then, the one I was most concerned about was Peter Osgood, who had good technique and excellent control of the ball, another top-class player who could really look after himself.

But it was a tackle from McCreadie in that first season in the top division, that changed everything for me. Until then, I had had a fairly innocent approach, certainly not cynical or aggressive, but I can remember the moment when I realised that that attitude just wouldn't work any more. We were playing at Chelsea, and McCreadie caught me with a bad, late tackle from behind. In fact, it was so late I had passed the ball to Norman Hunter and watched him take a shot at goal before I hit the ground. I sustained knee ligament damage, which kept me out for four weeks. As I was being stretchered off, I said to myself that I wasn't going to put up with this any more. I was twenty-four, married with a kid, and had responsibilities that I hadn't had before. Football was my living, and I felt I had to do whatever was needed to survive in the game. I just couldn't afford to be known as a soft touch.

As anyone can see from the old footage of those times, some of it quite terrifying, there was little or no protection from referees. And as a small, creative player, I was an obvious target. To change that perception, I had to get my retaliation in first. And I became good at it, recalling the words of an old American coach that you have to play with fire in your belly and ice in your head. I had been very nearly put out of the game for good by Johnny Watts, and it hadn't really changed my attitude. It took that tackle from Eddie McCreadie to make me get out there, and look after myself – like Peter Osgood did, like Mike Summerbee did, like Johnny Morrissey did – well okay, maybe not quite like Johnny.

And still the myth is more lurid than the reality. There's a story that has hung around for years, about a tackle I made, which supposedly ended the career of John Fitzpatrick of Manchester United.

Even Bobby Charlton gave it an airing in his autobiography, when he wrote that: 'John Fitzpatrick's career ended prematurely with a broken leg after a collision with John Giles.' I remember John as a young player at Manchester United before I left. I didn't know him personally, but he established himself in the first team a few years later. He was a good player, fiery, not short on confidence, and he knew how to deliver the verbals. His main contribution for United was to mark the likes of Alan Ball and myself out of the game. John would get stuck in, and he would get his assignment done by whatever means it took. He knew, as I did, the terms of engagement. If you give it, you have to take it.

I caught John on the half-turn with a bad tackle which was knee-high. Following treatment on the pitch, he finished the game. I did not break his leg.

His career was not finished that day. In fact, John played for a few more seasons. I later read in an article that he blamed Matt Busby for his premature retirement, because Busby had played him when he wasn't fully recovered from injury. And, in fact, John said recently in a newspaper article that if I was ever in his vicinity in Scotland, he would be delighted to share a bottle of wine with me. I would look forward to that.

I suppose the black-and-white myth will always be more attractive than the reality, which tends to be more complex, with shades of grey.

Even a man as intelligent as Ian St John was on Sky Sports a while back, reinforcing the myth of Leeds as the ultimate villains, presenting us as the cartoon baddies of that era. He was talking about this crucial season of 1964–1965, when we played Liverpool in the FA Cup final. They were the better team on the day, and though the game went into extra-time, they beat us well. But according to the Saint, Liverpool were aware of our colourful reputation, and they were ready for us. It is worth recalling that this was a Liverpool team that featured men such as Tommy Smith and Big Ron Yeats, and that the Saint himself was no shrinking violet. And yet he was making it sound like a western, in which the good Liverpool lads were forced against all their best instincts to take up arms against these bad Leeds lads who were on their way to shoot up the town.

I like Ian, and I respect him, and I hope that when I see him again we can laugh about this. And it was particularly strange, because I always felt there was a lot of mutual respect between Leeds and Liverpool. I can remember a lot of kicking-matches with various teams around that time, but I don't ever recall us having a kicking-match with Liverpool. And I have a pretty good memory for these things.

In a really tight match one day against Chelsea at Elland Road, down near one of the corner flags, and with our backs to the referee, I caught Eddie McCreadie with a late tackle. As he lay on the ground with a look of genuine surprise on his face, he said, 'What the hell was that for?'

I told him it was for doing my ligaments at Stamford Bridge, on that day back in 1964. McCreadie looked at me in total bewilderment.

It was 1972.

11

THAT MISTY SATURDAY AFTERNOON

IN 1965, there was a chance for me to qualify with the Republic of Ireland for the 1966 World Cup – at least, in theory, there was a chance.

I spent most of my career in football trying to reconcile the dream with the reality, at various levels, but, with the Republic, I was discovering that the reality would invariably win. And it would win virtually without a fight. By 1965, I had reluctantly begun to accept this as a fact of life.

My debut against Sweden at Dalymount had been one of the happiest days of my life, and it remains so. But when you're not yet nineteen, and you're getting your first cap in front of your home crowd, you're not really bothered about anything except the game. You're just trying to enjoy the occasion, and hoping that you can perform. You don't really care that you only found out about your selection because your pal went out and bought the *Mirror* that day, or that you're provided with a pair of shorts that go down below the knees.

The goal I scored on that day was not just a dream come true, it was better than any goal in any dream I had ever had. And yet by the time that the next international came around, against Chile a few months later, I was already waking up to the sheer strangeness of playing for Ireland at that time. My debut had been on a Sunday, and the team only met up on Sunday morning, so there was no training. The Chile match was a midweek fixture.

All the players who turned up had their own training gear from their clubs – there was none supplied by the FAI. So we'd be out at Milltown training in a variety of tracksuits and jerseys and shorts, here a bit of Sunderland, there a bit of Manchester United, over there a bit of Leeds.

Like most of the lads who were from Dublin, I would usually stay for the few nights with my family. This is how they ran things, when the Big Five was at the height of its power. With such a selection committee, even on the off-chance that they could pick the best players, it was impossible to have any real consistency in the selection. Even if they somehow managed to get it right, they would then sabotage the process by regularly changing the personnel on the committee – it almost goes without saying that none of these selectors had any meaningful professional experience that qualified them to pick a football team anyway.

Though it now seems completely mad, for a long time the Big Five was accepted as normal. Looking back, I feel that Jackie Carey, who was the 'manager' at the time, had the stature and the respect from his great playing career to try to change the system. He would have known how wrong it was when he didn't pick the team, but had to make the most of whoever was selected, leaving him at times in the Gresham on a Sunday morning, talking to players some of whom he had never met before, hoping they might be able to 'fizz it about'. Arthur Fitzsimons, the winger who was one of my boyhood heroes, recently showed me a letter that Jackie Carey had written to him before an international match in 1955.

It is poignant, written on the stationery of Blackburn Rovers, where Carey was the manager, containing sound instructions about the need for Arthur to help the full-back, and to play the simple ball and so forth. But it's very hard to coach by letter.

Eventually, it seemed that Jackie had become disillusioned with the Ireland job. His managerial career in the real world had gone into decline after a promising start at Blackburn. Indeed, he was supposedly sacked by the Everton chairman while they were sitting in a taxi, which has led to cries of 'taxi!' ever since, when a manager's position is being questioned on Merseyside.

So the FAI had ground him down until there wasn't much leadership coming from Jackie, and I quickly realised that there was no belief or confidence in the squad. It manifested itself at some stage during every international, but in particular when we played Spain in Seville in 1965, a qualifier for the 1966 World Cup. A mix-up in the draw had left only Spain and ourselves in a two-team group. So there was a play-off between us. And we actually beat them 1–0 in Dalymount, which meant that a draw or a win in the return leg in Seville would put us through.

In truth, we had no chance of getting a result in these circumstances. There was an inferiority complex in the dressing room, no inspiration from the manager and a hopeless atmosphere all round. After five minutes in Seville, there was an incident the like of which I have never seen before or since, and which astonishes me still. Ireland got an indirect free kick about twenty-five yards from the Spanish goal. The ball was pulled sideways to Mick McGrath who hit a great shot into the top corner of the Spanish net. We were on our way to Wembley, or Goodison, or Hillsborough or wherever the World Cup matches were going to be played.

Except we didn't celebrate the goal. Instead of leaping around and congratulating each other before getting back to the centre circle, we stood around stunned that we were actually ahead. It was as if we felt that we had no right to score against these guys. So muted was our response that the referee picked up on it, and started to assume that something must be wrong. Then the Spanish players also picked up on it, and ran to the referee to protest about the goal.

The referee disallowed it.

Twenty minutes later we scored again, and this time we were

able to celebrate with enough enthusiasm for the goal to stand. But we should have been two ahead at that stage.

We still didn't think we were entitled to anything but a beating from these aristocrats, and we duly lost the game 4–1. Afterwards, our lads were reflecting on the fact that Spain weren't really that good, that if we had done this, or if we had done that, it would be a different story. And, of course, they were right – Spain weren't brilliant, and if we had even had the confidence to claim our own perfectly good goal, we might have had a chance.

I detested this inferiority complex. I wasn't an eighteen-year-old kid in baggy shorts any more, I had played for Manchester United and now for Leeds, where they had no such complexes. I made a vow to myself that if I was ever the manager of the Irish team, whatever happened, we would never be beaten before we went out on the pitch, as we had been on that night in Seville.

But we were not out of the World Cup yet. Aggregate scores didn't count at the time, so ourselves and Spain had one win apiece, which meant there would be a play-off at a neutral venue, and the obvious place for the game was London. But out of this grew one of the darker legends of Irish football – a rumour which has never been denied – that the FAI came to a financial arrangement with the Spanish FA to play the game in Paris. The 'blazers' too had given up on us even before the game had started, and decided that, if nothing else, the FAI might as well make a few quid out of it. The choice of Paris gave a huge advantage to Spain. On the coach journey from the hotel to the ground, I sat beside the late Joe Haverty, and Joe was hopeful. 'As underdogs, we might have the French on our side,' he speculated.

By the time we got to the ground, all we could see were Spanish flags – no Irish flags, no French flags. We were on our own out there, whereas, for Spain, it was effectively a home game. And yet in the Irish dressing room in Paris, there was a better atmosphere than the one that had killed us in Seville. We knew that in that match, we had effectively gone two goals up, only one of which we claimed, so we didn't put them on a pedestal or fear them to the same extent.

Eamon Dunphy got his first cap for Ireland that night. He had moved from Manchester United to York, and was now at Millwall, and a good, skilful player who was now more experienced. We had Shay Brennan at right-back and Theo Foley in midfield, though Shay was much better in midfield than Theo, which, of course, the selection committee would not have known. But we were much more competitive in Paris, and when they went 1–0 ahead in the second half, Andy McEvoy had a good chance to equalise.

We lost the game on this occasion, but at least we had played. We were not aware until much later that we were only playing in Paris because the men in charge had sold us down the river. At the time, at Leeds, I was playing with a group of exceptional players, with a great manager who was picking and preparing the team in a highly professional way. In fact Don Revie, like most managers then and now, would have preferred if we never played any international football, because for him there was absolutely nothing to be gained from it, and potentially a lot to lose in terms of injuries, fatigue and bad practices in general which he had tried to eliminate at Leeds.

From this, I was coming into a situation where the draw would be made for a major tournament and the FAI would consider it a good draw or a bad draw depending on how much money might be made from the fixtures. The idea that we might actually qualify was too ludicrous to contemplate. It was nonsense. Nor was there any hope that this situation would change in the foreseeable future. Ireland has a proud tradition of producing great footballers and football men, and that tradition was being dishonoured at every turn. Weighing it all up, I didn't need much encouragement or excuse to miss a few matches. I am aware now – as I was then – of what an honour it is to play for your country, but I wouldn't be serving my country in any way by going along with this racket. I really didn't want to be a part of it.

For coming second in the league in the 1964–1965 season, Leeds qualified for the Fairs Cup, which is the rough equivalent of today's Europa League, but which was a lot harder to win. The second, third and fourth teams in the league qualified for it, making it more like the Champions League in terms of quality. And in the first game against Torino, there was another career-changing moment for me – in the most unhappy circumstances.

We beat Torino 2–1 in the first leg and drew 0–0 away to win the tie, but in Turin there was a nasty high tackle on Bobby Collins which broke his femur. Bobby would be out for the rest of the season. Although Don knew that I had played quite a few games in Bobby's role at Manchester United, strangely he opted for one of the younger lads, Rod Johnson, in that position for our next match against Sheffield Wednesday at Hillsborough.

I suppose I took it for granted that I would assume Bobby's role at some stage, so I was taken aback by this development. After a couple of games, I couldn't stand the frustration any more and I decided to talk to Don about it. When I had played regularly in that position for Manchester United I was only twenty-one. I had seen Johnny Haynes put on that extra-ordinary, even revolutionary, midfield display for Fulham at Maine Road, and had vowed to play in that way if I possibly could. But I recognise now that I was too young and inexperi-enced at the time to emulate what Haynes was doing. I had been neither mentally nor physically capable of doing what was needed in such a pivotal position. But having played on the wing at Leeds for almost two years, watching Bobby Collins who was such a fine exponent of the art of midfield play, I felt I had served my apprenticeship – and it was the best sort of appren-ticeship too, the type you receive almost without realising it, just absorbing it all by being close to a master.

I was about to explain all this to Don but, before I could speak, he told me he had already decided to play me in midfield for the following match.

'I will give you six matches and we'll review it after that,' he said.

The next match was against Northampton and we won 6–1. The team played magnificently. Then we won away at Stoke, and we won again.

We never got around to that six-match review.

We got to the semi-final of the Fairs Cup that year, but were beaten in a play-off by Real Zaragoza. The following year, we got to the final, where we were beaten by Dynamo Zagreb. The season after that we won the Fairs Cup, beating Ferencvaros in the final.

It almost seems too neat, too clear a progression. But even at the time, we had the distinct sense that we were getting better, that we were only going in one direction, that we really had something.

Europe was an education too. By playing the likes of Zagreb and Bologna and Zaragoza, we were competing against outstanding teams, and we had to cope with that, as well as adjusting to continental styles of refereeing. For example, we would assume that the home team would get any advantage that was going, and rather than whinging when this didn't happen, we realised we just had to be more careful in our defending. Europe was a huge adventure for us, and we had a hell of a run.

But perhaps the outstanding memory of that adventure for me was only partly related to the football. In 1967, we drew 1–1 with Valencia in the first leg in Leeds, and, two weeks later, faced the difficult second leg with what was considered a weakened team – injuries and illness meant that young and inexperienced players, such as Eddie Gray, Peter Lorimer and Terry Hibbitt, had to be drafted in. But I had another somewhat unrelated concern – our second child was due any day. So being out of the country for two days at this very advanced stage of the pregnancy could be regarded as unfortunate timing.

But Anne's timing was perfect. Just as we were waiting to go out on the pitch in Valencia, our much-loved club medic Doc Adams showed me a telegram. 'Baby Catherine born this afternoon'. I handed the telegram back to Doc Adams, feeling like I could conquer the world. After about twelve minutes I scored a cracker and we won 2–0 on the night.

Throughout this period in the mid-1960s, in Europe and at home, my football family was still evolving and maturing.

We finished second in the league again in 1965–1966, this time to Liverpool, and the following season we reached the semi-final of the FA Cup. And from then on, the line on the graph would keep going all the way up. In 1968, along with the Fairs Cup, we won the League Cup, our first major domestic trophy. And from then until 1974, we won more trophies than any other team, and were involved at the highest level every season.

Even though we became easily the most successful side of our time, we somehow got the reputation of being perennial runners-up. But, by then, we had already realised that almost everything we did at Leeds would be portrayed in the most negative light. Our nomination as the dirtiest team in the league, in the teeth of such fearsome competition on all sides, had taught us that.

Not that it wasn't factually accurate to say that we were runners-up in quite a few competitions. It might also be said of the golfer Jack Nicklaus that, as a matter of fact, he was a runner-up more often than anyone else. But then he also won more than anyone else, and that is the much more important fact.

You can only win if you are in contention, so if you finish second a few times, you're at least giving yourself a decent chance. In fact, almost anyone who wins a lot of things, also finishes second in a lot of things – because you can't win them all.

If I had ever doubted that I was in the right place, it was during this winning period that all doubt was removed.

On a misty Saturday afternoon a few weeks before Christmas, we played in front of a packed crowd at Elland Road against West Ham. All through the match, I had been getting the feeling that today, at last, I was realising that childhood dream, that vision I had seen in the picture they used for the Spot the Ball competition in the Sunday paper. I had already played a lot of games in the First Division for both Manchester United and Leeds, but none of them had given me this feeling, that I was actually stepping into that picture, living that dream.

Because in football, as in life, your dreams so rarely come true. Pros can become very cynical as well, broken down by too much reality, until the glory of scoring a goal and the roar of the crowd that they had dreamed about as kids, means nothing to them any more. And yet on that day, against West Ham, I could feel it all happening. The pitch was a bit greasy, just as I always imagined it to be. The atmosphere in the ground felt exactly as I imagined it would feel. But with about fifteen minutes to go, there was still one part of the vision that hadn't quite come alive. I hadn't scored with a perfect shot from twenty-five yards.

And then the ball came to me, about twenty-five yards out. I struck it with the outside of my right foot, catching it sweetly, a perfect contact which brought me back again to that first time I had ever kicked a ball, and knew I was kicking it the right way.

The ball flew into the net, a beautiful goal. And I remember thinking at that exact moment that this was what I had always been looking for, this feeling I had right now, on this misty Saturday afternoon. Even when I had come close to it on other days, there would be a couple of things that weren't quite right, or maybe just one thing – it might have been a windy day, for example, which made the ball come to me just a fraction wrong so that I blasted it over the bar. Only on this one day, did it all come true, exactly. Of course, there was one point of difference to the dream, the fact that I wasn't doing it for Manchester United at Old Trafford but for Leeds United at Elland Road.

Right now, that was probably the best part of all.

So there is the selfish thing, of being true to your own gift, and fulfilling the obligations you have to it. And there's the unselfish thing, whereby none of that matters if you're not doing it for the team. That goal against West Ham told me that the two things were working in harmony, as it should be.

We were getting stronger all round. When I took over in midfield, Mike O'Grady was signed from Huddersfield to replace me on the wing. And later in this pivotal period, the signing of Mick Jones from Sheffield United for £100,000 would make us better again. Excellent in the air, quick and with good control, Mick Jones was a sensitive man who'd get a bit embarrassed if he missed a chance or two, but he became invaluable to the team, and was seriously underrated. The likes of Peter Lorimer, Eddie Gray, Terry Cooper, Rod Belfitt and Jimmy Greenhoff were now coming through to the first team. Jimmy was an outstanding young wing-half when I joined Leeds, and was later converted to centre-forward where he would eventually go on to have a fine career with Manchester United due to his intelligence, quickness and first-class technique. For now, he was coming through with the other Leeds lads to replace stalwarts such as Don Weston, Jim Storrie, Ian Lawson, Alan Peacock and Willie Bell.

But though I was revelling in the role I had always wanted, it almost went horribly wrong. We were in pre-season training for the 1967–1968 season – a bit like the pre-season training of today, very tough, but with a lot less water. Indeed in passing, it should be noted that I would refuse any offers of water and wear a sweater over my shirt even on the hottest days, because I thought the whole idea of pre-season training was to punish yourself, to deprive yourself of all life's comforts so that you would feel the benefits all the more during the season.

But the problem in this pre-season for me was not thirst. It was a bit more deep-seated than that – in fact it was so deep-seated, it went all the way back to Ormond Square. I had suffered a back injury, and as is often the case with back injuries, it was hard to diagnose the true nature of the problem. Even though I could run – I could even sprint – I could feel something was wrong. I wasn't comfortable when I was playing, because my movement was restricted. And there didn't seem to be any end to it.

This was the most worrying part, the idea that I'd be carrying this injury indefinitely.

I had been to see the club specialist and he recommended a course of treatment but that brought no improvement. The medics can be very territorial, at Leeds as much as anywhere else, so they wouldn't have approved of me going outside their juris-diction for another opinion. However, at this stage, I was getting desperate. I wasn't playing at all. So I went to Don and suggested that I find my own specialist. I was also conscious of the fact that I was getting paid every week without playing, even suspecting that there were some who doubted the extent of my injury. So, to remove any doubts, I proposed that my wages be stopped.

Don was appalled at this suggestion, but he was open to the idea of seeking another opinion. He too had suffered with a bad back during his playing days at Manchester City, and he had continued to see a specialist, Mr Sidney Rose, who was, incidentally, a director of City.

So I went to Manchester to see Mr Rose, a small man with narrow features who stays in my mind as an enormously digni-fied person. He was always immaculately dressed, and had the manner of a professor, who measured every word he said. When he had looked at some X-rays, Mr Rose asked me in that precise way of his if I had ever jumped off walls as a child. I told him that I would often climb and jump off the high wall at the back of our home in Ormond Square, in the belief that it would strengthen my legs for football. Mr Rose's intuition was inspired.

Apparently, the impact of all that jumping had flattened my hip-bones. And that's what was causing the problem.

But the genius of Mr Rose did not stop with the diagnosis. He also knew the cure.

He recommended that I take the baths at Harrogate, which were quite close to Leeds, but which I had always assumed were only for the elderly and the infirm. On his advice, I took the mud and peat baths on Mondays, Wednesdays and Fridays, and the brine baths on Tuesdays and Thursdays. He told me to do this for six weeks, and he ruled out any training in that period. After the six weeks, he had another look at me, and told me to continue with the same treatment for another four weeks and to keep my quads in top condition, so they could take the strain and therefore avoid further back problems for the rest of my career.

The treatment worked superbly. I couldn't wait to get back. The torment of being injured is not just the fact that you can't play, it's the fact that you are cast out of your dreamworld for a short time, or perhaps for a very long time, excluded from all that juvenile banter and camaraderie, forced to live outside of that bubble where you belong. My own horrible experiences with injuries, the dread and the loneliness of it, have made me very unforgiving of Bill Shankly, for his attitude to players in that predicament. Shankly was a great manager undoubtedly for Liverpool, but he was quite savage towards players who were injured, regarding them virtually as carriers of the plague. Again I can see old players on television recalling Shankly's cold attitude to them when they were injured, as if it was another example of what a gas character he was. It must be easier to see the funny side of it, forty years later.

Even forty-four years later, the football image from that time which will never lose its power is that of England winning the World Cup. I had reconciled myself to the fact that Ireland wouldn't be in it – and probably wouldn't be in any World Cup for a long time to come – but I always thought that England had a good chance in 1966.

From the time that Alf Ramsey took over in 1963, I thought he had usually picked the right players. Which is not everything in management, but it's a hell of a start. He gave good players like Mick Jones and Mike O'Grady a chance, but ultimately he ended up with what can only be described as the best players in England, the likes of George Cohen, Martin Peters and Alan Ball.

Alan was a hugely influential player. I first played against him when he was at Blackpool in 1964. They beat us 4–0 that night and Ball, who was only nineteen, was outstanding. We played them again the following week and beat them 3–0 at Elland Road. It was the beginning of a rivalry I always relished. In tight situations, Ball was one of the quickest-minded players I had ever played against, and his technique was excellent. Don Revie was very keen to sign Alan at that time, but since Billy Bremner and myself already occupied central midfield, the addition of Alan would have made it very difficult to get a proper balance in the middle of the field. He went on to Everton anyway, so the problem never had to be addressed.

Alf caused some controversy when he declared that Martin Peters was ten years ahead of his time, but it turned out he was right. In my opinion Martin was never an orthodox midfield player, but a goalscorer coming from a deep midfield position, the first of his type. His successors in that role would include David Platt, Tim Cahill, Frank Lampard and Steven Gerrard.

Bobby Moore was simply a great player. He began in the game as a wing half, which in today's terms would make him a midfield player. But he didn't quite have the mobility and pace for that position. When he moved back to centre-half, he was much more effective as he was playing with the game in front of him, and his brilliant technique and reading of the game compensated for his lack of pace. He was also a great distributor of the ball and he could initiate attacks from deep positions. The bigger the challenge, the better Bobby played.

Like Bobby, Geoff Hurst started out in midfield, and was playing in that position for West Ham when I played against him for Manchester United in a youth tournament in Switzerland. I thought he was good then, but when he converted to centre-forward he became one of the best strikers in the game.

Jimmy Greaves was unlucky. Greaves was a genius, the best finisher I have ever seen. He had that ability to make scoring a goal look like the easiest thing you could do in this life. He tended not to do much in the game, apart from finishing – not that this was an insignificant thing to do. But if the team was playing poorly, as England were for the first two games of the tournament, it could seem as if Greaves was doing nothing at all. And so Ramsey went with Roger Hunt for a change. Greaves was England's first choice striker for about ten years, he only missed a few weeks – and they just happened to be the biggest weeks in the football history of England. Unlucky.

But the 'wingless wonders' was pure calculation on Ramsey's part. There is a myth about the 'wingless wonders', based on the notion that Ramsey decided to leave out the wingers just for this tournament. In fact, it was an idea that had been forming in the game for several years. With full-backs becoming physically smaller and more mobile than the more cumbersome types of the 1950s, wingers weren't getting past them the way that they had done. Stanley Matthews hadn't been up against these quicker guys like George Cohen or Ray Wilson or my fellow Dubliner, Tony Dunne. So his successors on the wing, such as Ian Callaghan, Terry Paine, or John Connelly who were in the England World Cup squad, couldn't be as effective as the wizards of old.

It has also been largely forgotten that Connelly played against Uruguay, Paine played against Mexico and Callaghan played against France in the group stage. So Ramsey wasn't against wingers, as such. He just decided that he could use the all-round contribution of Alan Ball or Martin Peters more than he could use wingers who were finding it hard to get to the by-line. And he was right. It wasn't some major philosophical issue with him, he just wanted as much as he could get from the players at his disposal.

I remember that night at Nottingham when the news came through about Nobby and Jack Charlton, and it confirmed for me that Ramsey knew what he was doing. Nobby wouldn't have been a fashionable choice, but he was the right choice.

Ramsey was a bit of an oddball – aren't they all? – but his judgement of a player was excellent, and there was a strong work ethic. Les Cocker of Leeds, who was a team trainer, made sure of that.

I wasn't in contact with Nobby during the actual tournament, but it was still a joy to see the bespectacled lad who had started coming to our house in Dublin in the summer of 1958, whose place I had taken in the 1963 cup final and who had been so generous about it afterwards, brandishing the World Cup.

I couldn't think of anyone I'd rather see get it than him.

I had reason to speak highly of Alf Ramsey in another situation, in relation to the Mexico World Cup.

It came about when Paul Reaney broke his leg and Paul Madeley, who could play almost anywhere, replaced him at right-back. When Alf picked his original World Cup squad, Madeley wasn't included. I don't think Alf realised just how good Paul was in that position, simply because he played in so many other positions as well. When Paul was called into the squad, I congratulated him on his selection, but he told me he was thinking of not going to Mexico anyway.

I was surprised, up to a point – Paul always had a mind of his own.

He told me that if Alf hadn't believed he was good enough

to get into the original squad, he felt he'd have no chance of getting into the team. He thought it'd be a waste of three or four weeks to sit around in Mexico and not play for England.

I disagreed with him. I firmly believed that Alf knew his stuff, and that if he had had the opportunity to watch Paul at right-back in training or in a practice match, he would have seen what Paul could do, and he would make him first choice. Paul listened to me, but he had made up his mind. He didn't go to Mexico.

Whether it was the right decision or the wrong decision, who can tell? But you can only admire the strength of character of the man, for sticking to his football beliefs in such a difficult situation. And when you consider that we had a fair few like that in the dressing room at Leeds, you get a better sense of what was happening for us at that period in the mid-1960s, why we were doing well and starting to make a name for ourselves. And why we would keep doing it, when all the others had come and gone.

12

THE BEST TEAM DREW

ANOTHER CUP final, the same hotel in Weybridge in Surrey. The last time I had stayed there was with Manchester United, when I learned for the first time from Noel Cantwell on the BBC that I'd be playing on the wing in the 1963 FA Cup final.

This time, it was for the 1968 League Cup final against Arsenal. Early that morning outside my window, I could hear the sound of pounding feet. I got to the window just in time to see a lone figure in a blue tracksuit running across the lawn. It was Terry Cooper. Apparently, the Wembley nerves had kept him awake, and he felt that a thirty-minute run before breakfast would help him to relax.

Terry scored the only goal of the game that day. It was a poor game, and the goal was bitterly disputed. From an Eddie Gray corner, the Arsenal goalkeeper Jim Furnell was challenged by Jack Charlton and Paul Madeley. The ball bounced out to Cooper, who volleyed it first-time into the roof of the net. We had won our first trophy. In fact, it was the first major trophy Leeds United had ever won, a reminder that the club had no tradition of success, no history that might have created an aura around us. We had to create our own aura.

But we were hammered in the press for our 'dull method play' in the final – apparently Arsenal had played no part in making it a dull match – and for the challenge on the keeper which was supposedly against the spirit of the game. Of course, there was nothing in the rules to prevent Big Jack standing on the goalline, and when you consider that this is now a routine part of every corner kick, perhaps they should have been lauding us for our original thinking.

Jack had been 'going under the bar' for England too, but it was only when he did it for Leeds that it became an ugly development in the game.

There is probably a lot more awareness now of how the media can seize on a cliché, on a half-truth or just on an easy line, and turn it into common knowledge. Back then, there was no debate.

It had quickly become an accepted fact that Leeds were aligned in many ways to the dark side of football and to the dark arts in general, a notion that is still doing the rounds forty years later.

Certainly, we had our superstitions. And while this is a very human foible, which is not exclusive to Leeds United, for some reason our superstitions seemed to get more attention than anyone else's. Actually, before I ever came to Leeds I was superstitious about magpies. It had probably been passed on to me by my mother. Throughout my playing career, if I was driving to a match and I saw a magpie, I would feel the need to get out of the car and wait around in the hope that another magpie would arrive to join the 'one for sorrow' to make 'two for joy'.

But in the superstition stakes, I was in the halfpenny place next to Don.

The first day I went into his office, I had my boots in a brown paper bag, which I put on the table. We were talking for a while, when Don pointed to the bag and said, 'What's that?'

I told him it was my boots.

'Get those fucking things off the desk,' he shouted. Apparently, putting your shoes on a table is bad luck. On his own arrival at Leeds, he had heard that there was a gypsy's curse on Elland Road, so he'd brought in a medium to lift the curse.

But there was more, much more. He had his lucky blue suit and tie that he wore at matches. He would make a special point of rubbing Terry Cooper's back with Algipan whether Terry needed it or not, even on a hot day. And when he walked out onto the pitch, he was always on Les Cocker's left side. Even stranger, when we played in Liverpool, he'd leave the hotel, walk down to a certain set of traffic lights, touch the lights and then walk back to the hotel.

Our results at Elland Road had improved greatly after the 'curse' had been lifted, and, for some reason, we tended to do well in away games against both Liverpool and Everton, but then getting rid of all the bad lads at Leeds and doing your home-work on the opposition may also have had a small bit to do with it. And it wasn't some lady with connections to 'the other side' who had done that.

It seems contradictory, to be obsessed with facts and infor-mation and technical detail, while also being deeply superstitious – it seems to be both highly sophisticated and very primitive – but such contradictions are not a Leeds thing. They are just a human thing.

Jack Charlton would be widely regarded as a practical man who wouldn't be wasting his time venturing into the spirit world, and yet Jack himself has described his own range of superstitions and rituals at that time. He would always put on his left boot first, followed by his right boot, then his jock-strap and then his shorts. He would take a programme and go to the toilet for about four minutes, and he would always leave the programme on the left-hand side of the toilet before he went back to the dressing room. He wouldn't put his Leeds shirt on, until he was ready to go out on the pitch. And he liked to be the last one out. He acknowledged that this was getting ridiculous, because it took him more than an hour to get ready.

Gary Sprake would wrap his cap around a doll, and take both onto the field. Paul Reaney liked to kick a ball against Don's trouser leg. Billy Bremner, who adopted numerous idiosyncrasies over the years, at one point became quite well known for taking a bath in lukewarm water half an hour before the start of a match. Norman Hunter was the last to comb his hair, after he and Jack Charlton had headed the ball to each other ten times without it touching the ground. And while warming up on the pitch, we would always split into certain groups.

Indeed, as I look back, given the result we got in the League Cup final, I'm surprised that no one suggested to Cooper that he should have a run before breakfast every day – certainly every day we had a match at Wembley. But perhaps there's a more rational explanation for his goal too – maybe it had something to do with the fact that Terry Cooper was a superb footballer, who was capable of almost anything on a football field, and who could perform on the big occasion.

Football is a deeply insecure business, and perhaps we cling to our superstitions for comfort, knowing it could all be over for us tomorrow. In fact, it is unlike most other occupations in the sense that the more experience you have, the more insecure you feel. Because the older you get, the more vulnerable you are to accusations that you are past it. Whatever you did last week doesn't matter, and can actually be used against you, to demonstrate that you used to be much better. You are acutely aware that the crowd which hailed you as a hero may turn on you and torment you.

All of which helps to explain why a player or a manager may have all sorts of progressive ideas about the game, and still subscribe to various forms of ju-ju. Certainly, I could live with these contradictions quite easily. I might be getting out of my car to wait for a magpie to appear but, in other ways, my approach to the task was quite scientific.

For example, I was getting into what is now called 'visualisation' in order to improve my own game.

The routine at Leeds was to train on Monday, to play golf on Tuesday, and then to do light training on Wednesday, Thursday and Friday. On a typical day after one of the light sessions, I would come home in the afternoon and have a lunch of steak or bacon and eggs or fish – just good, plain food. I never had a sweet tooth, and I actually stayed at my fighting weight of ten stone two pounds for about twelve years. I seemed to have control of my weight to the extent that I would know exactly what caused an extra few ounces, perhaps too many slices of bread. After lunch, I would read for a while, usually a novel by A. J. Cronin or a Bond book or maybe something by Daphne du Maurier – if I liked one book by an author, I would read them all. After reading another chapter of *Rebecca*, I would sleep for about an hour. And, when I woke up, I would start thinking about the last match I had played.

This was the visualisation process which probably had no name at the time, but which is now a recognised part of sports science in football, and especially in cricket, with experts who are getting paid fortunes. But when I was doing something of that nature at Leeds, just to improve my own game, I didn't really know what I was doing, much less that some version of it would one day become a lucrative occupation. It just seemed to work for me.

I could replay sections of a match in my head, the parts that involved myself. I could visualise the mistakes I had made, then I could visualise how to fix them. I wouldn't concentrate on the things I had done well, because that wasn't the point of the exercise. The point was to play the next match better than the last one. So I kept going back over a situation – for instance, being caught in possession – doing it often enough, and deeply enough, so that the next time that situation happened I could react automatically. It had become an indelible thing in my head, a bit like driving a car.

Because every time you play, you do something wrong. In fact, I never played in a game in which I got it all right – ever. But, by correcting mistakes from game to game, I felt that logically, the more games I played, the better I should become. And there's an old saying in football, that the day you think you know it all, is the day you're on the downward slide. So any time Anne would ask me how I'd played, I'd always talk about the mistakes I'd made, the things I needed to improve. I regarded the things I did well as just being part of my job.

Until I was twenty-eight or twenty-nine, I didn't feel comfortable on the pitch for the full ninety minutes. And then I would still keep finding mistakes that had to be eliminated.

It's called learning your trade.

The 'visualisation' might involve a problem with positioning. Always on the pitch, you do what you can see. Whatever the right thing to do is, you need to be able to hold the ball long enough, to see it. Ideally, you try to see it before you actually get the ball.

You get yourself into a position to receive the ball, facing where you need to be.

It is instinctual, but it is also an instinct that can be developed. At least, I felt it could be developed, by training my mind in this way. It worked for me, but it wouldn't necessarily have worked for my good friend Peter Lorimer, who would train his mind using other techniques, such as studying the runners and riders for the 3.30 at Epsom.

It is a strange life that we football men lead, in which most of the time we are very wrapped up in ourselves. And we each have our own way of coping, be it through reading books or backing horses or walking out of the hotel to touch the traffic lights.

I would finish my visualisation at about five o'clock, then maybe listen to records and watch television with the family. I was a great admirer of the *World at War* series and *The Forsyte Saga*, and as for David Attenborough's nature programmes, I could watch them all day. And I loved all the sports programmes, especially the tennis at Wimbledon and the British Open golf on the BBC – Jack Nicklaus and Rod Laver are two of my all-time favourites.

But I was away from home a lot too, wrapped up in the cocoon of football. We spent an awful lot of time in hotels, for home matches as well as the away ones. Trying to cover everything, Don would always want us to stay in a hotel even if we were playing in Leeds, not just to ensure we got a proper night's sleep, but to help us to comply with his instruction that we wouldn't have sex on the night before a game. It is a measure of the man's moral courage that he would put that proposition on the table in a room full of professional footballers.

All told, by most ordinary standards, it might be regarded as a pretty boring existence, certainly not a glamorous or a romantic life – at least not if you were doing it properly. But to me it was never boring because it was what I wanted to do. I didn't need will power or discipline to keep me at it.

I never heard of any of the other Leeds players using visualisation techniques. But I do know that Terry Cooper dreamed for three nights in succession that he would score the winning goal in that League Cup final. I could only look back at goals that had already been scored, but Terry could see it all before it happened.

We also won the Fairs Cup that year, though because of a fixtures pile-up the first leg of the final against Ferencvaros of Hungary wasn't actually played until August. We beat them 1–0 at home and drew 0–0 away a month later, but I missed a lot of it, as I was taken off in the home leg after a collision which knocked me out cold for a few minutes, and I missed the away leg through injury.

Winning the League Cup and the Fairs Cup in the same year was a major achievement, although the 1967–1968 season was seen by our critics as essentially one that was notable for the things we hadn't won – namely the league title and the FA Cup. We weren't given any credit for challenging for these trophies – finishing five points behind the winners Manchester City in the league and losing to Everton in the FA Cup semi-final.

We had grown accustomed to the bad press, but the Everton match featured something else to which we would become accustomed in the years to come. Gary Sprake screwed up in that game. He could be a hot-tempered lad and, late in that game, as he was kicking the ball away from the left side of the box, he also tried to kick Joe Royle. The ball went loose to an Everton player who knocked it back towards our goal, leaving Big Jack with no alternative but to handle it. The penalty was scored by our old friend Johnny Morrissey. It was one of Sprake's first major blunders in a big match.

People are often curious about how the other Leeds players would react when Gary Sprake would 'throw one in' and they would probably be surprised to learn that there would be no verbal attacks on the keeper, even in the heat of the moment in the horrible atmosphere of a losing dressing room. Jack would be the exception here, as he would be in most things, but it was also typical of Jack that he would do his haranguing in the open, out on the pitch. Jack would berate anyone who was annoying him, and then forget about it completely. But for obvious reasons, he was particularly down on Sprake. I don't think Jack liked goal-keepers in general, and Sprake probably summed up for him all that was wrong with the breed.

I wouldn't have a go at the keeper on principle, and most of the players would have the same attitude. We had a lot of respect for one another at Leeds, and in many ways we felt sympathy for him. Of course, it would drive us mad on a personal level, but we wouldn't be grabbing him by the throat and spitting abuse at him.

It was also a matter of respecting Don. The boss had picked him and, if anyone was going to do something about it, it was him. A manager like Don creates an atmosphere in which there is no backchat or challenge of that kind, it's an unspoken thing. We knew that he had his reasons for standing by Sprake. They were pretty deep reasons, maybe a bit complex, but you could still understand them at a certain level.

When Sprake first came into the team, Leeds were in the Second Division and not going well. He was one of the young lads that Don brought in, after which results started to improve. So Don felt that he owed him. And, of course, Sprake was a very good keeper in many ways, especially in those early days. His talent wasn't in question, just his temperament on the big occasion – and maybe a few small occasions too – not that there were going to be many small occasions given the level at which Leeds were now playing.

I do recall an ordinary league game in the 1970s, early in the season against Crystal Palace, when we were 1–0 up and winning well. One of the Palace players tried to cross the ball but miskicked it towards the near post where Sprakey, with nobody near him, let the ball go through his arms, off his shoulders and into the net.

The match ended in a draw and, afterwards, Don said to the keeper 'that kind of thing could cost us the league championship'. At the end of the season, it turned out that the point dropped on that day did actually cost us the league championship. All we needed was a steady keeper and we would have won a lot more trophies than we did – there is no point in pretending otherwise.

But we had managed to win the League Cup and the Fairs Cup in 1968. All these young, hungry lads who had been coming through at Leeds when I'd arrived, were now serious professionals who were getting a taste of glory. But they would not be satisfied with just a taste.

We felt we were ready to win the league. We were still on the way up, whereas Manchester United had been a better team the year before they won the European Cup, and in this season of 1968–1969 they were continuing to go in the wrong direction. We probably saw Manchester City as a bigger threat. Liverpool were still strong, but our players had been young when players such as Ian St John and Roger Hunt were at their peak, and we still had those same players, who had now matured. We hadn't suddenly emerged as contenders for the title, we had grown into it. But we still had to go out and win it.

We got off to a good start and then we became very, very consistent. We only lost two matches that season, one against Manchester City at Maine Road which I missed, and another at Burnley, which was always a tough game for us back then, and which was memorable for two things. The first was the fact that we were slaughtered 5–1, a humiliation that came out of nowhere, as if to prove that football will always surprise you, and the second was the sight of Ralph Coates sitting on the ball at the corner flag.

Now Ralph wasn't a bad lad, but with his team giving us a hiding, he got a bit carried away. So near the end, he found himself at the corner flag and sat himself down on the ball, to the acclaim of the crowd at Turf Moor. We did not join in their laughter.

Every dog has his day. And when you have your day, you shouldn't be doing what Ralph was doing. And I accept that Leeds famously showboated against Southampton several years later, but I think most people agree that we did it in with a certain style, which brought credit to us. Ralph was just taking the piss. We didn't forget about it, and Ralph got a fair bit of stick soon afterwards when Burnley came to Leeds and we destroyed them 6–1.

We made the most out of our eliminations from the League Cup, the FA Cup and the Fairs Cup and concentrated all our energies on the league campaign, but we never won anything easily. On paper, we still had a daunting run-in, which included games against City, Arsenal and Liverpool. Indeed, for the last ten games we could feel the pressure building, with Don telling us before every game, 'If we get anything today, we'll win it.' And we did get something, but would have to do it all over again in the next game.

But we beat City 1–0 at home, and Arsenal 2–1 away. So when we played Liverpool in the second last match of the season, we needed a point to win the title. This being in the city of Liverpool, no doubt Don made a special trip to those lucky traffic lights near the hotel. No doubt about that at all.

In the dressing room at Anfield, I beat him to it. 'If we get anything today, we'll win it,' I said jokingly. And this time it wasn't a line to concentrate the mind, it was a plain fact. Even Don laughed.

It was a Monday night, Anfield was packed. It wasn't a free-flowing game, but we did enough to get something and, in the end, we got a fairly comfortable 0–0 draw.

We had finally done it and were champions of England. We were wild with elation, but we were on somebody else's ground.

'Go down to the Kop End,' Don said.

We were a bit tentative about this. But Don was right. This was the Kop, where they knew their stuff, and they knew we'd won it, and they were going to take nothing away from us.

'Champions! Champions!' they chanted.

It was a fabulous moment, a fabulous feeling to be taking the applause of this truly great crowd. There was a lot of respect between Leeds and Liverpool, we had many big matches with them back then, played in the best spirit.

Bill Shankly was gracious, too, and typically funny when he came to congratulate us. Shanks got on very well with Don. Apparently, he would ring up Don at about eleven o'clock on a Saturday night to talk about the events of the day in football – and, frankly, I doubt if they spoke about any other subject in all the time that Shanks was making those calls.

So Shankly came into the dressing room. We all went silent, waiting for his verdict.

He thought about it for a moment.

'The best team drew,' he said. And through the laughter, we had a fair idea who the best team was, in his estimation. But it was done with humour and style, and it makes the memory of that wonderful night just a bit warmer.

We beat Nottingham Forest 1–0 at home in the last game to amass a record total of sixty-seven points. Our two defeats in forty-two games was also a record, though the fact that we had set another record for winning the league with the least number of goals ever scored gave our critics something to hang on to, to console them.

And Matt Busby was generous. Six years after I had left Old Trafford, Matt declared for the first time that letting me go was a mistake. Six years after I had walked away from his office and from my boyhood dream, with Matt happy to sell me to a provincial club in the Second Division, that club was now dominating Manchester United. Six years earlier, I had said to Anne that I would haunt him. I had haunted him. And he knew it.

Now I could let go of all that.

13

BATTLE OF IRELAND, BATTLE OF BRITAIN

IN IRELAND, they were still doing things differently. At a time when I was part of the Leeds team that had just won the First Division championship, and when the Republic wasn't exactly blessed with a large selection of top-class players to choose from, I was dropped. When the squad of sixteen was announced for an away game in Denmark at the end of that season, I wasn't in it. Obviously no reason was provided, but I heard a few whispers that I was omitted because it was felt that when I played for Ireland, I didn't play as well, or try as hard, as I did for Leeds. Whatever the reason for Ireland's poor performances, the Big Five considered themselves blameless.

Billy Newman of Shelbourne played in my position against Denmark. I have met Billy since, and found him a nice person, but even he had a laugh over that episode. I have also met the Big Five individually over the years and every one of them has assured me that they voted for me. After Denmark, they picked another squad for two games in Dublin, and, this time, I was included. But I pulled out on the grounds that I wasn't good enough to be in the original squad for Denmark, so I hadn't kept myself fit, and therefore I was unavailable for the summer games.

But the world had changed in many ways in the 1960s and, right at the end of it, things even started to change at the FAI. In September 1969, I played for Ireland in a friendly match against Scotland on a Sunday afternoon in Dalymount, and the main reason I played was that Mick Meagan had been appointed as manager. I liked and respected Mick, who was an excellent player for both Everton and the Republic. On the morning of the match, in the Four Courts Hotel, I started a discussion with some of the senior lads, Tony Dunne, Eamon Dunphy, Frank O'Neill and Alan Kelly, about our attitude to the selection committee and the need for a full-time manager. I knew I was pushing an open door here. Most other countries now had a proper manager and, in fact, England had appointed Alf Ramsey three years before they won the World Cup.

So Eamon composed a letter to the FAI on behalf of the squad, outlining our feelings on these matters. We were aware that being a member of the Big Five was a cherished perk for officials, a prestigious post that promised a lot of junkets. So in the letter, we suggested that they might keep the selection committee in place, but that the manager should be responsible for the selection of the team and all team matters. They could keep the glory, and all the trips, which we didn't mind, as long as the manager had the real power.

We handed in the latter to Charlie Walsh, who was the president of the association. 'Amazing, the first year I'm on the selection committee and you want to do this,' he said. But he, and everyone else, knew that we were on the right road.

Leeds signed Allan Clarke in the close season after we won the league. It was the right time to add to the squad, to keep our momentum going. The signing of Clarke completed the Leeds team, because Allan was a top-class goalscorer, quick, with a good shot in both feet, and was an excellent header of the ball. When one-on-one with the keeper, like all top strikers, he made the goal appear a mile wide. Jimmy Greaves could do the same thing, due to some mysterious gift that is bestowed on these lads, some quality of calmness or cleverness or confidence. By contrast a striker of lesser ability creates the opposite illusion, the sense that there is no possible way he can score in a one-on-one situation, that the goalkeeper has it all covered – I suppose the perfect example of that type of striker would be Emile Heskey.

I first encountered Clarke when he played for Fulham. He'd made an impression because he was mouthy, and clearly wasn't intimidated by Leeds' reputation. He got myself and Billy going that day, but we had to admire his cheek. He then played for Leicester, scoring more than his share of goals in a poor side that was relegated, but that also got to the FA Cup final in 1969. Don believed that if Allan could score in a struggling team, he could score a lot more for the champions.

Clarke also had a reputation for being an awkward type at Fulham and Leicester, where he had been the star man. But when he came to Elland Road, he was with Les Cocker on the touchline watching the rest of us training, and Les was giving him a running commentary, 'That's Billy Bremner, he's a star . . . that's Peter Lorimer, he's a star . . . that's Eddie Gray, he's a star . . .' Les went through the whole squad, describing us all as stars, to emphasise to Allan that he was now just one star among many.

He joined us for a campaign that would have an epic quality, but not in the way we might have expected. As champions, we were naturally hoping to challenge for the league title again. But Everton got away from us in the early stages, and finished up winning the league comfortably. We were learning that the levels of concentration and performance required of league champions were difficult to reproduce at the start of the following season. The dreadful fear of failure is gone, to be replaced by a certain calmness that comes from the knowledge that any damage done at this stage can be repaired in the run-in, the decisive phase. So when Everton took advantage of our slow start, our priorities switched to the FA Cup and the European Cup.

That cup final of 1970 between Leeds and Chelsea is now

regarded as a classic, a great drama with many twists and turns in the first match at Wembley and in the replay at Old Trafford. I can understand that, and I'd agree with most of it.

Whenever there's a television programme remembering the 1970s, they usually show a few scenes of Eddie Gray tormenting the full-back David Webb and then Webb scoring the winner in the replay. I've seen myself a few times, about twelve yards out from the Chelsea goal, hitting it on the volley and Webb somehow getting it over the bar. It is a match that brings back so many memories for everyone, of that period in the 1970s when the FA Cup final was probably the main event of the entire television year. Of course, it has also generated a fair amount of nonsense.

I recall one programme with a commentary by the actor Dennis Waterman, which looked back at this contest between ourselves and the Chelsea lads, and which reinforced all the myths about Leeds, and indeed about Chelsea, that had become established in the public mind as facts. Supposedly, it was a battle between two contrasting styles, between two different ways of looking at the game – it almost goes with saying that the Chelsea way was seen as far superior.

Those guys were down the King's Road enjoying a few beers while we country bumpkins were taking it all too seriously, too obsessed with getting a result to appreciate the things that really matter in football, and in life itself. According to their showbiz friends, those Chelsea guys weren't taking it seriously at all – and apparently this was exactly the right attitude. In this hackneyed version of events, they were great blokes who knew how to have a good time, and we were basically a shower of bastards.

All the half-baked prejudices of several years were thrown into the pot for this one. It was all concentrated into this one decisive battle which would eventually be spread over two games of 120 minutes, in the south at Wembley and in the north at Manchester, and in the end a winner would emerge. And it wasn't just a question of winning the FA Cup, it would be a sort of moral victory in this battle for the soul of the game. In the minds of their supporters, Chelsea, raising their pints of lager in the pub while Leeds were out there in the rain doing push-ups, had their priorities in order.

Now there was a certain amount of truth in the idea that Leeds were more dedicated and more hard-working in general than Chelsea. In fact, that Chelsea team was far less successful than it might have been. Like all the others – Everton, City, Arsenal – they had their moments for a couple of seasons but, unlike Leeds, they couldn't keep it up.

So it is clear that whatever we were doing at Leeds was working better than whatever they were doing, or not doing. It only starts to get a bit silly when the conclusion is drawn from all this, that it was actually Leeds who were the misguided ones at that time, and all those other lads had it just about right.

You can still see this point of view represented in nostalgic pieces about the 1970s, which celebrate the more flamboyant players such Frank Worthington. And clearly those lads were talented. But it's worth making the point also, that Frank Worthington played for Leicester City. And there was a reason for that. There were things you could do at Leicester City, that wouldn't have much place in a team that was trying to win something. And, ultimately, while the fans enjoy the tricks and the flicks, you'll find that the fans will get a far deeper enjoyment from being in the thick of things, not just for a couple of months, or even a couple of seasons, but for ten seasons in a row.

We went into that Wembley final after three matches against Manchester United in the semi-final, and with the two legs of the semi-final of the European Cup against Celtic starting the following Wednesday – the Battle of Britain, as it was being called. Our squad had about sixteen players, and, like any other squad at the time, we could do without an end-of-season fixture pile-up. Especially as these games were so intense, generating such massive levels of interest. The Battle of Britain would see 136,505 people jammed into Hampden Park for the second leg.

We said nothing about it at the time, but, towards the end, we were most certainly exhausted. In most years, you can win the FA Cup by playing six matches in total and we still had five matches to go after we reached the semi-final, with a fair bit of extra-time on top of that. And when the European Cup semi-final was thrown into the mix, it meant that we had seven of these huge matches in a row with either glory at the end of it all, or devastation.

But we weren't complaining, this is what we had always wanted. And it was Chelsea, after all, standing between us and the cup.

There had been a fair bit of needle between Leeds and Chelsea even before I came to Leeds. Chelsea, then managed by Tommy Docherty, had come up from the Second Division the year before us. We were both young teams, and, throughout the 1960s, a fair amount of bad feeling had built up between the players, which wasn't the case between the Leeds and the Arsenal players, for example. Certainly I always got on well with the Arsenal lads, before and after, if not during, the matches.

But there was a special sort of animosity between ourselves and Chelsea. I had that bit of 'previous' with Eddie McCreadie. And John Hollins, who would usually mark me, could do a bit. Peter Osgood, the most dangerous of them all, hated Norman Hunter – really hated him. And Ron 'Chopper' Harris had made a name for himself.

In 1967, the rivalry had gained an extra edge in the FA Cup semi-final, when they were leading 1–0 through a header by Tony Hateley until late in the game, when we got a free kick about five yards outside the area. I squared it to Peter Lorimer, who sent it like a bullet past the keeper Peter Bonetti. The referee Ken Burns disallowed it, claiming he did not give the signal for the kick to be taken, as the Chelsea defenders were not standing ten yards from the ball. Yet it is clear from television pictures that several seconds had elapsed between the time the referee awarded the kick and the moment I took it, and that the Chelsea players themselves seemed to think they'd had enough time, because none of them appealed to the ref when the goal was scored, and a couple of them had their heads in the hands in grief. Anyway, they went on to lose the final 2–1 to Spurs.

Though they enjoyed being seen as the playboys of the King's Road, the Chelsea players knew that Leeds had actually been winning things, while they were otherwise engaged. In that rivalry between the two young teams, we had gone ahead of them, and there wasn't much chance of us being caught. In those years, when they had a lot of talented players, Chelsea never once made a run for the league. City, Everton and Arsenal may have burned brightly for a short time but Chelsea didn't really burn at all, except the odd time in the cup.

But this was the cup final, so they would fancy themselves against us, on the day. They would revel in the occasion.

Personally, I regarded all the preliminaries as something to be endured. I know that the television people must do their job, and that it's not really their problem if the likes of me regard what they're doing as a pain in the arse. So I would just try to switch off from it. You're nervous in these situations, and you don't want to be bothered by someone talking to you before the match.

It's too easy to get carried away. Coming out of the tunnel, I wouldn't be looking for my family in the crowd or waving to them. My enjoyment would come from winning a cup final. Then you can start looking for your family, looking for your friends.

I can't recall which member of the royal family shook my hand as we lined up before the match. I have received a winner's medal twice, from the Queen, but I have great difficulty recalling which of the royals was introduced to me, or I to them, during the prelims. In 1970, my mind may have been elsewhere, thinking about the state of the pitch, which had just been destroyed during the Horse of the Year Show. We knew that the pitch had been in a poor state for the League Cup final, in which Manchester City had beaten West Brom, but it was only when we walked out onto it an hour before the match that we realised the true extent of the damage. It was really just a big field of compacted mud, with almost no grass on it, nowhere near the great arena of green turf that would normally be such a novelty at the end of the season. Yet the terrible state of the pitch is probably one of the things that made that final so distinctive, so memorable.

Nor was it even in the month of May, the traditional cup final time, because everything had been moved back a month to allow England to acclimatise for the World Cup in Mexico. There was also the fact that the game seemed to go against some of the popular wisdom.

The first goal, headed in by Jack from a corner kick, with the ball skidding past McCreadie and Harris on the line after a bad bounce, seemed to reinforce one cliché at least – Jack had 'gone under the bar' again. But, eventually, it was impossible to ignore the reality that it was actually Leeds, of 'dull method play' fame, who were doing most of the entertaining. In particular, there was Eddie Gray on the wing, killing David Webb, the full-back, and dominating the game from that position in a way that hadn't been seen since the Stanley Matthews final of 1953. Not that we had any interest in 'entertaining' in a shallow sense, we felt that we played good football most of the time anyway, and that this is where the true entertainment lies, not in the 'nutmegs' and the overhead kicks. We didn't want to be one of those teams which only knew the tricks of the trade, not the trade itself. We knew what Eddie could do, and we had seen him doing it many times, but Eddie became something of an overnight celebrity, because of his spectacular performance on the big day.

We were all over them, really, leading 1–0 just before half-time. And then Sprakey turned the game. I was standing near Peter Houseman when he went to take a shot from about thirty yards out and my immediate reaction was one of relief. Even with a perfect shot from there, I felt that Houseman had little chance of scoring, and it seemed to me that his was actually a poor shot, that he didn't catch it properly. So that was all right.

But as I turned away, I saw Sprakey letting it get past him somehow, and it became the equaliser. It was horrible. Goals dictate games, and now Chelsea would be thinking, We've had a bit of hiding, but we're level. They would be happy men, as they headed back down the tunnel, while we were choking on this latest sickener.

We had reverted to type in one way at least, with the keeper throwing one in. In a tight game, you can't give away soft goals. If a team is going to score, it should be a good one. Coming in level at half-time, we were like a golfer coming down the stretch in a major, who'd missed a few putts he should have got – it's hard to win after that.

But the Leeds lads were able to pick it up again in the second half and, late in the game, I crossed for Clarkey to head against the post, with Mick Jones reacting well to knock in the rebound. We really thought we'd won it this time – everyone did – but with a couple of minutes left, Ian Hutchinson headed a good goal from a Hollins cross, and we were facing extra-time, another thirty minutes charging through the mud. I suppose I must have been exhausted, at this stage, though, in truth, I was able to put these thoughts of fatigue to the back of mind, with the cup still waiting to be won.

I had a chance in the first period of extra-time to put us ahead again, to win the FA Cup for the first time, for Leeds. Eddie Gray, still creating chances, pulled it back to me. I was about twelve yards from goal. I saw it coming and I knew what I was going to do. I was going to volley it. I was going to volley it with two things in mind. The first thing was to get the ball on target, the second thing was to hit it downwards and into the ground so that the mud would help it to stay low.

I did exactly what I had wanted to do. It came to me about waist-high and I caught it perfectly, directing it downwards and on target. But the ball didn't stay low as I had anticipated. It must have hit the only half-decent yard of grass on the pitch, because it bounced normally, allowing David Webb, a broken man after what Eddie had done to him all afternoon, to stick out a leg and to make a good clearance over the bar.

A good clearance for him, that is.

We jogged around the pitch afterwards, the two teams together, on a shared lap of honour. We knew that when hostilities resumed in the replay, it might well be a kicking-match, but, for now, even with Chelsea, when the match was over, that was the end of it. In fact, years later there was a funny scene in a hotel in Florida, when, completely by accident, I bumped into one Eddie McCreadie. Our kicking-matches a long way behind us, I had no problem with Eddie, and Eddie had no problem with me. We were just two old footballers trying to enjoy ourselves in Florida, two old rivals who probably had more in common with each other than we had with anyone else down there. I'd say that if I met most of those Chelsea players now, we'd probably just have a laugh about it.

But in April 1970, we still had another cup final to play. And it would not be suitable for viewers of a nervous disposition.

In the meantime, there was the small matter of the so-called Battle of Britain. Again I could claim that we were not exactly in the whole of our health at this stage, and that we were further wearied by the disappointment of not winning the cup final, but then Celtic had actually lost their own cup final on the Saturday to Aberdeen. Ultimately, there were no excuses here.

Regardless of what state we were in, we probably would have been knocked out anyway by this superb Celtic team. They won both games and, over the two legs, they beat us well. It was a soft deflected goal from a George Connelly shot in the first minute, that gave them a 1–0 win in the first leg at Elland Road. We just couldn't find a way through them after that, and we were discovering what an impressive side they were. Jock Stein had won the European Cup with most of these lads, and it was no accident. Up in Glasgow, Billy Bremner actually equalised for us with a terrific shot from thirty yards in front of the biggest crowd ever assembled in the one place in the history of European football. There was an eerie hush for a few moments in Hampden, but then the deafening noise of 130,000 Celtic fans started again, and eventually we couldn't keep them out. John Hughes equalised just after half-time. Then he was in a collision with Gary Sprake, who was taken off injured and replaced by David Harvey. But it made no difference really, who was in goal. Bobby Murdoch scored the winner on the night, after a one-two with Jimmy Johnstone, who tormented us from start to finish. Even a defender as accomplished as Terry Cooper couldn't get near him. Johnstone was magnificent, as were their midfielders Murdoch and Bertie Auld, already mentioned in despatches as a hard man of such prowess, he would put Johnny Morrissey himself in the shade – though like Morrissey, as a player he was top-class.

The Celtic players had a lot of class off the pitch too. There was plenty of mutual respect, and there was no gloating on their part, though they had been seriously underrated in the run-up to the tie. The press had called it the Battle of Britain, but it didn't feel like that. Maybe the fact that Leeds had players from Ireland, Wales, and Scotland itself, made it feel less like a hate-filled Scotland v England match than it might otherwise have been.

On the other hand, the match that was about to resume the following Wednesday at Old Trafford felt a bit more like the Battle of Britain, if not indeed the War of the Worlds.

*   *   *

It is said that approximately 28 million people watched us lose to Chelsea that night.

And some of them may even have been supporting us after our tremendous display in the first match had gone unrewarded. But after ten minutes it was clear that Eddie Gray wasn't going to be repeating his Wembley heroics. He was 'done' by Chopper Harris, who had switched with David Webb, moving from centre-half to full-back to spare Webb a repeat of the nightmare. After he had been kicked on the back of the knee, Eddie stayed on the pitch, but could contribute little to the cause.

Most of the other twenty-one players out there, responded in full-blooded fashion. It was a wild night and some of those tackles will be shown until the end of time. Even Chelsea's keeper Bonetti was hampered by injury when we got the opening goal, Mick Jones scoring it after a terrific run by Allan Clarke. Bonetti would go on a few months later to replace Gordon Banks in the World Cup quarter-final against West Germany, which England lost, and for which Bonetti was blamed for doing a Sprake on a soft shot from Beckenbauer. I think that Bonetti was perhaps over-criticised for that, and I generally rated him highly as a keeper. He was a brave lad too, and at Old Trafford he needed to be.

Big Jack blames himself for the equaliser, which is odd, because Jack was never to blame for anything. He says he was waiting on the Chelsea goalline for a corner kick to come over, when one of their players – probably Ian Hutchinson – whacked him in the thigh with his knee. After the corner was cleared, Jack proceeded to chase Hutchinson over to the right. Then Jack saw that the ball had been knocked in long to our box, but with his leg still dead, he couldn't get back in time to stop Osgood's diving header.

He also recalls kicking open the door of the dressing room, gutted after the match which had been won by a header from Webb, of all people. I only remember the appalling pain of losing, the devastation of ending the season with nothing after we had come so close, played so hard and so long. So long, we thought it would never end.

As Chelsea celebrated in front of their fans and the 28 million other people out there, we wandered off to the dressing room. We didn't collect our medals. Partly, we weren't sure if the prize-giving procedure was the same at Old Trafford as at Wembley – there was no precedent for this – mainly we just couldn't be bothered. We probably should have gone up to get those medals but we didn't want to be there. We wanted to get the hell out of Old Trafford, as quickly as we could manage it. We had seen the European Cup and now the FA Cup getting away from us – in every sense we were on the floor.

The Chelsea lads might be having a tipple or two, we just wanted to go home.

We got hammered for that too but we were past caring about our critics, secure as they were in their smugness and their ignorance. They say we won a lot of friends over the two games of that great epic, but then we couldn't see any good reason why they weren't our friends in the first place. We had played some outstanding football against Chelsea, but it wasn't as if we had suddenly discovered how to do all that on the coach on the way to Wembley.

We were shattered. But it was in such moments that I feel the real greatness of this Leeds team would always emerge. We wouldn't go away and settle for less. Don would tell us that we'd have to start again, that we could come back from this.

Only Leeds could come back from this.

14

UNNATURAL AND INSANE

Around this time, I lost all my money. Like a lot of people in sport or in showbusiness, I walked right into it, thinking I was doing the smart thing, the sensible thing. But, in fact, I didn't know what I was doing at all.

It wasn't that I had big ideas. I just felt that I needed to start some sort of a business for the future, for when my football career was over. Footballers were on good money at the time by any normal standard, but we wouldn't be able to live for the rest of our lives on what we were earning from the game – and if we thought we could, we were very much mistaken.

So that's how I got into the insurance business. I was approached by a Dublin businessman to form a partnership. It would involve a special scheme for footballers. For example, a footballer needed a pension at the age of thirty-five rather than sixty-five. And I knew a lot of footballers, and a lot of footballers knew me, so it seemed like a good idea at the time.

And while all this seemed sensible, in theory, I soon learned that I really had no idea of the practicalities of running a business. I didn't have the time to give it the attention it needed, and even if I'd had all the time in the world, I hadn't the experience to do it right. They say you should keep all your eggs in the one basket, and keep your eye on that basket. I didn't keep my eye on that basket.

I had formed a partnership, rather than a limited company, which was another mistake.

Without getting tangled up in the details of company law, in my case this meant that if things went wrong, I would be personally liable. Since I was a well-known professional footballer who would clearly have a few quid, this meant trouble.

I was getting well paid, but I did not exactly have limitless amounts of cash at the time. When I joined Leeds in 1963, I was on about £60 a week. By the late 1960s this had risen to £100 a week plus bonuses. We had a nice detached house in Headingley which had cost about £9,000 with a mortgage. And now we were getting visits from the bailiffs.

Playing in the 1970 cup final in front of 28 million people might be regarded as a stressful experience, and losing it was a horrible blow, but the thing that was dominating my thoughts at this time was the insurance business.

I was thirty, and I was broke. And the debt-collectors were at the door.

At most, I had only three or four years left in football, in which I could earn the sort of money I had been earning. But it was all I had. It was the only way out. I was at least lucky enough to be able to focus on playing, on the one thing I could do to clear up this mess.

I felt worse for Anne, who had to deal with all this trouble that she had done nothing to cause. We had three kids now – Jimmy had arrived in 1968 – and suddenly our happiness and our peace of mind had been ambushed by this foolishness on my part. I just felt so embarrassed, so silly, so stupid. Everything we had worked for, was going down the drain. But I couldn't crack up. Apart from anything else, we just couldn't afford it. And along with Anne's support on the emotional side, on the business side I received the support of a man to whom I will be forever grateful.

Ronnie Teeman was one of the leading lawyers in Leeds, with a great reputation. He was recommended to me by a mutual friend, a man called Tunc Osbay, who ran a disco in Leeds, and who had availed himself of Ronnie Teeman's advice in a time of trouble. Tunc, originally from Turkey, knew I had this problem, and he told me that Ronnie Teeman knew I had this problem, and he strongly urged me to go and see Ronnie.

I was reluctant to see him. Again I was just so mortified about this whole thing, for a while I just couldn't deal with it rationally. I kept putting off this visit to Ronnie Teeman until I couldn't really put it off any more, until the demands for money just wouldn't stop coming, until it finally sank in that I really had nothing to lose.

Ronnie was about ten years older than me, but about the same size, a dark-haired bespectacled man and a sportsman, with a slight preference for rugby league over football. But he loved all sports, and he understood how a footballer could get himself in to the situation I had found myself in. He knew that we live in this parallel world, in which we are largely protected from all these dangerous and boring things like insurance and pensions, a dreamland which we leave at our peril.

Even more importantly, he knew how a footballer could get himself out of this situation.

Or at least he knew how to organise things so that the situation could eventually be resolved. I don't know how exactly he did that, because he told me just to send anything to do with the business straight to him, and he would deal with it – I don't know exactly how he did that either, because his office seemed to be overflowing with paper. But Ronnie somehow knew where everything was, and what it was doing there.

All I knew was that we could now get on with our lives with some sense that this thing was being looked after, by someone who knew what he was doing. Essentially, he pulled it all together, and made it manageable in a way that would have been completely beyond me. So that all I had to do was pay up. At a certain stage, simply handing over all your money has a pleasant simplicity to it, as long as someone else is reading all those documents that only give you headaches. From now on, I wouldn't have to be dealing with people calling to the house for money, they would be called in by Ronnie, who was experienced enough to know how to handle these things. I was starting to realise that I wasn't the first person that such a thing had happened to, that businesses go wrong, you try to get the best advice and, at the end of it, you have to start again.

Ronnie had – and still has – a terrific sense of humour, but when the work started, he was serious. He made it clear that I should be under no illusions. I knew those bailiffs wouldn't just go away, that they would have to be paid, that it would cost me. And it would cost me a lot. But Ronnie, by being so good at his job, still took a lot of the heartache out of it. I will always be grateful to him for what he did for us, and to his wife Shirley too, who was eternally patient as she answered many phone calls to the house during those troubled times. Ronnie was a hero, when I needed a hero. And we got through it in the end. He and Shirley have been great friends of ours ever since.

At Leeds we were also picking ourselves up and starting all over again. I was still able to concentrate on my football, regardless of anything else that was going on. Maybe all that visualisation I'd been doing was standing me in good stead, helping me to focus when I needed it.

We got sixty-four points that season, only three short of our own record tally of sixty-seven, but Arsenal got one more. Don must have been wondering about that curse which was supposedly lifted from Elland Road, after our home game against West Brom towards the end of that season which featured an incident so strange, it still looks like something out of Orson Welles' *Great Mysteries*.

It was a goal scored by Jeff Astle for West Brom, a goal which to this day defies all rational explanation. And even before that goal was scored, there had already been an odd incident, when a Leeds goal, a header from Mick Jones, was disallowed for some minor infringement. West Brom had been leading 1–0 and when this 'equaliser' was disallowed, it inflamed the Leeds crowd who'd been getting a bit paranoid – probably with good reason – about bad decisions against Leeds in general.

But the real madness was still to come. After an attack of theirs, which we cleared into their half, one of the West Brom players, Colin Suggett, was feeling a bit tired, and was walking back towards the action. The ball was now with Norman Hunter, and I went to receive it from him. But Tony Brown intercepted Norman's pass and knocked the ball twenty yards ahead of himself. As Suggett was still walking back on his own, the linesman correctly flagged him offside – in those days the offside decision was clear-cut, with no players being deemed 'active' or 'non-active'. Brown had seen the offside flag and had stopped running. He was looking at referee Ray Tinkler, assuming that the game would now be stopped and would resume with a free kick to Leeds for offside. But astonishingly, Tinkler waved play on. So Tony resumed his run before slipping the ball past Sprakey to Jeff Astle, who might also have been adjudged offside, but who ran on to score a perfectly illegal goal. Tinkler had completely lost it at this stage, and we were stuck with his ridiculous decision. There was pandemonium.

And in that wild atmosphere, the crowd invaded the pitch. We were just about to enter the era of the football hooligan, but this particular pitch invasion wouldn't come under that heading at all. It wasn't quite men, women and children, but certainly there were a lot of middle-aged, middle-class men involved, ordinary respectable people who had been driven mad by this blatant injustice. There were no drunken skinheads with swastika tattoos, these were the ordinary people of Leeds displaying their righteous anger. After about fifteen minutes of bedlam, the match resumed. And Leeds scored, but we couldn't get the equaliser.

The good goal that had been disallowed, and the bad goal that had been allowed, cost us this vital game.

There was fierce criticism of the referee, and not just from Don Revie. The illegal goal was shown again and again to an incredulous audience of millions on *Match of the Day*, and for a few moments it seemed that Leeds were actually receiving some sympathy from the press and the general public. But that couldn't last for long, and by Monday it was generally felt that Ray Tinkler had taken enough abuse, that he was only human after all. At which point most of the sympathy transferred from us to him.

For the crowd disturbances, we would be forced to play our first three home games of the next season away from Elland Road. Of much greater significance, was the fact that when you look at the final league table for that season, you can see that the point which we were denied against West Brom, would have enabled us to catch Arsenal.

And it wasn't just a matter of numbers, it was the fact that Arsenal had taken great encouragement from our defeat, adding to their momentum during the run-in.

Perhaps feeling that the gods were smiling on them, Arsenal went on to win the double, with Charlie George's famous goal beating Liverpool in another legendary Wembley final. Except this one was played at the right time of the year, and on grass.

I don't think Arsenal were as talented as we were, but they had qualities that were completely admirable. They went on a tremendous run that year, from around Christmas. At one stage we had been about seven points ahead of them, and at no stage did we collapse. They won the league that year, not because we cracked up, but due to their own character, their own ability to keep getting the results all the way till the end. Indeed, we beat them during the run-in, but they just kept going, notching up the 1–0 wins that are so difficult to achieve under that sort of pressure. Perhaps the last game of their league campaign was the most difficult, away to Spurs, of all people. But they won that too, 1–0.

At Leeds we had the height of respect for the Arsenal lads for what they did that season.

We saw them as good, solid pros who did their business and did it well – players like Pat Rice, Bob McNab, George Armstrong and, of course, Peter Storey, who left his mark on all of us. And there was Bob Wilson, who was probably the best goalkeeper in Britain during that season.

But the driving force behind their success was the captain Frank McLintock. He had started his career around the same time as I did, and had been converted from wing-half to centre-half. But it was his leadership qualities that made the difference for Arsenal that year. Apart from keeping their noses in front of us to win the league, they had to come from two goals behind to equalise against Stoke City in the FA Cup semi-final at Hillsborough, with Storey getting both goals, the second a late penalty for which he held his nerve to send Gordon Banks the wrong way. They won the replay easily. And they then went a goal down to Liverpool in extra-time at Wembley, before coming back on a hot day to score two goals and to break through a psychological barrier, as well as a physical one – winning the Double had been done only once in the century, by a very special Spurs team.

We were always striving for it at Leeds – to win everything in fact – which gave us an extra appreciation for what Arsenal had achieved. And it was McLintock who ultimately got them through it, making him a deserved winner of the Footballer of the Year award.

In fact this was unusual in itself, because we had a certain attitude at Leeds to the Footballer of the Year award, since the time that Big Jack won it in 1967.

Not only was Jack not the best player in England that season, he was far from being the best player at Leeds and, in truth, he was one of the worst. A lot of the England players who had won the World Cup played poorly the following season, mainly due to a natural comedown after the incredible high they'd been on, and also because of fatigue – they had been training and playing when most other players was resting. So Jack, even by his own admission, was an absurd choice for the award. And for years afterwards, in five-a-side matches, we would have a vote afterwards to decide who'd been the worst player. The 'winner' would get a yellow jersey and be named Footballer of the Year.

But Frank McLintock was the real Footballer of the Year in 1971. Any time I run into Frank these days, we joke that he was my lucky mascot. I got three winners' medals at Wembley and, every time, Frank was on the other team. He played in that fine Leicester side with Gordon Banks in goal, which was beaten by Manchester United in the 1963 FA Cup final. He played for Arsenal when Leeds won the League Cup in 1968 and the FA Cup in 1972.

I thank him for that, but not for being Arsenal's inspiration during their magnificent season of 1971.

We won something ourselves that year. For the second time, we won the Fairs Cup, beating Juventus in the final. Then, as now, they were a big club, with big players like Helmut Haller, who had scored for West Germany in the 1966 World Cup final, and Roberto Bettega. Both matches were drawn – 2–2 away and 1–1 at home – but this was the first year in European football in which away goals counted double. And there was a further complication in the away match in Turin, because the game had to be played twice.

During the first game, we were going well, drawing 0–0. But it was lashing rain, which brought up something of a dilemma for the Italians. According to local custom, if a game was abandoned, the spectators only got a refund if a game lasted for less than fifty minutes. So in the first half, even with the downpour and the increasingly poor state of the pitch, Juventus weren't calling for the game to be stopped. But in the second half, unhappy with the scoreline and the way the match seemed to be going, they unveiled their full repertoire of acting skills, playing up to the referee at every opportunity about the difficulty of playing football in the conditions, throwing the ball on the ground to show that it wasn't bouncing properly, and all that carry-on. And it worked. The match was abandoned after 51 minutes at 0–0, which meant that we had to stay in Turin and start again the following night.

In midfield, I was up against one Fabio Capello. I would end up having played against him three times in a short period, twice against Juventus and once against Italy in the first match that the Republic ever played at Lansdowne Road. Eamon Dunphy also played in that match, but I don't recall Capello being overly impressive. Clearly he was a good player, to be at Juventus, but not exceptional.

Still he scored the second goal that night in Turin, Bettega scoring the first. We equalised through Paul Madeley, and again through Mick Bates. The 2–2 draw was a better result for us than the 0–0 would have been, so, in the end, the play-acting of the Italians backfired.

This was the last season of the Fairs Cup, or the Inter-Cities Fairs Cup to give it its full title. In 1972, it became the UEFA Cup. Whatever it was called, it hadn't been a priority for us at this stage, but it was still a consolation though.

We were living at the top now, where the margins are frighteningly thin. When you win something, it is only to be expected; when you come second, it is seen as a catastrophe. But for the Leeds lads, it was the right place to be, the only place.

We didn't know it at the start, or even at Christmas, but in the 1971–1972 season we were heading for a climax that would leave us not knowing whether to celebrate the good of it all, or sink into despair.

In the Leeds dressing room, after qualifying for the League Cup final in 1968. Back row, left to right:
Bob English, Don Revie, Terry Cooper, myself, Billy Bremner, Paul Madeley, Paul Reaney, Gary Sprake,
Norman Hunter, Mick Bates. Middle: Peter Lorimer. Front row, left to right: Eddie Gray,
Jimmy Greenhoff and Rod Belfitt.

High spirits on the train, after winning the League Cup in '68, from left: Mick Jones, myself, Peter Lorimer,
Norman Hunter, Terry Cooper and, centre Billy Bremner. Playing the toy piano is Don Revie's daughter
Kim. Far right is Jack Charlton, in his own world.

With Billy Bremner after
Leeds drew with Liverpool
at Anfield to clinch our
first league title in the
'68/'69 season.
"Champions! Champions!"
the Kop chanted.
A wonderful moment.

A proud moment with my son Michael and Les Cocker with the first division Championship trophy afterwards.

Taking the penalty that clinched victory for Leeds over Sunderland in the fifth round of the FA Cup, 1967. It was in the last five minutes of the second replay.

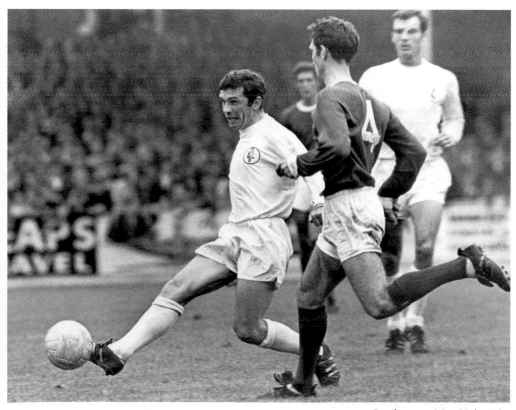

Leeds versus Man Utd, 1969.

1972 FA Cup final, victory against Arsenal. Clockwise from left: Mick Bates, Paul Madeley, Eddie Gray, Paul Reaney, myself, Allan Clarke, Billy Bremner, Peter Lorimer, Norman Hunter, and Jack Charlton in front.

With my son Michael (right) and nephew John Stiles (Nobby's son) after the win.

Brian Clough leads us out at Wembley for the infamous Charity Shield match in 1974, against Liverpool, led by Bill Shankly (right).

In the player–manager role for West Brom c 1976.

Ireland versus England
friendly, on the
Dalymount pitch with
Bobby Charlton, 1964.
Bobby was the greatest
player I ever played with,
or against.

Leading out the
Ireland team as
player–manager
for a friendly
against Austria.

With Steve
Heighway, and
18-year-old
Liam Brady
making his
debut in a
tremendous 3–0
win against the
USSR, 1974.

Rep of Ireland versus West Germany, 1979.

The RTÉ panel, from left to right: Ronnie, Liam, myself,
Bill, Eamon, Graeme, Ray and Kenny.

I've known Eamon Dunphy since we were kids. We never realised we'd end up on television together, because there were no televisions in Ireland back then. But we're both proud of the reputation of the RTÉ panel.

These days I mainly kick the ball around with my grandchildren, but I still give them a good run for their money! Clockwise from top left: Conor, myself, Dominic, Sarah, Charlotte, Luke, Craig, Ciara and Matthew

Coming towards Christmas, we found ourselves in an unusual place. We were down the league. Because of the ban carried over from the West Brom debacle, we had to play our first six matches away from home, at neutral venues, so we'd had a slow start. It just wasn't happening for us, and Don called a meeting with the players. 'Let's forget about the league and concentrate on the cup', was the message. At which point, we suddenly found our form, and started to play some of the best football we played in my time at Leeds. In fact, between that Christmas and the summer, we played football as good as I've seen played anywhere in the world. We shot up the league and found ourselves back in contention for the title.

It is a period which is immortalised in *Match of the Day*'s highlights of our 7–0 destruction of Southampton, when we decided to showboat.

There were flicks and back heels and all sorts of trickery, and we kept possession of the ball for forty odd passes, each one greeted by a burst of acclaim from the crowd at Elland Road. It is a game that people reminisce about, and that they want to discuss more than any other game I played at Leeds United. Which is a bit off-putting for me, because I remember it as one of our more insignificant games, and I didn't enjoy it all that much. Certainly not as much as the millions who still remember it so fondly.

Basically, we were just bored. I had wanted to come off the field at 6–0. So we kept ourselves and the crowd entertained with the showboating, and I think even Southampton felt we'd earned the right at 7–0 to play whatever way we wanted to play. But what we did on that day was actually the direct opposite of what gave me the most satisfaction.

For me, the real enjoyment came from playing in a game that was really tight, where you had to perform under pressure, doing your stuff at the height of the battle and helping to turn the game in your team's favour. That was the buzz for me.

Later on that season, we were a goal down against Spurs in the sixth round of the FA Cup at Elland Road. We played brilliantly, and went on to win 2–1.

I don't want to be a sourpuss, but that is a game that sticks in my mind – and nobody ever talks about it. So I'd just like to redress the balance a bit here. I'd love to see that game against Spurs replayed on television again and again. But I see it only in my own memory.

That win helped us on our way to Wembley, where we beat Arsenal 1–0 to win the FA Cup for the first time in Leeds' history. Allan Clarke's perfectly placed header from a Mick Jones cross from the by-line, brought us the trophy that we felt we left behind us against Chelsea. We were driven by the desire to put that right, and I guess the presence of Frank McLintock on the other side removed any doubt about the eventual outcome.

And yet we couldn't celebrate, because on the Monday night we were playing Wolves at Molineux, needing only a draw to win the league, and to do the double just a year after Arsenal had done it. Our superb form in the league after Christmas had put us in this position, and now just forty-eight hours after winning the cup, we had to finish off the job. Really, it was unnatural and insane. Before the Wembley game, we had played on the previous Saturday and then the Monday. So with Wolves to come, we were looking at four games in nine days, four games of historical significance for the club.

After winning the cup, there was no night out at the Savoy Hotel, with entertainment by Max Bygraves. We just got on the bus, which took us straight up to our hotel in Wolverhampton. Leeds made a request to the FA to postpone the Wolves game until the Wednesday. The extra two days rest would have made all the difference. But the Home Internationals between England, Scotland, Wales and Northern Ireland were due to start that week, so the FA said that if Sir Alf Ramsey agreed, it was all right with them. And Alf, the cute old bugger, agreed that Leeds could play on the Wednesday night but with one important stipulation – he wanted the England players Norman Hunter, Allan Clarke and Paul Reaney in Wales no later than midnight on Monday. Which left us with no option but to play on the Monday.

Alf had no intention of doing Don any favours. The club managers held the power at the time, to decide whether a player would report for international duty. And Alf remembered with resentment the way that Don had persuaded some of the England players to pull out of games, on the pretext of illness or injury. Alf had a long memory.

With all these bad wishes ringing in our ears, we faced Wolves in the last game of the season, just needing that one point to win the double, on the same night that Liverpool needed a win at Arsenal, to take advantage of any slip-up on our part. Derby County, meanwhile, were already on holiday in Majorca, awaiting developments. If we lost and Liverpool didn't win, then Brian Clough's side would be champions.

Wolves were up for it, certainly, but I don't think it was anything to do with a particular grudge against us. They were playing the last game of their season in front of a packed house of about 50,000, with millions around the country paying attention. They also hadn't played for about ten days, a crucial factor at that stage of the season. So while we were feeling the effects of too much football, they were fresh. Certainly, I hadn't recovered from the cup final by Monday, and we'd also lost Mick Jones with a dislocated elbow.

In the white heat of Molineux, Wolves took the lead, then they went 2–0 up, and now, desperately fatigued, we were looking at the double slipping away from us. Billy Bremner got one back for us, but in the end we just couldn't get the point that we needed.

I should add that there were claims that two Wolves players, Danny Hegan and Francis Munro, had been offered bribes by

Billy. It was claimed that Billy had phoned Munro in his hotel
and offered him five grand to throw the game, while, in his
version of events, Hegan alleged that Billy had said to him during
the game, 'Give us a penalty and I'll give you a grand.' Billy sued
the *Sunday People* which had printed Hegan's allegations, and he
won record damages of £100,000. Perhaps what really annoyed
Billy was not just the abuse he got from rival fans after the story
appeared, but the suggestion that Billy Bremner, the ultimate
competitor, would feel the need to bribe his opponents. And to
emphasise the nonsensical nature of the claims, Derek Dougan
of Wolves, who scored the second goal in the match, actually
gave evidence on behalf of Billy.

Yet it was typical of some of the madder notions that have
attached themselves to Leeds over the years, put about by those
who seek any explanation for our success apart from the blatantly
obvious one that, for a long time, we were just better than anyone
else. Bob Stokoe would claim that when he was manager of
Bury back in 1962, Don Revie had offered him a bribe of £500
to 'go easy' in a relegation match, a claim that was entirely un-
supported by any evidence, and one that I wasn't aware of Stokoe
making until the mid-1970s, when Don was a deeply unpopular
figure after failing as England manager. Don must also be regarded
as a total failure in the match-fixing stakes, apparently unable to
find anyone who would take a bribe to throw us the right result.

Looking back, I think that even Leeds' worst enemies would
concede, that we didn't get to where we were, with lines like
'give us a penalty and I'll give you a grand'. Brian Clough might
have said that we won all those medals by bloody cheating, but
that wasn't the sort of bloody cheating he meant. He was in the
Scilly Isles with his family while we were losing at Molineux,
which, combined with Liverpool's failure to beat Arsenal, meant
that his Derby County, with fifty-eight points, had won the league
for the first time in their history. They were also the seventh
different team to win the league since Liverpool had won it in

1966. The Derby players would already be celebrating in Majorca, while we were boarding the bus in Wolverhampton.

To describe the atmosphere on that bus as funereal, would be to paint a picture that is far too cheerful. And it was a long journey back from the Black Country, nearly three hours. Personally, I was shattered. You couldn't talk to Don at all, he was so disappointed. A grand reception had been prepared for us at the Queen's Hotel in Leeds, a victory celebration for the double winners, except without the second part of that double, everybody on the bus felt that they couldn't face the party atmosphere and they just wanted to go home.

Well, not quite everybody.

Peter Lorimer, my good pal, was sitting beside me on the bus, and he had a somewhat different attitude to these things. Over the years, some of us hadn't been too happy with Peter's approach, which was, as the saying goes, to treat success and failure as equal impostors. The rest of us felt that failure alone was the impostor. But, even in defeat, Peter would soon be seeing the world in a cheerful light again, whistling softly as he combed his hair in the mirror, already looking forward to a night out.

Along with Mick Jones, Mick Bates and Eddie Gray, he was one of the gambling lads who once formed a syndicate to buy a horse – though they had some odd arrangement which meant that they actually hired the horse, paying the training fees rather than buying it outright. For this, they got a terrible time in the dressing room, not least on the day after training when they all got dressed up to go to the races to see their hired horse running for the first time.

Next morning over breakfast, I checked the results in the paper. The lads' horse had come last. Again, they were taunted without mercy, as they described how the trainer had promised a better run next time. A few weeks later the horse ran again, and I duly checked the morning paper to see that there was a big D after its name. We found out that this meant the horse had died. And while the horse had our deepest sympathies, Peter and the other members of the Leeds syndicate provided us with a lot of laughs that day, and for many a long day after that.

He believed that in a short football career, you had to enjoy it when you had the chance to enjoy it. And I now believe that he was absolutely right about this, and the rest of us were wrong. Indeed, when I became manager of the Republic, largely influenced by what I'd learned from Peter, we would always have a singsong and a drink after the match, win or lose. And I'm really glad now that we did that.

But there wouldn't be any singing on that bus home from Molineux, on that awful night in 1972. The mere fact that Peter was sitting beside me, instead of playing poker with the other card-players on the bus, was a sure indicator that nothing could lift the pall of gloom. And this despite the fact that just two days previously, we had won the FA Cup.

It was this that was bothering Peter the most, the fact that we had won the cup and we hadn't celebrated it. The very idea of it offended him at the deepest level.

If it had happened the other way round, and we had finished second in the league, before going on to win the cup, we'd have called it a good season, not another 'Leeds failure'. Even if we hadn't won the cup at all, to finish second in the league was a decent enough achievement in itself.

'Fuck this,' he said as the bus approached the Queen's Hotel. 'I'm going in for a drink.'

I thought about it and I realised he probably had a point. We had won the cup, and that was no small thing. We had beaten a really good Arsenal team at Wembley, at the end of a season in which we had played some magnificent football, and it was wrong to end it like this, everyone on the bus home under a cloud of misery.

'I'm going in too,' I said.

We looked around the bus for possible drinking companions, but there were no takers. And so it was that Peter Lorimer and I went into the Queen's Hotel in Leeds, to celebrate the winning of the cup, and anything else we could think of. We were greeted sympathetically by the many staff members who had been preparing the great homecoming. We walked on towards the banqueting room, where the tables were laden with food, and the bar was open. And there we sat, drinking and talking. I had Bacardi and Coke, Peter had whiskey.

We didn't really have a great night, the two of us there in the deserted hall.

But we still felt that it needed to be done.

It was a gesture.

15

DRINKING SUNDERLAND'S CHAMPAGNE

THE FOLLOWING season, Leeds beat Wolves in the semi-final of the FA Cup. The only goal of the game was scored by Billy Bremner. What goes around comes around.

On the face of it, our opponents in the 1973 final, Sunderland, wouldn't be able to live with us. There was a feeling out there that, by beating Wolves, we had already won the cup. And now we would just have to go through the formalities at Wembley against a Second Division side who were just happy to be there and to enjoy the occasion.

The Leeds lads didn't think like that though. We appreciated the fact that they had good players like Dave Watson, Jim Montgomery and Dennis Tueart. But most observers felt that we would have too much for them, and understandably so. Nobody thought this was going to be a great epic like the final against Chelsea, when we had gained a few admirers for the quality of our football and the cruelty of our defeat.

This time, in the minds of everyone, we were clearly the bad guys, who were going to turn the cup final into something of a non-event by hammering little Sunderland. It couldn't be any other way. And, of course, we did hammer Sunderland on the day. We slaughtered them. We did everything we could possibly do to them, except one thing – we didn't score a goal against them.

They scored a goal against us. And that was that.

The big moments from that day are known to all – the miracles performed by Montgomery, the shock of Porterfield's goal, the sight of Don's old enemy Bob Stokoe racing across the pitch at the final whistle to embrace his keeper. To me, the whole thing still has a horrific quality, the biggest disappointment of my career. It wasn't one of those horrible experiences that you might learn something from, except this one thing – as I watched the Sunderland players going up the steps to collect the cup, I finally knew what people meant when they said that something 'felt like a bad dream'.

And we'd had a few of those already. But sometimes when you lose the league, you don't know you've lost it, on the day. You may realise six weeks later that that was the moment when you lost it, but it's not quite the same as standing on the pitch at Wembley looking at Second Division Sunderland receiving the cup, realising that it's actually happening to you right at that moment, and knowing what's in front of you – all the jeering, the gloating, the demolition.

In my case, they'd be saying I was past it. For the younger lads, playing for Leeds in itself would be enough grounds for mockery. And it continued to feel like a bad dream, which was somehow getting worse as we sat in the dressing room and Bobby Kerr, the Sunderland captain, came in with the cup.

Bobby wasn't a bad lad, he wasn't trying to rub our noses in it, but it was still a totally surreal experience as he handed the FA Cup around to us, so we could take a drink from it. One by one, we all had a sip of the Sunderland champagne. Nobody told Bobby to fuck off. Which on a day of miracles was probably the most astonishing of them all.

And then the scene of this rambling horror story shifts to the Savoy Hotel, where the Leeds victory dinner was due to take place – a familiar enough arrangement at this stage, except, this time, there'd be a lot more than myself and Peter Lorimer at it. All the wives and girlfriends would have stayed at the hotel on the Friday, and everyone would have been ready for a fantastic night. If only we could have scored a goal against Sunderland, just the one. If we had scored one, we would have scored all day. And then we'd all be looking forward to our big night at the Savoy, instead of dreading the very thought of it.

Don was in bits. When everyone had sat down in the banqueting hall, he stood before us and he tried to make a speech. It was so sad for a man who was so driven, to have to face this. He started speaking, but he couldn't do it. He just broke down.

About ten days later, he told us he was leaving.

He told us in Greece. We were there for the Cup Winners Cup final against AC Milan. I had had to get there via Moscow, where I had played for the Republic against the USSR on the Sunday, before making my way to Salonika for the final on the Wednesday night – a long journey. And, at this time, when everything that could go wrong was going wrong, I picked up a hamstring injury in Moscow. As soon as it happened, I knew that I wouldn't be able to play against AC Milan. And perhaps, even worse than that, I knew I would have to break the news to Don. I wasn't relishing this encounter with the man I had last seen breaking down in front of everybody at the hotel, bearing in mind that we were already missing Billy Bremner and Allan Clarke through injury and suspension.

When I got to the hotel, straight away I thought it was odd that he wasn't there to meet me. Normally he'd be waiting for me, to see how I was. He'd be anxious about any injuries I might have picked up on international duty, which was the bane of his life.

Instead, a couple of the lads – Norman Hunter and Mick Bates – were waiting for me. And they looked anxious, for reasons that I would soon discover.

But, first, I went to find Les Cocker, to tell him about my injury. When I had told him I couldn't play, I was surprised that he didn't say something like, 'You'd better see the boss.' It would be completely uncharacteristic of a man with Don's obsessive attention to detail not to want to know everything, as soon as it happened, at all times.

It was Norman and the lads down in the lobby, who provided the explanation.

'There are big rumours that the boss is leaving and going to Everton,' Norman said.

I looked at Norman and Mick Bates who had been at Leeds with Don since they were kids. They were shocked, dispirited, confused. I had great difficulty myself, trying to take it in. I felt that the first thing we needed to do was to find out exactly what was happening, from the only man who really knew.

'The best thing we can do,' I said, 'is go to his room now, and just ask him straight out if he's going.'

So Norman, Mick Bates and myself went up to Don's room. He was sitting on the bed.

I knew I had to ask the hard question, but I already knew what the answer would be. The fact that Don still hadn't said anything about my injury said it all.

'There are rumours you're going to Everton, and obviously the players are unsettled,' I said.

'Yes, I'm going,' he replied.

And then, just as he had done at the Savoy, he broke down and cried.

We appreciated his honesty. We knew he wasn't going to fob us off in that situation, and he didn't. Don said that the only reason he hadn't told us already, was that he hadn't wanted to upset the players before the game. He had planned to tell us afterwards. And, anyway, the deal with Everton wasn't done yet.

But the lads were devastated. They'd grown up at Leeds, participating fully in the family atmosphere which Don had created, and which had formed such strong bonds of friendship and solidarity when the going got tough.

I suppose I was a bit more distant from Don, on a personal

level. I had arrived at the club a bit later than Norman or Mick or Paul Madeley or Paul Reaney or Billy. So while I got on well with Don on a day-to-day basis, I wasn't as friendly with him as Norman or Billy were.

I didn't really believe in having a close personal relationship with the manager. I had seen at Manchester United the way that Matt Busby would do a bit of socialising with Noel Cantwell when he was captain, or with Maurice Setters and Dennis Viollet, and I didn't think it worked. Matt may have wanted to keep the captain close to him, but, regardless of that, when the time came, those lads still had to leave abruptly. It ends in tears.

Manchester United was my family club since the age of fourteen. Like Mick Bates and Norman Hunter, I had thought it was going to last for ever. But the time came when I had to leave, to face that devastation and to start again. I realised then that, in football, when you have to go, you have to go. The Leeds lads were learning that now.

And when you looked at it a certain way, it started to make sense. There was the bitter disappointment of the defeat to Sunderland and his breakdown at the Savoy. There was also the plain fact that Don had never been on more than £15,000 a year at Leeds, which played its part in his open disdain for the chairman and the directors throughout his time at the club, and his eventual decision to move on. But in a complex way, I think that Don's personal feelings for the players also influenced his desire to move to Everton. I wonder if he had formed the view deep down that maybe the critics were right for a change, that some of the lads really were finished, and that we wouldn't be able to stay at the top level with this particular team.

He loved those lads, and the feeling was mutual, and in the mood of despair after the cup final, I think he saw a day coming when he would have to tell some of them that it was time to go. And he couldn't face that.

*   *   *

In contrast to this emotional drama, the Cup Winners Cup final itself was a sick joke.

We'd heard rumours before the match about the referee, one Christos Michas. And when AC Milan went ahead after five minutes with a goal by Chiarugi, who scored direct from an indirect free kick, it seemed as if Michas had that result on his coupon. A good goal of ours was disallowed, a penalty wasn't given to us for a blatant handball and Norman Hunter was sent off. Bizarrely, the home crowd started to support Leeds, who took a lap of honour at the end, while missiles were thrown at the Milan players in view of the assistance they had received from Michas – and for their own negativity. Michas would never referee another match, and he would ultimately become quite famous for match-fixing but, in relation to this match, any objections from Leeds were brushed aside by UEFA. The controversy has struggled on to recent times, with Richard Corbett, the former MEP, collecting signatures in 2009 on a petition to be handed in to UEFA, demanding that the result be annulled and the trophy be awarded to Leeds. This does not interest me greatly.

Of course, if the dark forces which decided that game had only known the state Leeds were in, emotionally and physically, they might have felt there was no need for a bent referee on top of that. Or maybe they would have gone for it anyway. For insurance.

Losing that cup final didn't break our hearts as the other one had done, but it certainly contributed to this aura of doom which had attached itself to us in this period. At this stage, we were starting to just assume the worst, so that we weren't surprised when it inevitably happened.

But the thing about Leeds, is that we always stuck together. When most teams experience such huge disappointments, a crack usually starts to appear. There are recriminations, in public or in private. With the Leeds lads, nobody broke ranks. We took it together. And we would come back from it together. Always we could come back.

Sometimes maybe you need those disappointments, to show how strong you are.

And there was one more twist left in this season, this time of the happier kind. The papers got hold of the story that Don was leaving, and Everton pulled out of the deal, fearing that they might be charged by the FA with making an illegal approach.

Don was staying.

I was about to get into management myself. We had a family holiday back in Ireland that summer, in County Wexford where my friends, Tony Byrne and his brother Johnny, had a place near Courtown. I've known the Byrnes since we played football together in Ormond Square, and, in fact, Tony went on to own the Tivoli Theatre, or the Tivo, one of those cinemas we had gone to, and been ejected from. Anne and I and the kids loved this part of Wexford near the sea, and we ended up buying a plot there ourselves and building a bungalow. For years, I would look forward to the peacefulness of this place, to playing golf at the Courtown club and enjoying the sea, but not actually swimming in it very much. I was cowardly about the coldness of the water of the Irish Sea, and could only be persuaded to have a dip in it very, very occasionally.

But I'm sure it all helped me to recuperate after that traumatic 1972–1973 season. There was a new beginning too, with the offer from the FAI of the job of player-manager of the Republic. Liam Tuohy had taken over from Mick Meagan, when Mick resigned after a short time in charge. Liam was a real football man, and one of my heroes when he had played for the great Shamrock Rovers team under Paddy Coad. He had a relaxed attitude and I enjoyed playing for him. I was even getting fewer accusations from high up and low down that I wasn't trying or, hilariously, that I was playing only for the money – at the time, the match fee was £50.

So it was a surprise when Liam resigned for personal reasons, and I was disappointed to see him go. I was equally surprised when two senior FAI officials, Fran Fields and Des Casey, approached me, asking me if I would be prepared to take charge of the team. The thought had never even occurred to me as I was still only thirty-two. I felt it was a bit premature. But then I felt that I might as well do it, instead of someone else coming in and doing it in a way that I felt was wrong. There were no outstanding candidates out there.

I talked it over with Don, who had no objections. So, I decided to say yes.

But I let Des and Fran know that because of my playing obligations with Leeds, there would be certain restrictions on what I could do. I knew there would be difficulties scouting players and travelling to watch the opposition. I didn't have a written contract with the FAI, but Fran and Des explained that the finances were very tight. We agreed that my fee would be £1,000 per match. Money wasn't the issue and, indeed, over the seven years that I was manager, I never earned more than £6,000 a year in the job.

But I was excited about the new challenge.

Straight away I had to put aside my thoughts about the dangers of the manager and the players getting too friendly. I couldn't just turn around and pretend that I wasn't already a pal of Eamon Dunphy's or that I hadn't joined in singsongs all over the continent with Ray Treacy playing the banjo – it was all too late now for that. I couldn't make this announcement: 'I'm the manager now, I can't be your mate.' But I felt that you can still establish boundaries, and that you can turn the situation that already exists into a plus. You're not dealing with players' contracts either at international level, you're not deciding their personal terms. So you can make a virtue out of the social side of it, basically making

sure that everyone who comes to play for Ireland is having an
enjoyable experience – but of course, not too enjoyable.

I have never seen such determination in a bunch of players to
put right all the things that had gone wrong, as I saw in Leeds
when I got back. Even Don seemed refreshed after the break.
There was no more speculation about him leaving. He called a
meeting of the players. 'We will try and go through the season
unbeaten,' he announced. No one shuddered, no one muttered
that it couldn't be done, no one doubted that we were able to
conquer this challenge.

Indeed if there were any doubts, they probably lay deep
within the man who was setting this most ambitious target for
us. Because as the years went by and as Leeds matured, I think
Don was so close to the situation he didn't fully see that matu-
rity and improvement in the team. His emphasis was still on the
dedication and the doggedness and the attention to detail, rather
than the sophistication and the skill we had acquired. For example,
I remember a game against Burnley at Turf Moor where we were
winning 1–0 with eight minutes to go. I was in possession of the
ball in the old inside-right position, forty yards from their goal.
Allan Clarke made a run through the inside-left position and
the pass was on for me to put Allan through on goal. It was a
relatively easy pass, but I under hit it and a Burnley defender
intercepted it. We still ran out 1–0 winners.

But Don approached me in the dressing room afterwards and
said, 'Do you remember that ball you hit for Allan? Do you think
you should have tried it?'

'Oh definitely,' I replied. 'It wasn't a difficult ball and nine
times out of ten I would've put Allan through. We'd have been
two up and the game over.'

But Don wasn't so sure.

'I'd prefer if you'd knocked it towards the corner flag,' he
said.

It was clear to me then that Don didn't have the same confidence in the players that the players had in themselves. Matt Busby would have endorsed my decision in a similar situation, and I believe Matt's philosophy might well have been more suited to the players we had become. Conversely, I don't think Matt could have created that Leeds team with the players Don had at his disposal during the early days. In truth, Matt Busby, Jock Stein, Bill Shankly and Brian Clough were all brilliant managers in their own way, but none of them was perfect.

Don believed in gamesmanship, in breaking up the game, in taking the ball to the corner flag with time running out, though I have noted with amusement that far from condemning teams who do this today, commentators can be heard praising their professionalism. If we were 1–0 up after five minutes, as far as Don was concerned, that was enough. That insecurity of his, so clearly to be seen in all the superstitions, never really left him, even when we had become quite a different team, a better team.

We started the 1973–1974 season brilliantly, beating Everton at home, Arsenal away and Spurs away in the first week. We didn't quite go unbeaten all season, but we set a new record of going twenty-nine games undefeated, on our way to winning the title. It was a stunning campaign.

Don himself couldn't quite get his head around it. Over the years, after a bad performance, he had a line that he used to throw at us, 'If you lads are not going to do it, I'll get players that will.' To which we would mutter darkly among ourselves, 'There's the fucking chequebook out again.' He would then stand in front of the mirror, combing his hair – for how long it was hard to say, but certainly longer than was needed.

Then, on Monday, we would just start again. Now, after a home match against Stoke City, our tenth match of the season and the second one in which we had actually dropped a point

(Stoke equalised in the last minute), Don greeted us with this, 'If you lads are not going to do it, I'll get players that will.'

And he gave his hair the usual thorough combing.

That season was a towering achievement for the lads. For me, it wasn't so good. I picked up an injury after about ten games, when I felt a tear at the back of my left leg. I assumed it was a hamstring strain, but even after the normal rest and treatment for that type of injury, the discomfort persisted. I couldn't get a proper diagnosis and the weeks flew by, with my frustration increasing. The team was playing superbly. New lads such as Joe Jordan and Gordon McQueen were starting to show what they could do.

Gordon was a young, immature lad when he came down from Scotland, but he was good in the air and quick. When he came into the side originally, he would run with the ball and some-times get carried away when the crowd started cheering. Billy and Norman and I would try to restrain him, and it was a struggle for a while, but we knew he was a really good player.

Joe Jordan was playing at Morton when Bobby Collins himself recommended him to Don. Joe had a great attitude, was highly ambitious and always prepared to learn. Much quieter than Gordon, he was quick, athletic, naturally aggressive and brave. In one of his first games for Leeds reserves, he had his front teeth knocked out, but was undeterred. When Mick Jones was forced to retire through injury, Joe was ready to replace him, and went on to become one of the leading centre-forwards of the day. Though he had an aggressive image, he was a true gentleman off the pitch, one of the most genuine and reliable people I have ever met.

So the Leeds lads were doing great, and all I could do was watch. I was back in a situation similar to the one with my back problems a few years previously. And I came up with the same solution. I spoke to Don and went to see my old friend Mr Rose in Manchester. Unfortunately, legs were not his specialist subject, but he put me in touch with a Mr Shaw, a somewhat different character, more outgoing and informal. I would talk to him a bit more than I talked to Mr Rose, perhaps because he couldn't quite figure out what was wrong with me, and we needed to talk it through.

He injected the injured area and outlined a fitness programme. If there was no improvement within four weeks, I was to come back and see him and he would have to perform an exploratory operation.

There was no improvement, so I needed the operation, which was to take place in Manchester. The pre-operation injection was supposed to sedate me, but really, it just brought a wave of depression over me. Probably for the first time in my life, I began to think seriously about my future.

I was thirty-two, and there was a possibility that I would never play again. I now had four children – Chris came along in 1973 – and I was a long way from financial security, or anything remotely resembling it. Already my efforts to plan for a career beyond football with the insurance business had succeeded only in making everything much worse than it might otherwise have been.

Those drugs they gave me before the operation seemed to be bringing all that stuff up for me, instead of blanking everything out.

I had had a couple of serious injuries, but I had managed to avoid the sort of long-term problems which had blighted the careers of other players. I never suffered with my knees, for example, the sort of thing that gives players arthritis in later life. I would just have the scars from operations. I didn't even wear shin guards, because I didn't believe in them. I didn't like playing with them, and, anyway, they didn't really protect you from anything serious. I didn't mind the kicks and the cuts, it was a tight hamstring that would worry me. And probably what worried me the most, was the sort of thing I had now, the injury that lingered on mysteriously, with no guarantees at all that I would ever be right.

As I waited for Mr Shaw to wield the knife, I also thought about my own obsession with the game, the tunnel vision that Sue Hunter told me about, how everything we did as a family had been built around my career, and what was going to happen in the future when there was no career in football or maybe in anything else either.

But right now, I was at the mercy of Mr Shaw, his skill with the scalpel, and his verdict.

'There are three hamstring tendons that are connected to the back of your knee,' he said, after the operation. 'One of those tendons became detached.'

He had never encountered such an injury before. The proposed solution was quite complex. The damaged tendon would be cut, shortened and sewn onto one of the other undamaged tendons. All I really wanted to know was whether I could play again. Mr Shaw couldn't make any promises.

'Will this be OK?' I asked.

I remember his exact words.

'There's no reason why not,' he said. Which wasn't exactly a loud 'yes', but which I took to be broadly optimistic.

I seized on his optimism, and added a bit of my own. It was all I could do. I worked really hard in unsupervised training sessions, morning and afternoon. By the end of March, I was regaining full fitness. But I had worked so hard that when I got into the team again, there was no zip in my play. I just felt drained. Having put me back in the first team, Don quite rightly left me out after a few matches.

At that point I thought it was all over for me.

If anything, the excellent form of the team was making me feel even more surplus to requirements. I was travelling with the squad, which meant that I wasn't even playing with the reserves, and only doing light training. Which turned out to be the perfect treatment, because I was giving my body the chance to recover. This was what I needed.

Just when I thought I was finished, it transpired that everything I was doing was repairing the damage. And when Don picked me for the last match of the season against Queens Park Rangers, I felt really good and played well.

He only played me because sixteen appearances were required to qualify for a league winners' medal and I had only played fifteen. He was doing me a favour, for old time's sake.

And while I was delighted to qualify for the medal, as it turned out, I was even more delighted to realise that I could still compete at this level, that I wasn't finished after all.

A year after we had been humiliated in front of the world at Wembley, Leeds and Don Revie were the champions again. Sunderland and Bob Stokoe were still in the Second Division. What goes around comes around.

16

'REVIE TO TAKE ENGLAND JOB'

POLAND DREW with England at Wembley, putting them out of the 1974 World Cup. And, four days later, in my first game as player-manager of Ireland, we beat Poland 1–0. Regardless of the fact that our game was only a friendly, and Poland may still have been high on the improbability of it all, it set the right tone. It was only the Republic's second home win in six years. And, in fact, things had become so rundown, we wouldn't play another match for seven months.

There may have been a few innocent souls who thought that the team which beats the team which knocks out England must be a great team indeed. But those of us who were closer to it, were just delighted with the positive start. In truth, all of us were still a bit dazed from the English defeat.

I remember being both appalled and strangely impressed by Brian Clough's performance as a television pundit on the night. Having called it completely wrong by dismissing the Polish keeper Tomaszewski as a clown, he apologised afterwards to the English people for his error of judgement. As if it was all about him.

I thought, This guy is good – at something. I just couldn't quite figure out what the something was.

And as a Leeds player, I wasn't at all surprised that Norman Hunter was quick to take full responsibility for the mistake that led to the Poland goal. You never had to chip away at Norman to get him to own up to a mistake, he was too honest for that.

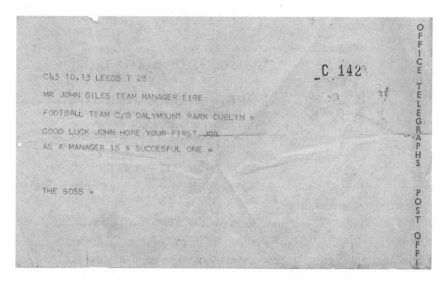

Don Revie sent me a telegram wishing me luck in my first match as player-manager of the Republic of Ireland team, 1973.

And in this instance, I might have expected Peter Shilton to say something about the shot that he let under his body. After Norman missed that tackle on the halfway line, there was still a fair bit for Poland to do before the ball was smashed into the net. But Norman took all the flak anyway.

His willingness to take responsibility was part of a culture we had developed at Leeds, a togetherness that I was hoping to bring to the Republic. There are things that the crowd never sees, but are well known to your fellow professionals. For example, if I saw Paul Reaney in trouble on the ball, I could go back two yards to receive the ball from him, and then I could be in trouble. Or I could just move two yards in the other direction, and abdicate my responsibility, and no one would know anything about it. At least, no one in the crowd or in the television commentary box would know. But my team-mates would know. Paul Reaney would certainly know – and these were the people I wanted to impress, not the crowd. Because these are the people I'd be relying on in a similar situation, to get me out of trouble.

We were playing a European Cup match one night and were winning 3–0. We were well on top. With about ten minutes to go, Norman got the ball and knocked it out to Paul Reaney, not to me, though I had come to receive it from him.

'What the fuck are you doing?' I said.

Norman had just got bored.

'I haven't had a kick for ten minutes,' he said. He had got more satisfaction out of the ball to Paul Reaney than the simple ball to me. And Norman knew this as well as I did. So after the game, I felt that this was the right moment to clarify it for both of us.

'When we're playing at Derby,' I said. 'And the pitch is bumpy . . . and you're having a bit of a nightmare . . . and you receive the ball and I'm ten yards away from you, are you glad to see me?'

'Dead right I am,' Norman said.

And he knew what was coming next.

'I'm there on the good days and the bad days,' I said.

And Norman would be there on the good days and the bad days for me too. Again it involves that balance between selfishness and unselfishness, between being true to your own gift, and fulfilling your obligations to it, but always with the unselfish motive of doing it for the team.

It was a culture which had developed at Leeds over ten years and, by contrast, I would hardly have ten days with the Republic of Ireland. But there were still certain things that we could establish, to change the existing culture, the deep-rooted attitudes which had always held us back.

In the summer of 1974, just after Leeds had won the league, the Republic embarked on a three-match trip to South America, during which we played Brazil, Uruguay and Chile. Apart from occasional training sessions, which we were now having at Bisham Abbey in north London, this trip which the FAI had somehow arranged, would be the first real opportunity I would have to work with the Irish lads.

At Leeds, we had that winning mentality, which was one thing that Ireland had never had. When the squad of about sixteen gathered at Bisham, I recalled that horrible night in Seville, when Ireland scored first and we didn't even have the confidence to claim the goal that was rightfully ours, and I said that I would never allow such a thing to happen again. From now on, if we had the opportunity to win, I wanted us to take it. I didn't want us to be looking back at the ifs, the buts and the maybes.

I knew that if you cut out the ifs, the buts and the maybes, then you have a winning team – *if* I'd got back that time, I might have stopped that goal . . . I was going to follow it in *but* I didn't follow it in . . . *maybe* if I'd done that, we'd have won the game.

Just fucking do it, was my attitude.

You've got ninety minutes out there in which to do it, and that's enough.

I'm sure that a lot of Irish people were terrified at the prospect of us playing Brazil in the Maracana in May, just before they went off to Germany to try to retain the World Cup which they had won so brilliantly in Mexico. It was a daunting prospect, which made it all the more important that we go out there with a positive attitude. If we were defeatist about this one, then we would surely be slaughtered.

Though the great Brazil team of 1970 had broken up, they still had the likes of Rivelino and Jairzinho. But we stood up to them, and, in fact, we gave them a game to such an extent that they were delighted with such a lively contest. They needed proper games to prepare for the World Cup and, apparently, we were the only opponents who had tested them. In fact, they were so pleased with it all, they took the extraordinary step of inviting me, as the manager of Ireland, to be their guest in Germany, an offer I was happy to accept. I had recovered fully from injury and I enjoyed the game on a personal level, as it confirmed that my encouraging end-of-season performance at QPR wasn't a false dawn. They scored a couple of good goals, then Terry Mancini scored with a header from my free kick. Terry was one of the more notable arrivals under the 'great-grandmother rule', and you can still hear tales of him not recognising the Irish national anthem. But playing for Ireland was good for him, and he was good for us. Otherwise it was a 'conventional' Irish squad, with experienced Irish-born players such as Ray Treacy, Paddy Mulligan, Joe Kinnear, Tony Dunne, Jimmy Conway, Eoin Hand and Eamon Dunphy, though the keeper, Peter Thomas, who played in the League of Ireland with Waterford, had been born in England – Alan Kelly, our outstanding keeper for several years, had a bad shoulder injury which would cause his retirement. Our other keeper on the tour, Mick Kearns of Walsall, became the most important member of the squad in a way that no one could have foreseen.

We went to the Copacabana Beach on the day after the match, and Don Givens went in for a swim. Nobody thought that anything could possibly be wrong, because Don seemed to be about ten yards away from us, certainly not far enough out to get into any trouble. But Mick Kearns somehow sensed that all was not right with Don. He went in after him and pulled him out, almost certainly saving Don's life. But this being a group of footballers, it wasn't long before a potentially horrendous incident was turned into the big joke of the day, with Don thankfully being able to see the lighter side.

The young Liam Brady was spared this disturbing experience. I had seen him playing for Arsenal at Leeds towards the end of the previous season, and I was enormously impressed by him. I knew straight away that I wanted him to go on this tour, but his manager Bertie Mee refused permission. He was being protective of his eighteen-year-old star, but I think he was being overprotective and, moreover, he hadn't bothered telling Liam about any of this. Liam was very annoyed when he eventually found out about it. I'm sure it wouldn't have done him any harm to play against Brazil at the Maracana, if nothing else.

To the folks back home, a mere 2–1 defeat by Brazil must have seemed like one of the greatest moral victories in Irish sporting history, given the levels of fear they would have felt beforehand. And there was a time when most of the players would have seen it as a moral victory too, but, as far as I was concerned, those days were gone. There was no such thing as a moral victory any more. What had happened against Brazil is that we had got beaten by a better side on the day. But we had done a lot of things we wouldn't have done in the past – basically, we had a go at them.

In Montevideo to play Uruguay, there was this sinister feeling in and around the hotel that everybody seemed to notice, but that no one could identify. Rio had been terrific. I had made it clear to the players that I was giving them personal responsibility for how they looked after themselves, to which they responded really well, with everyone having a wonderful time, but not too wonderful. Uruguay was different, and to this day I can feel what I can again only describe as something sinister – some sense that if you left the hotel and went out for a walk, you might never come back. Which may have contributed to a 2–0 defeat, and a feeling that if we'd done this, or of we'd done that . . . it was disappointing, we were back to the ifs and the buts and the maybes.

But in Santiago, against Chile, we got a result. A real result, a 2–1 win against a decent Chile side that was on its way to Germany with high hopes. They were a rough mob too, getting stuck into us from the start, with the referee a 'homer' who was letting them get on with it. But we matched them. And we took the lead, when Eoin Hand 'went under the bar' like Big Jack, to score from an in-swinging corner. Then they made it 1–1, and instead of disappearing back into our shell and letting them kick us around for the rest of the day, we came back straight from the kick-off for Jimmy Conway to score the winning goal.

I think there was a growing sense of disbelief back in Ireland that we weren't getting massacred down there in South America, and when we actually won a game, it was a big deal. You can talk to the players until you're blue in the face about what you're trying to do, and the values you want to instil, but when you win, there's no need to explain.

It had been a really valuable trip for me, and for the Ireland lads who were hopefully coming with me. As a start to this new career of mine as an international player-manager, I could hardly have asked for better.

And yet that trip is remembered mainly for the contribution of Eamon Dunphy, who didn't actually play in any of the games – and not, I hasten to add, because I had lowered my opinion of Eamon as a player. He was still a very good and a very skilful player, and I had intended to play him in that first match back in October against Poland at Dalymount, but his manager at Millwall, Benny Fenton, hadn't released him to play in it. And Eoin Hand had done very well in his place, in what would now be called the 'holding' role. As I was now fit again, I'd picked myself in the other midfield position. But it was Eamon who had brought another dimension entirely to the trip, by making us aware of the human rights issues which were involved here. In Chile, the democratically elected government of Salvador Allende had been overthrown six months previously, in a CIA-backed coup which had installed the dictator Pinochet. It was said that thousands had been killed, many of them in the stadium in which we were due to play, the Estadio Nacional. At Bisham Abbey, anti-Pinochet protestors had given Eamon leaflets, and he had distributed them among the players. In an ideal world, we would all have been more politically aware. But footballers, far from living in an ideal world, don't even live in the real world that everyone else lives in, their own families included.

Eamon would have been exceptional in his awareness of these issues, not just in the Ireland team, but among the overwhelming majority of his fellow professionals. He came with us anyway to South America, and as far as I was concerned, he was still a valued member of the squad. Indeed, he was one of the senior players who had done much to change the old system, not least by composing that letter to the FAI which resulted in the abolition of the Big Five. He suffered for his stance on Chile. When he got back, he did a newspaper interview about the controversy, and about why we shouldn't have gone. It got blown out of proportion, resulting in the FAI banning him from playing for Ireland *sine die*. Eamon wouldn't have been the most popular guy anyway, with the FAI, due to his efforts over the years to make things better. It took us a while to figure out that *sine die* meant that no date had been set for his reinstatement, that he could never be picked again, until the ban was lifted.

As far as I can ascertain, it remains in place to this day.

I also became a victim of injustice as a result of this brutal decision. It arises from the custom whereby a player received a statuette when he played twenty-five times for Ireland. It was a prestigious award in those days when far fewer international matches were played, certainly by Ireland. Eamon had played twenty-three times for Ireland when he was suspended *sine die*, leaving him two caps short of the statuette.

And ever since, when we're having a drink with Graeme Souness or Ossie Ardiles, or any of the visiting RTÉ panellists, he does a hilarious routine about this, concluding that I, and I alone, am personally responsible for denying him his statuette.

It was while I was in Germany as a guest of the Brazilians that I found out that Don Revie was about to become the manager of England. I was strolling down the street in Frankfurt with Ronnie Teeman, when Ronnie stopped suddenly. He had noticed a headline in an English newspaper at a newsstand: 'Revie To Take England Job'.

We were both stunned. There had been no indication that this was about to happen, no speculation at all. The last time I'd seen Don, we had just won the league and he was in good form and seemed to have no plans other than to keep doing what he was doing at Leeds. Certainly England needed a manager, but I didn't have Don down for it. So I was now manager of Ireland and Don was manager of England, another state of affairs I wouldn't have foreseen.

The news about Don also had other immediate implications for me. For a start, my contract was due for renewal, and I really needed to sort that out with Don before he left. Luckily, I had my advisor there in Frankfurt, on the spot, and Ronnie took the view that I should get back to Leeds straight away. Certainly, I didn't feel like strolling around Frankfurt any more, with all this drama going on at home.

I'd made the odd visit to the Brazil camp, where Rivelino recognised me and was friendly, but otherwise there was a language barrier. I had been knocking around with members of the RTÉ crew such as Jimmy Magee and Tim O'Connor. I had also visited the Scotland camp, where several of the Leeds lads were staying – Billy Bremner, Peter Lorimer, Gordon McQueen, Joe Jordan, David Harvey. There was much talk of how Rod Stewart had been out to see them, and how Jimmy Johnstone had joined in singing, sounding more like Rod Stewart than Rod Stewart himself.

But after ten days, I was happy enough to be going home to watch the World Cup on television – and to find out exactly how my life was going to change again. Back at Leeds, Don was still to be found in his office, so I went in to see him. It was no great emotional encounter, just businesslike as it always had been. There was never much small-chat between us, after five minutes our conversation would just dry up. But before we discussed my contract, Don told me he was glad that I'd come back, because he was recommending me as his successor at Elland Road. I had trouble taking this in, as it was a possibility that had never, ever crossed my mind. As far as I was concerned I was still a player. And though I was thirty-three at the time, my desire to keep playing had, if anything, been sharpened by my recovery from injury and my good form during the trip to South America. I told Don I'd need to think about it.

As it happened, there wasn't much need for that. A few days later, Don phoned me to say that the board had rejected his recommendation. He sounded very surprised himself, but then he was probably learning, too, that everything would be different now at Leeds. Managers try to give the impression that they own the club, that they are in control of everything, and on very rare occasions they are. But with Don on the way out, all that was changing. As for myself I had never actually said that I wanted to do the job. There would have been a lot more to talk about, before that happened. Nor had I gone to see the directors or engaged in any of the ducking and diving that is essential if you really want to stake your claim.

And when Don had given me the board's verdict, I realised that I had been turned down for a job that I hadn't applied for – the sort of thing I was getting used to at this stage, from the men who ran football.

We could look at this using common sense. We could reflect on the fact that Don had been an extremely successful manager at Leeds for fourteen years. And as a result, he might be the man most qualified to recommend his successor. That would seem logical – which is probably one of the reasons why it didn't stand a chance in this situation.

I believe that whoever Don recommended would have been the last person the directors wanted for the job. Because football is like no other business. Indeed if the chairman Manny Cussins, who owned the Waring & Gillows chain of furniture stores, had had a chief executive running those stores who was as successful as Don had been at managing Leeds United, he would have done everything humanly possible to keep him there. And failing that, more than likely he would have given the job to whoever his successful chief executive had recommended.

But this was football, to which the directors would not apply the same high standards that they would apply to the selling of wardrobes and three-piece suites.

I firmly believe that they could have easily persuaded Don to stay at Leeds. They could have made him an offer he couldn't refuse, certainly a lot more than the £15,000 a year he was getting. And I'm convinced he would have taken it. In fact they made a settlement of something in the region of £100,000 with his successor, which I'm sure Don would have found more than acceptable. But, in truth, the board wasn't sorry at all to see Don going. To understand why they were glad to see the back of him, even though he had been so successful, you have to understand the complex relationship that exists between a manager and directors.

Let us take a hypothetical situation: An ex-player is appointed as manager of the club. Like all young managers, he won't be treated with the greatest respect. To get the conditions he knows he needs, he will sometimes have to eat humble pie. The more successful he becomes on the pitch, the stronger he becomes in the boardroom. And he will never forget the early days, the disrespect. The taste of all that humble pie lingers.

The most important man in any football club is the manager. As his level of success increases, so does the club's wealth, and the role of the directors is diminished. In fact, they become virtually redundant. They are not happy with this situation, which leads to resentment and jealousy of the manager. In return, the manager treats them with disrespect or even with outright contempt.

Yet, despite his power and influence over team matters, the directors retain control over one thing that is very important to the manger – his salary. Because of their resentment towards him, his salary does not reflect the success he has brought to the club. By refusing legitimate requests from the manager for an appropriate increase in his salary over the years, the directors can screw him for all the disrespect he has shown to them.

I believe that this is essentially what happened at Leeds. After fourteen years, Don was nowhere near being financially secure. So when this far more lucrative offer came from the FA, and when it became clear that Leeds had no intention of matching it, he was left with no option but to leave. Believing that continuity was needed to maintain the club's success, he naively thought that the board would accept his recommendation of a senior player.

But the directors, who had been redundant for so long, were now back in a position of power. And they were going to make the most of it.

At some level, I could even understand their resentment of Don, having witnessed his treatment of them at close quarters.

Once we were coming back from a European game, and we landed in Middlesbrough. The lads got their stuff off the carousel in the airport, but one of the directors had bought a huge amount of wine, and it still hadn't come through.

Don turned to him and said, 'Don't you think we are going to wait around here all night for you and your wine. And if there is any delay you have to give every player six bottles each or we're off.' Don spoke to him with such disdain in front of everyone, you would almost feel sorry for the fellow.

On another occasion, we were on the coach coming back from a game, when Don went up to the front and asked, 'Does anyone want to stop for fish'n'chips on the way home?' Only one hand went up, belonging to one of the directors. Don totally ignored him, turned his back and said, 'Straight home, driver.'

I saw an example of the board's resentment of Don too. I recall one director, in the company of myself and a few other players, asking us in all seriousness, 'How is it that Don gets all the publicity and the credit at this club, and we never get a mention?'

But they got him in the end.

And they got me too, because in their desire to erase the memory of all those slights and insults, to erase his memory from the club altogether, they weren't going to hand the reins quietly to his preferred candidate. In looking for a successor, not only would they not accept Don's first choice. The man they would go after would be Don's last choice.

17

THE ENGLISHMAN AND THE IRISHMAN

BRIAN CLOUGH was a genius. He got a lot of things right. Like all men of genius, and like all the great football managers, he also got a few things wrong. And to be perfectly fair, I think that we got a few things wrong about him too.

Long before he came to Leeds United, we knew that he hated us. I don't think he hated us all as people, I think we just represented everything that he hated in football. And one thing tended to lead to the other. Even when Derby were a very good team, we generally had the upper hand on them, which drew a certain admiration from Clough, but also deepened his hatred, the idea that we were capable of so much better, but apparently chose to do it all the wrong way.

There had been one famous incident in which he had behaved spectacularly badly towards an individual Leeds player. When Peter Lorimer was given the Yorkshire Personality of the Year award, Cloughie of all people was given the job of presenting it to him. In the heart of Leeds, in front of an audience the vast majority of whom supported Leeds United, he first delayed proceedings by announcing that he was going out for a piss, and when he came back, he had a go at Peter for diving.

But, again, I don't think it was about Peter Lorimer, as such, it was about the team he played for, and all the things we meant to Brian Clough, things which offended him to the depths of his soul. For example, we did not have much respect for referees.

Like a lot of other teams, we believed that gamesmanship and manipulation were part of the professional game. It was a game within a game. It may have been considered cynical, but we were a winning team and we could see nothing wrong with what we were doing. It was the culture of the time.

Clough was alone in going against that culture. He believed that all referees should be treated with the utmost respect, that whatever decisions they made were final and should not be challenged. There could be no eye-for-an-eye mentality, or as we saw it at Leeds, an eye-for-an-eyelash. Feigning injury, or diving to influence the referee's decision were to him unacceptable. I have never seen or heard of any manager before or since Brian Clough – and that includes Matt Busby – who believed in and demanded such a high standard of discipline from his team.

And I now believe that Brian Clough was right. It took me a long time to fully appreciate his football philosophy. But, eventually, I too realised that the better the discipline of the team, the better the chances of success. Fewer sendings-off, fewer suspensions and the goodwill of referees will always lead to more favourable decisions, which, in the final analysis, increases your chances of winning tight matches.

He was right about all that.

But if he thought he could change our ways by confrontation, insults and insensitivity, then he was completely wrong. One of the many misconceptions about Clough's days at Leeds is that we were lying in wait for him, conspiring against him, doing all we could to ensure that he failed. This is to misunderstand the huge level of self-interest in footballers, who may regard the arrival of a new manager as an odd appointment, even a completely mad appointment, but who ultimately want to keep winning things. If he fails, they are hardly going to succeed. Regardless of any ill-feeling that has occurred in the past, players know that a new manager is probably going to be there for a good while, which triggers that self-interest in them, the need to make the best of the situation.

Normally, a new manager would seek an immediate meeting with the players to explain what he expected of them. When Clough signed his contract, the players were back in pre-season training. He had been on holiday in Spain when the directors appointed him. So he flew to Leeds to sign the contract, and then he flew back to Spain to complete his holiday. On his return, that meeting still hadn't taken place – in fact he hadn't communicated with any of the players for three days. Billy Bremner, as captain, approached him to suggest that a meeting with the players might be a good idea. Clough agreed. As experienced players, we knew it would be mutually beneficial to the manager and the players to work together. So before this meeting, despite all the bad things that had been said over the years, the mood of the squad was quite positive. As we sat waiting for him in the players' lounge, we felt we were in this new situation and we might as well get on with it. And then we heard his opening gambit, 'Right, you fucking lot . . .' he began.

I have seen it reported, in fact and in fiction, that he opened with the word 'Gentlemen' but that was not the case.

'Right you fucking lot . . . As far as I'm concerned you can take all the medals you have won and throw them in that bin over there.'

That positive mood among the players was starting to fade.

It has also been reported that he told us we had 'done it all by bloody cheating' but I don't remember that bit. Nor do I recall him saying that in addition to our medals, we could chuck all our caps and all our pots and all our pans into the biggest fucking dustbin we could find. I'm not sure why people feel the need for the pots and the pans and the biggest fucking dustbin, to embellish that line about throwing the medals in the bin. Like a lot of things to do with this period, the truth was strong enough. What actually happened, and what was actually said, should be enough for anyone to get the message.

Certainly the Leeds lads got it, first time.

There was silence. I was sitting beside Norman Hunter. Clough pointed to Norman and said, 'Hunter, you're a dirty bastard and everyone hates you. I know everyone likes to be loved, and you'd like to be loved too, wouldn't you?'

Norman had no such feelings.

'Actually I couldn't give a fuck,' he replied truthfully.

Then Clough turned to me and said, 'You, you're another one. You're a dirty bastard. You go over the ball.'

'So . . .?' I replied.

As he turned away from me, he added, 'It's not my fault you didn't get the job.'

Next he landed on Eddie Gray.

'Eddie Gray, if you were a horse you'd have been put down years ago.'

This was definitely the wrong thing to say in a room full of players who had been close to Eddie Gray since he was about seventeen, who loved the man himself and his attitude to the game, and who had huge sympathy for all the physical and mental pain he had suffered as he struggled to maintain his fitness.

Eddie himself was still thinking straight.

'Hang on a minute,' he interrupted. 'Didn't your career end prematurely because of a bad knee injury?'

'Yes,' Clough said.

'Well, then, you of all people should know how I feel,' Eddie said.

It ended on that note, and with the meeting over, so too were Brian Clough's prospects of success at Leeds United. At a certain level, I can understand what he was doing. He was trying to dominate us, as he dominated the players of other teams he had managed. He would get them first to defer to him, and then he would mould them with the force of his personality. He had done this at Derby, and he would do it later at Forest. When he took them over, they were struggling and unsuccessful clubs with a group of players who were less talented and less assertive than the ones he found at Leeds. Clearly, this style of domination had worked for him before, and later in his career it would work for him again. But we just found it silly, rude and insulting.

We had just won the league. I sometimes have to remind myself of this, when I think back on those times, because there is this perception that we were mostly a bunch of broken down old cynics on the way out. That we were standing in the way of a fresh new manager who had the enormous task of reviving this club which was degenerating under the weight of all these bad lads with their bad habits.

Again, for the record, a few weeks before the arrival of Brian Clough, we had won the English First Division, setting a new record of going twenty-nine games undefeated. We were an experienced team of top-class professionals who had been winning major trophies for a long time, and we were proud of our achievements. And at this meeting he had treated us with the utmost disrespect.

He was a bit like an entertainer doing his act in front of the wrong crowd.

And yet, even if that ugly meeting had never happened – and having thought deeply about this over the years – I now believe there's no way it could ever have worked for Clough at Leeds.

For a long time, I thought that if he had lasted about three months, things might have turned out all right. Now I realise that we were coming from different planets. We believed in what we were doing, totally. And to him we were demons. And we weren't going to work that out in a few months. For me, and I think for Brian Clough too, it would take years.

*   *   *

And still I played for him. I played in all but one of the games he was in charge for, and I tried 100 per cent. Despite not having a good relationship with him, part of me wanted to please him and to gain his approval. In fact, I played really well for him. At that stage of my career, I was both surprised and confused by my own response to him. I actually felt there was some chemistry developing between us towards the end. Which gave me some inkling of the genius which the man undoubtedly possessed.

If he could have that effect of me, how much stronger must it have been on the players that his assistant Peter Taylor found for him over the years, the sort who wanted to play, not for themselves, but for him? I don't know if Taylor would have had a calming influence on him at Leeds, but I do know that even without Taylor, Clough had this strange power.

It had worked with many players but, in my opinion, it was best demonstrated by the transformation of John Robertson at Forest. He was a lad with ability, but he had played mainly in the reserves before Clough arrived. Through the manager's influence, he became a great player, capable of dictating a game from the left wing. Robertson received the approval of Clough in a way that, say, Martin O'Neill never did. Martin has also spoken about this desire he had to please Clough, and how he never managed to do it. And yet in trying for that approval, he too ended up giving the manager what he wanted.

But Clough had more than just these perverse powers of motivation. By not dwelling too much on the technicalities of the game, he didn't complicate it, and like Matt Busby, he had the courage to allow his players the freedom to take responsibility and to express themselves.

So I played for him, even when it seemed pretty certain that I wouldn't be playing for long. It was obvious from the start that I wasn't in his plans. Neither were Terry Yorath and Joe Jordan, who had both played a major part in winning the championship, partly because he saw us as being too aggressive. He didn't fancy the keeper David Harvey either, for reasons best known to himself.

He had other reasons for wanting to get rid of me. In one biography, he was quoted as saying: 'Rightly or wrongly, I got the impression that Johnny Giles was behind much of the hostility and opposition towards me.' Rightly or wrongly – wrongly I would maintain – this is why he wanted me out from the start, and also because Don Revie had recommended me to the Leeds board before they gave the job to him. He saw my continuing presence as undermining his authority.

I could understand that part of it. Managers are always a bit paranoid at the best of times – often with good reason – and when a new man arrives at a club, he usually decides that he'd better get rid of a few lads as soon as he can. For whatever reason, if he's going to make the changes he feels are needed, these early days are the time to do it.

Of course as a player, you don't have to go anywhere. Clubs can agree terms, but unless your contract is up, you still don't have to go. You may believe that the manager will suddenly see the light and realise what a good player you are, but it's usually pretty clear that you have no future under a new regime.

In my case, there was no doubt about it. When a request came from Bill Nicholson to interview me as a possible successor to him as manager at Spurs, Clough gave me permission to go down to meet him, and he asked me to see him on the following Monday to let him know how I had got on. If someone wants to keep you, they don't let you go down to Tottenham to have a chat about your future prospects.

I'm sure that Clough saw the request from Nicholson as an answer to his prayers, even though all parties knew that Tottenham's search was only in its early stages, and there was no possibility of an immediate commitment from either side.

So I met Bill Nicholson in London on the Sunday. In an odd

and poignant echo of Don's attitude when he was leaving Leeds, Nicholson thought he had a responsibility to pick the next manager – and the authority to get it done. It would turn out that he was sadly mistaken. He too had been a great manager of a great Spurs team, and he probably thought that his choice of successor would have a certain weight. Again, I hadn't applied for anything, I was just listening. Bill understood that, and so we talked on the basis that there were several other candidates, and he'd be talking to them too. He promised to keep in touch about the job.

I went to see Brian Clough on the Monday, as arranged, to tell him how it had gone.

As I approached his office, he walked out. Without a word he walked past me in the opposite direction, as if I wasn't there.

Morale was low going into the Charity Shield match against Liverpool, and it was about to go down a bit farther. Kevin Keegan seemed to be in a strange mood that day. From the start, he gave the impression that the world was against him. He had been involved in two heavy tackles in quick succession on the edge of the box with Billy Bremner and Norman Hunter. I was protecting the ball which had broken loose, and Kevin challenged me from behind. He was all over me with his arms and legs which I hated. I lost control and as he came around the side I whacked him in the face. Bob Matthewson was the referee. I had a lot of respect for Bob and we'd had a good relationship over the years.

'Sorry about that, Bob,' I said. I deserved a red card but Bob gave me a yellow. Soon, Billy was following up the altercation by giving Kevin a few verbals. Kevin lashed out and Billy responded and there they were, having a punch-up in the sunshine at Wembley, in front of millions of television viewers who were seeing the Charity Shield live for the first time, with all the proceeds going to good causes. Bob Matthewson sent off both of them, and as Kevin made his way to the touchline, he took off his shirt and threw it down. Billy, for some reason, did the same. A national outcry ensued.

They were both fined £500 and suspended for eleven games. For years afterwards, I was accused by Liverpool fans of starting it all, and I'm certainly not proud of my contribution, but I do believe that Kevin was in a most peculiar state of mind on the day. Certainly, there was no history between us, and I regard Kevin as one of the game's great players. He wasn't as naturally gifted as a Cruyff or a Eusebio but he had an energy, a zest and an optimism that was extraordinary. He was quick, he was an extremely good header of the ball, and he scored more than his fair share of goals. There was always a total honesty about his play. And my admiration for him would grow in 1976 when he informed Liverpool that he was moving abroad at the end of the following season. At the height of his powers, he did not accept the culture of the day. Although there was no freedom of contract, Liverpool agreed to let him go for a fee of £500,000. I loved Kevin for that. And it had a happy ending for all parties when Liverpool went and signed Kenny Dalglish for slightly less than they got for Keegan. Though he had started at Scunthorpe, the big grounds didn't intimidate Keegan or inhibit him in any way. If anything, the huge crowds and the famous grounds only inspired him. Except on this day at Wembley, when for a few minutes it all unravelled.

So remarkable was the fighting, it has almost been forgotten that this was not just Brian Clough's official debut as Leeds' manager, it was also Bill Shankly's last match in charge of Liverpool. This can now be seen as a pivotal time in English football. At this point, Leeds and Liverpool were the two outstanding teams in the country. And we were evenly matched, though they were the younger team. Manchester United had been relegated the previous season – truly, I never thought I would see the day when Leeds United would win the title in the same year that

Manchester United went down. But it happened, just six years after they won the European Cup. Indeed it is a measure of how fragile and fleeting success can be in football that, with the exception of Arsenal, all the other clubs who dominated the scene at certain stages since the war, have been relegated. The great Wolves team was relegated within four seasons of winning their last trophy, the FA Cup in 1960. Portsmouth had won two league titles but were gone by the end of the 1950s. Big clubs like Spurs and Manchester City won league titles and cups but they also went down. Decisions are made on a daily basis that can make or break a club.

So as we walked out for that Charity Shield, we probably didn't fully realise just how vulnerable we were, how close to the edge.

Arsenal's double-winning team had gone into decline, and Alan Ball had left Everton, who were also fading. Brian Clough, of course, had left his title-winning team at Derby to spend some time down at Brighton and was now trying to bring his magic to Leeds.

We were at the crossroads. Liverpool had appointed from within, with Shankly handing over to Bob Paisley and the boot-room, 'sensible and sound men' as he called them. Leeds had done the exact opposite, appointing from without and going for a man who has been described in all sorts of ways, but never to my knowledge as 'sensible and sound'.

The big decisions had been made, as they led their teams into the sunshine at Wembley that day, Shankly leading out Liverpool, a club that would develop into the dominant force in British and European football for a generation; Clough leading out Leeds, a club that would be going in the other direction for a long time to come.

But Shankly himself was making a terrible mistake. He gave his life and his soul to Liverpool Football Club, an old-fashioned football man who believed that everything he did was for the benefit of the club. And yet, right to the end, he would do as he had always done, favouring the men who paid him over the men who played for him. When Ian St John was nearing the end of his career, he was left out of the team for a match at Newcastle. He only learned this when he was talking to Jackie Milburn, the legendary Newcastle striker then working in the media. St John was naturally very upset. He had been a great player for Shankly and he deserved to be treated with more respect. But Shankly himself, for all his own greatness, was about to have many sad days of his own. After he finished as manager, he continued to visit the Liverpool training ground, until eventually he had to be advised to stay away. I'm sure this was very hurtful to him, but it was the best thing for the club. As a man who had put the club before everyone and everything, I'm sure the irony of the situation was not lost on him.

Bill Nicholson was gone too, and Spurs are still looking for a way back to the top, fifty years after he took them there. Bill called me a few weeks later, as he had promised. He had done everything the right way, in his dealings with me. Bill Nicholson was a gentleman. So it must have gone hard on him when he had to phone me up to inform me that without his knowledge, Terry Neill had been appointed by the board. The man who won the double with Spurs was left to make these embarrassing calls, apologising to anyone he may have offended.

As soon as the new season began, Clough was already struggling. He had brought in two Derby players, John O'Hare and John McGovern, whose arrival didn't really compensate for the displacement of Joe Jordan and Terry Yorath. Duncan McKenzie was also bought from Forest, a very talented player, but not a Leeds player. Billy Bremner, even if he hadn't been suspended, was injured, and he would never play under Clough again. And if morale was bad, our results were worse. We won only one of our first six games. The board members were in despair over what was happening and called a meeting of the players to discuss the deteriorating situation. This was more nonsense on their part, a sham.

It was the board's responsibility to decide whether or not they wanted to dismiss the manager. They hadn't consulted the players when they were making the appointment, but rather than admit they had screwed up, they were now attempting to shift the responsibility on to us.

We were brought into the players' lounge that day, along with Brian Clough, as a PR exercise. They wanted us to criticise Clough while he was there, so they could say that they were left with no alternative but to dismiss him. If they just wanted to find out what the players were thinking, they could have called in a few of us, on an individual basis. But that wasn't their true purpose. They needed something exceptional to sack a manager they had appointed only forty-four days previously. So they created this scenario whereby the players rebelled, so the board had to get rid of him.

Billy pointed out that we weren't going to start criticising Brian Clough with him standing there in the room, still the manager. So Clough left the room. But even if he had stayed, the board would have achieved their aim that day. And, over time, it really worked for them. By calling that meeting, they established the perception of player-power as the reason for the dismissal of Clough.

But the bad-mindedness and bad decision-making which had led to this was theirs – all theirs – and now they were left with only one decision they could make. Later that day, Brian Clough was gone.

After he left Leeds, I never spoke to Brian Clough again. When I was player-manager of West Brom, and we were playing Forest, the club he went on to manage, we might have had a few words at the City Ground one day. But it didn't happen.

West Brom had won 2–0, and afterwards I was standing in the corridor with the journalists, doing an interview. A joke was made and there was laughing, at which point Brian Clough walked past us. I thought, by the look on his face, that he had believed I had just made a joke about him, but I hadn't. Later, I spoke to one of the Forest people, asking if I could have a word with Clough to clear up any misunderstanding. The word came back that Clough didn't want to see me. On three other occasions after that, at games between West Brom and Forest, we never spoke.

Over the years, I think he slowly began to change his mind about what had happened at Leeds. He would have spoken to people who knew what had actually happened, rather than people who just wanted to sell a story. I was also complimentary towards him in my column in the *Express*, quite rightly too, as his achievements with Forest and at Derby were immense. I had no hard feelings about Brian Clough. It would take about twenty-five years for him to officially soften his position, which he did in his 2002 autobiography *Walking On Water*. 'I never did get to know John Giles, still don't,' he wrote. 'I wish things could have been different at Leeds and we could have got our heads and our talents together over a longish period of time. Who knows? Giles could have been my Peter Taylor.'

He was also very complimentary about my playing abilities: 'He could grab hold of a match, tuck it in his back pocket, and carry it around with him. He didn't need to find space; it was as if space found him.'

Apart from the fact that I found this very flattering, coming from him, it gives a perspective on another version of our relationship which is now widely accepted as fact, because of David Peace's book *The Damned United*.

In Peace's version, Clough is also quoted saying nice things about me, telling me that God gave me intelligence, skill, agility and the best passing ability in the game, qualities which in

Clough's opinion helped to make me a very wealthy young man – a line which I read with rueful amusement. But then this imaginary Clough adds that the same God did not give me six studs to wrap around someone else's knee.

Brian Clough never said anything like that to me. Nor did he describe me either to my face or, to the best of my knowledge, in any other context as 'The Irishman', which is his nickname for me throughout *The Damned United*.

But there's a lot more about this book that I found objectionable.

I had been hearing about it for some time, and mostly the people who mentioned it to me were complimentary about it. Essentially, they said it was a good read. They seemed to be under the impression that it was a lively and generally accurate account of what had happened during Brian Clough's forty-four days at Leeds. And, clearly, most reviewers regarded it as a very fine book, one of the best novels written about football.

I suppose in some arty-farty sense it may now be acceptable to write a novel in which actual living people are mentioned by name, and placed in entirely fictitious situations, saying things they never said, and thinking things they never thought, and doing things they never did. But as one of the people misrepresented in this way, I do not find it remotely acceptable.

If someone wants to write a novel, based on real events, they can do what they have always done in that situation, and create a work of fiction in which the names of people are changed and situations and conversations are obviously invented, so that readers are always fully aware that there's a distance between what's on the page and what actually happened. That approach had worked for a very long time, and I assume there was a good reason for that – basically because it was just considered a cheap shot to make up things about living people, to put words in their mouths that they never said and that wrongly portrayed them in a bad light. You couldn't do it in a newspaper, it would be considered out-of-order and absurd. So why should you be able to do it just because literary critics think it's fine?

Certainly *The Damned United* portrays me in a bad light. I come across as a sort of a winking, scheming leprechaun – The Irishman who always seems to know something that Clough doesn't, always one step ahead of him. I took legal action against Peace and the publisher, Faber & Faber, in which I succeeded in having parts of the book removed which misrepresented me, with the publisher paying costs and damages.

I have no wish to give another outing to the lines to which I objected. But to give an idea of the sort of fabrications that appear in the book, I should mention a scene in which Clough is playing with us on the training ground, and Norman Hunter and I contrive to give him a suicide pass which ends up with us 'doing' him, an incident that never happened. And I could pick out a few more of them, but it is this recurring image of The Irishman constantly plotting and scheming that I found most offensive. As if the events of those forty-four days weren't dramatic enough in themselves, they needed to dress me up as the cartoon villain.

Another reason I took action against it, was that I am the only one of the main characters who is still alive. Don Revie, Billy Bremner, Brian Clough himself, are no longer around to represent themselves. The Clough family found the portrayal of Brian to be deeply offensive. Though I was supposedly his arch-enemy, I contributed to *Clough*, a documentary made by Yorkshire Television with the co-operation of the Clough family, which sought to correct the impression that the Brian Clough who managed Derby and Forest and Leeds was the raving madman who appears in the pages of *The Damned United*.

They too would have been aware that *The Damned United* was becoming the official version of events, that it was being read as the true story of what happened, rather than a piece of fiction. In fact Peace's book – and the movie based on it – have worked so well as commercial products, that, these days, you are as likely to see the Leeds United of that era described as 'The Damned United', as you are to see their proper names. The made-up story has actually knocked the real story out of the public's mind. Not that the author didn't conduct a lot of research. At the back of the first edition, he names nearly forty books which gave him some assistance in his project, from Eamon Dunphy's *Only A Game?* to *The Loneliness Of The Long Distance Runner*.

But he still didn't do enough research, in my view. He never talked to me, though I was there for those forty-four days and I am easily contactable. I would have been happy to talk to him. Norman Hunter, Allan Clarke, Paul Madeley, Paul Reaney . . . none of these men were asked for a contribution, though Margaret Drabble is acknowledged as a source for *The Ice Age*.

So it seems to me that if Brian Clough himself had a look at *The Damned United*, he would say it was done by bloody cheating. The author wants to have it every way, like the makers of films who announce that their movie is 'based on a true story', and then proceed to invent as they see fit. Which led to further complications when this book was made into a film.

After I had taken action against the book, the part of The Irishman in the movie was reduced to a level that is relatively harmless, just irritating. I watched it on DVD, not as a hostile witness, but as an ordinary viewer, someone who saw every movie made between 1956 and 1960, and one or two since. I wanted it to be good. And I felt that there were good things in it, such as the performances of the actors Michael Sheen as Clough and Colm Meaney as Don Revie, though the story didn't allow him to portray any of the warmer aspects of Revie's character. Jim Broadbent was terrific as the old Derby chairman Sam Longson. It did capture some of the atmosphere of the 1970s, but, eventually, the bullshit just got too much for me.

Apparently, it also got too much for Dave Mackay, who received an apology for a scene which suggests that Mackay broke a players' revolt in support of Clough at Derby in 1973. Unfortunately, Dave Mackay was not at Derby County at the time, having left to become manager of Swindon Town in 1971. Which again raises the question of why they felt the need to make these things up – some of them totally ridiculous – when what actually happened is so interesting in itself.

There is a perfect example of this in the film when the Leeds lads are shown swaggering off the team bus which is parked a hundred yards away from the ground. This never happened. In my entire time as a professional footballer, I never got off a bus a hundred yards from the ground, because there were too many people around and it wouldn't work, and, anyway, there was no point.

So when Leeds are seen doing this strange thing, it is explained by the Peter Taylor character that this is one of Revie's superstitions – he always does this for an away match in the cup. Now, we had a lot of superstitions at Leeds. We were famous for them. You could have filled half the movie with Revie's superstitions, and it would have been quite entertaining in it own right, so when I saw that they'd gone and given us one that we never had, I really had to laugh – why on earth would they do that?

Then you start to think of all the terrible football movies – there is hardly any other type really – and you get the sense that there's something about football that movie makers have never been able to grasp. They're always trying to add stuff, that it doesn't need. And when they start contriving it, they lose it altogether. When they're making the film of the book more stuff is added, more contrivance. They don't seem to be able to get across the idea that Brian Clough hated Leeds for all sort of reasons mainly to do with the football we played, so they invent this little scene in which Don Revie shunned Clough when Leeds came to play Derby years before in a cup match. They have Cloughie all excited about this visit by the great Don Revie, preparing two glasses of wine to share with this man whom he admires so much, and, on the day, he is totally humiliated when Revie more or less ignores him. From that day on, we are led to believe that Clough vowed that he would have his revenge on the man who had made him feel so small.

When you see them making up that sort of thing, it helps you to understand why, for example, they so rarely manage to make their professional footballers look even vaguely like actual professional footballers. I don't think I'm being vain when I say that the lads in *The Damned United* look like the members of a pub team at the bottom of their league. That sort of thing doesn't seem to inspire the film-makers enough to get it right. Instead, in *The Damned United*, they take all this dramatic raw material about football and football men and they start looking for a love story.

And of course they find it.

They bring us the love story of Brian Clough and Peter Taylor. They think that that's what it needs. Maybe they're trying to make the film appeal to people who mightn't be interested in football, in which case maybe they should just take out the football altogether.

You'll hear it said that the essential truth is ultimately more important than mere factual accuracy. And I would agree with that. But I also believe that football reveals the essential truth better than all these people are able to do. And I don't think they understand that, which may explain why they're always getting it so wrong.

Football has no script, no formula. Yet it reveals character and tells us much about the human spirit in victory and defeat and in just striving to get better. It is enormously important in the lives of people.

And there's a deep truth, as well as factual accuracy, in all sport. Because there's no way you can spin your way out of a defeat, the numbers are there for all to see. There's no way your

PR advisor can convince people you won the race, or finished first in the league, when you actually finished second.

In football if you haven't got it, you can't make it up.

Even the little epitaph at the end of the movie doesn't ring true. The line about Brian Clough being 'the greatest manager the England team never had' is just silly. They also give the impression that, in the end, he triumphed over his hated rival Revie, who failed as England manager, and ended up in the football wilderness, while Clough got together with Taylor again and took over Nottingham Forest, a small provincial club, and went on to win the European Cup. Twice.

This may be factually accurate but it is not the essential truth. Because it is also factually accurate to say that by the time he became the manager of England, Don Revie had already won major trophies, and won a lot more of them than Brian Clough, from equally humble beginnings. And if they'd kept going past all the astonishing things he did, it would also be factually accurate to say that Clough's career at Forest ended in sadness and relegation.

So they're at it again. They take the careers of two great football men, and they choose to diminish the achievements of one, in order to give a boost to the achievements of the other – and there is no need for it.

Leeds had just won the league title for the second time when Don, the outstanding candidate, was appointed to the England job in 1974. But a few things prevented him from emulating his club success at international level.

For a start, he didn't have as many good players at his disposal. He couldn't select Peter Lorimer, Eddie Gray, Billy Bremner or myself. Don was also a day-to-day man, who created good habits and a good attitude. As an international manager, he didn't have as much time with his players. He also assumed that players from other clubs would have the same approach and attitude as the Leeds players he had developed, but that wasn't the case. And the simple things we did at Leeds to pass the time – the famous carpet bowls and the bingo – were ridiculed by the national squad. It was essential for Don to win over the international players to his way of doing things, but he didn't, and the results on the pitch reflected this. He wouldn't be the only England manager to realise the enormity of the England job, but he was the first in a long line after Sir Alf, and that didn't help either.

He told me later that, towards the end, he was convinced he was about to be sacked, and that the FA had already decided on his successor. Therefore, he felt it reasonable to talk to another employer about his future. But unfortunately for him, it became public knowledge that he was negotiating with the United Arab Emirates while he was still under contract to the English FA. This was seen as treason and he was slaughtered in the press. Had the public been aware of his imminent sacking, they might have been more forgiving, but they weren't, and it gave his enemies the opportunity to compose the critical verdict that dominates his legacy.

When I was granted a testimonial, he was manager of England and I was manager of Ireland. I asked him if he would bring a Don Revie X1 to Dublin in 1976 for the game and he agreed without hesitation. There was no suggestion or request for any remuneration, untypical of so many other more respectable managers of that time.

And some readers may have noticed that I have got to this stage without mentioning the word 'dossier'. Almost every article about Leeds in the 1970s, from *Shoot* to the *Daily Telegraph*, would mention the 'dossiers' compiled by Les Cocker and Syd Owen that Don would use to give us the lowdown on the opposition. The impression given was that there was something almost sinister about it. In fact, any manager who was any good would go through the strengths and weaknesses of the opposition, highlighting anything that might be to his team's advantage – their keeper is vulnerable on crosses or weak on his left side.

But, eventually, we became familiar with most of our opponents, so the 'dossiers' were no more than a formality, just to remind us of things we knew anyway. They were not our obsession, they were the obsession of others who were always under the impression that there was some secret formula to success, and that we had somehow got hold of it.

And when it all went wrong for Don with England, the dossiers and the bingo and the carpet bowls were transformed by the same foolishness into the formula for failure.

In his late fifties, Don Revie was starting to enjoy life outside football, when he was struck down by motor neurone disease. I went up to Kinross on the east coast of Scotland to see him not long before he died. Already he had lost the use of his arms, and he warned me not to make him laugh, as I tended to do. At that stage, it didn't take much to leave him exhausted. We talked as we had always talked, not very deeply as he would talk to Norman or Billy, but friendly and respectful. I knew I would probably never see him again.

I got the impression that just before he was incapacitated by that awful illness, he was happier than he had been for a very long time. After all those years of total dedication to football, he had been able to relax for a while, playing a bit of golf in Spain, just taking it easy for a change. He had been so driven, he had never had the time for these things.

Having become a manager myself, I was now more aware of all that went into it, in a way that I hadn't been as a player. I had a better sense of what he had achieved.

He was my manager for eleven years, so I got to see all sides of him, his strengths and his weaknesses, that insecurity of his. Matt Busby, Jock Stein, Bill Shankly and Brian Clough had their own greatness, their own weaknesses, but if I had my time over again, I would rather play for Don than for any of the others.

He died in 1989 at the age of sixty-two, just at the end of the football season. His ashes were scattered on Elland Road.

18

'I HOPE YOU'LL ALWAYS FEEL AS INDEPENDENT AS YOU DO NOW'

O N THE night that Brian Clough was sacked, Norman Hunter was at the club, having a meeting about his testimonial, when he met Manny Cussins. He was told by Manny that the board was about to offer me the manager's job. Norman rang me to tip me off.

But Manny didn't call that Thursday night. Instead he phoned at seven o'clock the following morning. He wasn't the most articulate of men at the best of times, so when he came on the line, he said without any preamble, 'I say I say I say, will you take the job?'

I told him I couldn't give him an answer there and then, that there was a lot to talk about before I could make that decision. We agreed to meet at the ground at nine o'clock.

And there was a lot to talk about too. This was my first contact with any of the board since they had rejected Don's suggestion that I should be offered the manager's job, and I wasn't too pleased about that. Clearly, there would have been a presumption on their part that I was keen to get such a prestigious position, but I had mixed feelings about it. I certainly had ambitions to go into management when I finished playing – but I also really wanted to continue playing. I knew that if I took the job, I could not be a player-manager at a major club like Leeds.

I hadn't become the sort of hardened old pro who had lost

touch with the magic of playing. Even at the age of thirty-three, I was hanging on to the dream. For me, football always came back to that. So I had to decide – and decide pretty quickly – if it was worth missing out on two or three years of playing, to take on one of the biggest managerial jobs in England. I was still wrestling with this as I drove into the ground. And when I passed the treatment room to go upstairs to the boardroom, I bumped into Billy Bremner.

I knew he was having treatment for a calf injury but I was still a bit surprised to see him at the club so early. I was on my way up the stairs when he joined me.

'I told them that if they didn't offer you the job, I was going to apply for it,' he said. I was preoccupied about the meeting, so what Billy said didn't really register with me. Sure enough, Manny and the directors were assembled in his office, but as soon a I sat down he surprised me, 'Look, what we want John, is for you to continue just being a player,' he said.

'Hang on,' I said. 'I already am a player. You rang me at seven o'clock this morning to ask me if I would take the manager's job. Now you're telling me you want me to continue as a player. So what is this all about?'

Then, it started to get ridiculous. He told me that they wanted me and Syd Owen and Billy to take the team for this Saturday. I told him there was no way I would do that. Then Manny started waffling about 'things happening'. Nothing he said was coherent or made much sense to me, but one thing was clear – I was no longer being offered the job that I'd already been offered a couple of hours ago.

Soon I was back in the car driving home. I was still befuddled by it all. Then, I started to rerun that conversation I'd had with Billy. But it still didn't dawn on me.

I got home and Anne asked me what had happened. I actually said, 'I don't know.'

And then the pieces started to drift together. Suddenly it hit me, as it should have done earlier: Billy . . . had . . . applied . . . for . . . the . . . job.

In my mind, which wasn't really focused on what he was telling me, I was still assuming that Billy was saying he'd apply for the job in certain circumstances. But it transpired that after the chairman had phoned me at home, a club employee, who was friendly with Billy, had told him about my meeting in the boardroom at nine. That's why Billy was at the ground when I arrived. Billy had been to see the directors and had applied for the job while I was on the way in. Which explained the board's change of heart between seven and nine o'clock. And I could now see their dilemma. Billy's application had effectively scuppered things as far as I was concerned, because it would split the dressing room. Now, they couldn't offer the position to either of us.

I would have had no objection to Billy applying for the job, but it had never entered my head that he was interested. I was thirty-three and felt it might be premature to give up playing, but Billy was only thirty-one. He had just captained Scotland to the World Cup finals of 1974.

We were due back at the ground at one o'clock that day for training and, before I arrived, the other players asked Billy to confirm that he had applied for the job. When he said that he had, he got an icy response. Billy decided not to travel with the team for the next game.

I was amazed at him. Had I known of his interest in the job, I would have withdrawn any interest of my own. I can only imagine his reasons for doing what he did. He was close to Don, and it's possible he might have been hurt by Don's recommendation of me as manager, rather than him. Maybe he felt it undermined him in some way, as the public face of Leeds.

My relationship with Billy was strained for a period, something that had never happened before. There had never been any rivalry or animosity between Billy and me in all our years playing together. Part of the reason we were so effective, is that we always covered for one another. In fact, I often laugh when I hear them talking these days about the 'holding' role, or the midfielder 'sitting' in front of the defence protecting the back four, even though it is completely impossible for one player to 'protect the back four'. I had a 'holding' role if Billy was going forward, and vice versa, otherwise there was no 'holding' to be done. We weren't trying to hold, we were trying to play. It was all about getting the right balance between us, and by an eerie coincidence, we both ended up scoring exactly 115 goals for Leeds from midfield.

This sad situation lasted for a short while, until Billy withdrew his application, but by then, the board was already seeking alternatives.

Then there was another twist. I was informed that the board had decided to offer me the job again – but only on a 3–2 majority, and after much debate. When I heard this, I immediately informed Manny Cussins that I didn't want to be considered a candidate. I was no longer interested, because if I was to take on such a difficult job, the very least I needed was the full support of all the directors. As much as they didn't want a divided dressing room, I didn't need a divided boardroom. Especially one for which I had little regard or respect.

Twice I had been turned down for a job at Leeds that I hadn't even applied for. And twice daily thereafter, for five more years, I thanked my lucky stars that I was able to continue doing what I loved doing the most – playing the game.

There were times when going from Leeds to play for the Republic had not been the most inviting prospect, but around this time it became a merciful release. I never thought I'd see the day when an Ireland match would give me a break from dealing with incompetent football administrators, but this was how it seemed to me in the autumn of 1974, as we prepared for a European

Championship qualifier against the USSR. This would be my first competitive match in charge, so I could joke that I was playing under a good manager for a change.

It was also Liam Brady's first match for Ireland, and though he was only eighteen, you didn't need to be a genius to see that he had it. And that being the case, though I had wanted to bring him on that tour to South America, I didn't believe there was any point in delaying his international debut. But this meant that I had to leave out Eoin Hand, who had done really well for me on the tour, and scored against Chile when he 'went under the bar'. This was a term which would now become infamous among the Ireland players, because on the night before the USSR match, I called a players' meeting in the hotel, just to run through pre-match meeting arrangements, what time we would leave for the ground, and so on.

I had no intention of talking about team matters, but Eoin for some reason introduced the football side when he asked, 'Do you want me under the bar tomorrow?'

I had already decided that Liam would play instead of Eoin, and when I announced the team the next day, the players remembered Eoin's assumption that he would be playing, and the line, 'Do you want me under the bar?' From that day on, it became the standard line for players who assumed they were in the team, but weren't. Eoin, who was always a good team player, took it very well.

As to why I didn't just tell Eoin the day before that he wasn't playing, an experience at Leeds had taught me that you're probably better off leaving it till later. It was the famous case of Asa Hartford, who has been signed by Don from West Brom. He trained with us on the Friday morning, and then he had to go for a medical in the afternoon. We were wondering which of us he was going to replace. Without doubt, the one who was left out was going to be very upset, to say the least. But Don wouldn't tell us. It emerged the next morning that Asa failed his medical because of a suspected hole in the heart and was returning to West Brom. No one ever knew who was to be left out. By waiting overnight before naming the team, Don had avoided a very embarrassing situation. I took this as a handy tip, for the future. That's why I didn't tell Eoin.

Liam was outstanding in the match, which is now regarded as one of the happier days in Ireland's football history. We won 3–0, with Don Givens getting an excellent hat-trick. The highlights of that game at Dalymount are still shown frequently on RTÉ, with commentary by Jimmy Magee. It was the first really big result we'd had in a very long time, and it was all hugely exciting. In South America, apart from being pulled out of the sea at Copacabana by Mick Kearns, Don couldn't buy a goal. Soon, he would add to his three against the Russians by scoring another four against Turkey in a 4–0 win in the last competitive match played by Ireland at Dalymount, before the move to Lansdowne Road. He was like a man reborn.

But his three against the heavyweights of the Soviet Union would linger longest in the memory, and, on the night itself, they triggered massive celebrations among the Ireland squad. We were staying in the Central Hotel, where I had also had my wedding reception, and we were joined by various legends of the Irish folk scene. Ray Treacy, a keen music fan and a fine exponent of the banjo himself, was friendly with Paddy Reilly, Patsy Watchorn, Tommy Byrne and Luke Kelly, who were all soccer lovers and delighted to accept Ray's invitation for a few drinks and a singsong back at the hotel.

I had known Luke myself from way back. Indeed my father knew his father, who was also a football man, and a drinker – to know my father, he'd have to be a drinker. Luke was the same age as me, and had been a centre-half with Home Farm when I was with Stella Maris. Apart from his name, Luke, which was quite unusual at the time, he was unforgettable because of his red hair and the fact that he looked like a really hard nut. But his appearance was totally deceptive. Luke was one of the gentlest centre-halves I ever played against.

I got to know him well over the years. Back in the early 1970s, I went to see The Dubliners in Leeds, and Luke announced from the stage that if I was in the audience, I should come backstage after the show to meet him. Which I did. We went for a meal later on, and thereafter if Luke was playing in that part of the world, he would come and stay with us. We would play golf, which may surprise a few people who never associated Luke with the Royal and Ancient game. But mainly he loved his football, and he would always come to Elland Road whenever the Dubliners were in the area.

We had many great nights but this night in the Central Hotel after beating the Soviet Union was special. The match had been in the afternoon, so we had an early start to the celebrations. There is no better feeling than enjoying a good win. Back then, we all had our party pieces: Terry Conroy would sing 'To Dream the Impossible Dream'; Mick Martin gave us a memorable 'Step It Out Mary My Fine Daughter' and Noel Campbell did 'Massachusetts' by the Bee Gees. Eoin Hand's party piece was 'Green Valleys' and there was a debut performance by Liam Brady of 'Ruby Don't Take Your Love to Town'. I wasn't really a folkie, so I would stick to my repertoire of Nat King Cole or Johnny Mathis numbers.

I would also have a crack at 'Don't Cry for me Argentina', and that night I think I sang 'The Twelfth of Never'.

Eamon Dunphy was still suspended *sine die*, or until the Twelfth of Never, so we had to make do with Luke Kelly performing Eamon's favourite, 'Raglan Road'.

Ray Treacy had many songs, but he excelled at 'Whiskey in the Jar', accompanying himself on the banjo. He still maintains that of the forty-two caps he got for Ireland, the banjo was responsible for thirty of them. I recall a day when we were going to the airport and Ray announced he had forgotten his boots. I asked him if he had his banjo. He said he had.

'That's OK then,' I said. 'Don't worry about the boots.'

I hasten to add that we had a very strict and disciplined approach to training before a game, and we would soon be assisted in our preparations by Mick Byrne, who was able to strike that perfect balance between getting the job done, and enjoying the more light-hearted side. Mick was very helpful to me, with his enthusiasm, his ability to get on with the players, and the fact that nothing was too much trouble for him. He would soon be a permanent feature of the Ireland camp, becoming nationally famous around the time the Republic qualified for Italia '90.

But in that campaign for the European Championship of 1976, we would narrowly miss out on qualification, at a time when only the group winner got through. We were beaten 2–1 by the Soviet Union in the return leg, for which they took the extraordinary step of playing the entire Dynamo Kiev side against us, on their home ground.

The Soviet Union seemed to be actually worried about us, which was progress in itself.

The Leeds board finally succeeded in appointing a new manager, Jimmy Armfield. I had been messed about by them, with all these high-profile wranglings putting me in a difficult position with any new manager. So I began to seriously consider my future options. I had been eleven years at Leeds and, at that time, it was the custom, if not an automatic entitlement, to be granted a testimonial match after ten years. But there was an exceptional situation at Leeds, because most of the players had been at the club for ten years or more. And while I was older than Norman Hunter, Terry Yorath, Paul Madeley and others, they had all signed professional forms for the club before I had, which put them ahead of me in the testimonial queue.

There was a backlog too because Jack Charlton had been due his testimonial first. Having signed for the club back in the 1950s, he had been due his match by the early 1960s but as the club had become more successful, it had become more beneficial for Jack to postpone his big day. As it turned out, it was 1972 before he had it.

Younger readers may have difficulty understanding the importance of being granted a testimonial in those days. Compared with most workers, players were on good money, but none of them in my day accumulated enough to be able to support themselves or their families when their playing careers were over. With no freedom of contract, players usually stayed at the one club for much longer than they do now, and some never changed clubs at all. So a testimonial represented the only opportunity for players to get some degree of financial security. But nothing was ever guaranteed, and some players even lost money on their testimonial after bad weather or some ill-luck kept the crowds away.

After the managerial fiasco, I had a meeting with Manny Cussins, asking for a letter of assurance from the board that I would get a testimonial match whether or not I was still at the club. A testimonial actually cost the club nothing, but I sensed a reluctance on his part. He promised to discuss it with the directors at the next board meeting and come back to me. Weeks passed, I knew there had been board meetings but I'd heard nothing back. It was during this period that Jimmy Armfield arrived.

Manny had a ritual of coming in to the dressing room to wish each player the best of luck before a home match, and coming in afterwards to congratulate or console us. He would go around the room pinching us on the cheek, with an 'I say I say I say'.

When he was performing this ritual before a European Cup match against FC Zurich, I asked him about my letter of assurance. He just fobbed me off, and went on to the next player. But I waited until after the match, and when he had completed his post-match ritual, I cornered him near the exit. He tried to dismiss me again, claiming the letter was in the post. I had a lot of pent-up anger after all that we'd been through at the club, and this was bringing it to the boil.

'Don't fucking give me that letter-in-the-post business,' I said.

Jimmy Armfield was becoming aware of the commotion and, doing his manager bit, he tried to intervene.

'Leave it with me, John,' he said. 'I'll try and sort it.'

I didn't want to be starting from scratch with Jimmy on this.

'This has nothing to do with you Jim,' I said.

There followed a visit to the secretary's office and a convoluted exchange at the end of which I saw a letter confirming that Manny was still stalling me.

When I got back to the dressing room, Manny was gone.

Ronnie Teeman was in the players' lounge. Assessing the situation, Ronnie told me to go down to Jimmy Armfield immediately.

'Tell him you're retiring,' he advised. And that's exactly what I did.

Jimmy was shocked.

'You can't do that,' he said.

'Why? What's stopping me?' I asked. I gave a him a brief summary of my request for a testimonial and how I was getting the runaround.

'Some players at the club have their priorities all wrong about testimonials,' Armfield countered. Which amazed me, and brought up even more of that pent-up anger.

'Oh is that right?' I said. 'You were at Blackpool for a long time. Didn't you get a testimonial?'

'Yes,' he said.

'Then it was OK for you,' I shouted. 'But after eleven years, my priorities are all wrong?'

Of course Jimmy, who had just arrived at the club, had no great allegiance to me. But his lack of understanding as an ex-pro really upset me.

'I'm telling you now, I'm finished,' I said, and I walked out of his office.

I didn't report for training for the rest of that week, but, on Friday, Jimmy phoned to tell me the travelling arrangements for the next day's game against Coventry. I reminded him that I had retired, and repeated that I wouldn't be going to Coventry.

'What am I going to tell the press?' he asked. 'Will I tell them you have the flu?'

'Tell them what you like,' I said.

I knew that Jimmy and Manny wouldn't want my dispute with the club to become public, and clearly they had nothing to gain from this new situation, in which I was essentially on strike. So it was no great surprise that, a few days later, I received the letter guaranteeing me my testimonial match. I was glad the matter was resolved, but I was still angry and disheartened at the club's meanness of spirit.

After all that needless confrontation about what should have been a swift and positive response to a simple request from a loyal player, ultimately I never had that testimonial match at Leeds.

Jimmy' attitude throughout this episode did not fill me with optimism for my remaining days at Elland Road. He was frustrating, to say the least, largely because he had difficulty making important decisions. Duncan McKenzie summed him up best. 'Jimmy's indecision was final,' he said.

I don't want to be too harsh on Jimmy, because he's an amiable sort of a guy. It's just that I probably didn't need that sort of a guy in charge at the time. And I don't think Jimmy entirely believed in me either.

Our league form was inconsistent but we did better in the cup competitions. We reached the sixth round of the FA Cup, where we lost after three replays to Ipswich. But we reached the final of the 1975 European Cup, which wasn't too bad for a side that was supposedly on the way out.

We played Bayern Munich in the final in Parc des Princes in Paris. This was the great Bayern side that had won the European Cup the previous year and would go on to win three in a row. With Franz Beckenbauer, Gerd Müller, Sepp Maier and Uli Hoeness, they had provided the backbone for West Germany when they won the 1974 World Cup.

And still we dominated the first half. I felt that if we could get in front, they would collapse. But we never did, partly because of one of the worst refereeing decisions I have ever seen – and I've seen some. Allan Clarke beat Beckenbauer and was through on goal when Beckenbauer went through Allan to get back at the ball. It was a clear-cut penalty, but the ref gave a corner.

Revived by this, the Germans came back to beat us 2–0.

It turned out, that this was our last hurrah.

I didn't know it at the time, but it was also my last game for Leeds United.

Jimmy Armfield had arranged an end-of-season week in Spain for the squad. It was a strange interlude for me, because instead of playing golf, having a few drinks and taking it easy, I was uptight, distracted by some news I had received – West Brom were interested in me becoming their player-manager. It was a huge decision for me, because even though I hadn't particularly enjoyed the previous season, I wasn't sure I wanted to move to West Brom.

Eventually, I decided that if Jimmy would agree to give me a two-year contract, I would stay. He assured me that he wanted me to stay, but said that he could only offer me one year. I wasn't happy with that.

I had just played really well in a European Cup final, and felt I could contribute for another two years. I wasn't looking for favours. But it again seemed that Jimmy's indecision was final.

On my first day back home, I received a phone call from Jimmy, telling me he'd agreed terms with West Brom, and then, typically and confusingly, he added that he didn't want me to go. I knew I couldn't take another year of this. A manager doesn't agree terms with another club unless he wants you to go, even if his name is Jimmy Armfield.

My mind was made up. I was going.

The procedure usually involved the buying club agreeing a fee with the selling club, and then coming to terms with the player. The usual signing-on fee for a player of my experience was £25,000. When I spoke to the West Brom people, they told me the clubs had agreed a transfer fee of £50,000. I was informed that instead of West Brom paying me the signing-on fee of £25,000, Leeds would pay it to me out of the inflated transfer price of £50,000. This sounded like bad news. Remembering all the grief I'd had, trying to get a guarantee of a testimonial, I was immediately suspicious of this complicated arrangement. My disquiet deepened after a meeting with Jimmy. I told him that West Brom had informed me that Leeds were to pay me my signing-on fee.

'I don't know anything about that, but I will have a word with the chairman and come back to you,' he said.

A few days later, he told me that the club had agreed to give me a paltry £5,000 payment from the £50,000. I told Jimmy to tell Manny what he could do with his £5,000. But Jimmy wasn't going to make any such representations on my behalf.

'You should speak to the chairman yourself,' he said.

Manny Cussins agreed to meet me. In all these horrible dealings, I realise I was unlucky that Don had left when he did, otherwise he would still have had some power in the club, and would have done what he could for me. Instead, I was standing face to face with Manny Cussins, in his office, bargaining for my future. I wanted to keep it simple.

'You bought me for £33,000,' I began, 'and after 525 appearances over twelve years you are now selling me for a profit of £17,000. You're offering me £5,000. I don't think that's fair.'

Manny cut me down straight away.

'We paid you good money over the years,' he said.

Naively, even innocently, there was an expectation from players of my generation that after long and loyal service, the club would look after you. I thought they would. I believed when the time came to leave, the directors would show some appreciation. I had helped the club to win the FA Cup, the league, the League Cup and the Fairs Cup. At the end of all that, I sort of expected that the directors would say, 'Thanks very much for what you've done for the club. In recognition of your services, we are giving you a free release and you can make your own financial arrangements with West Brom. We wish you well for the future.'

Something like that, anyway.

But that's not what Manny was saying. 'We paid you good money over the years', is what Manny was saying.

It came out of him so cynically, it was one of the most infuriating things I've heard in my life. It annoys me now just thinking about it.

I grabbed him by the throat.

'You miserable little fucker,' I said.

Maybe he thought I was going to choke him, right there in his office. But I let him go.

I walked away from him, leaving him a bit shaken, maybe his glasses at the wrong angle, but nothing he wouldn't get over – already he was probably putting it down to my stupidity and that of footballers in general. As I left his office, I just wanted to get away from the likes of Manny, with their condescending attitude towards the players who had built that place for them, the players that these businessmen would never understand.

What he was telling me was that I had been an idiot. Which reflected the attitude of businessmen in general – when your day is done, it is done. I had served my purpose and these smart men were going to do nothing they weren't strictly obliged to do. They would never understand the spirit of a professional footballer, how the fulfilment of dreams is the essence of a player's life, and how much of himself he gives to the cause.

They would never comprehend that you can't put a price on these things, that when a player is doing what it takes to win the semi-final or the final of the FA Cup, he is doing it with his heart and his soul, and he is not looking at the bottom line.

In Manny's world, if that's what you did, you were a fool. And when you were finished, it counts for nothing. Any expectations of respect, affection or generosity of spirit are regarded as nonsensical. Certainly they are not the right bargaining tools.

But I had one good man on my side, who knew how these characters worked, and knew how to deal with them. Ronnie Teeman explained to me, that if I just refused to go to West Brom, Leeds would have to sign me and pay me for another twelve months, or release me on a free transfer. Either way, they would lose the £50,000 fee. So that became my strategy.

I went back to Manny and I told him I was staying. He immediately came up with an improved offer. Leeds reduced the fee by £15,000 and agreed that the team would play a testimonial match for me, free of charge at The Hawthorns. West Brom would then guarantee my signing-on fee of £25,000 from the match proceeds, and they said they were happy with the reduced fee.

Manny had one more condescending line to add. 'I hope you'll always feel as independent as you do now,' he said.

Still putting me in my place.

'Don't you worry about that,' I said.

*   *   *

I ran into Manny a few times after that, and I always tried to avoid him, but during Paul Reaney's testimonial reception at Nouveau, the nightclub run by Tunc Osbay, Manny came to my table and stood behind me. He did that thing of his, pinching my cheeks as he said, 'I say I say I say lads, we should never have let him go, should we?'

I was already in a bad mood after someone told me they'd overheard one of the club's directors stating that he disagreed with testimonials for players 'on principle'.

And fortified by a few Bacardis, I turned to Manny and said, 'Weren't you the chairman who sold me?'

'Yes, that's right,' he said.

'Well you were the one responsible for me going. So fuck off and don't annoy me ever again.'

There was loud laughter from the players at the table. I turned around, but there was no sign of Manny.

And I never saw him again.

A football ground at the height of summer can be a lonely place. On the day that I called in to Elland Road to collect my boots and a few other bits and pieces, it felt like I had the place to myself. Maybe somewhere on the premises there was someone doing the laundry or cleaning the canteen, but I didn't see anyone. And I don't think anyone saw me, as I parked outside the ground for the last time as a Leeds player. Or was I a West Brom player? I suppose I had already crossed over that line contractually, but as I called in to Elland Road on that day, I was still torn. I was travelling on my own that day to Birmingham, a place I knew nothing about, and soon my family would be joining me. In so many ways, we would have to start all over again, and it wouldn't be easy.

I went in to collect my stuff from the cubby-hole. I had never imagined it would turn out like this, that I would be walking all alone through this deserted building, on my last day at Leeds.

Back in the days when I would be doing my visualisation, one of the things I visualised, in a sentimental way, was my last game for the club.

The ground would be packed, of course. It would be at the end of the season, and it would be well known that I was leaving. So there would be a proper send-off, and we'd all make a day of it. I would be able to thank the crowd for all their support, they could savour all the memories of the successful years we'd had together. Anne and the kids would be at the game, the families of the other players would be there, it would be a party atmosphere. Later, we'd go to Tunc's place for a good few drinks and have a laugh as we always did.

In the mind's eye, it was never like this, collecting my boots on a dead day during the close season. The way it had turned out, there would be quite a few people at Leeds who probably wouldn't even know I was gone. But I was gone all right, taking my boots with me through these empty corridors which on so many days, and so many nights, had seemed like the most exciting place in the world.

It was one of the saddest days of my life.

19

'JOHN, YOU'VE GOT TO PUT UP WITH THAT TYPE OF THING'

JOHN OSBORNE told me there were two players he had really hated in the game.

One was Emlyn Hughes. The other was me. And if he had to pick the one he hated the most, it would be . . . me.

John was the goalkeeper at West Brom, but I had first encountered him back in 1956 at Tolka Park when he played for the England schoolboys team that beat us 1–0, with Barry Bridges scoring, and John actually playing at left-back.

John would become a good friend of mine – he passed away in 1998 – but when I arrived at West Brom, I had been warned he could be bit troublesome. As a keen young manager, I had asked the players to come back a week early for pre-season training. Which they all did, apart from John. When he eventually appeared, I told him that since he had a year left on his contract, I was offering him the opportunity to stay at home, and have his wages posted to him. John decided he would prefer to come in and train. Maybe it was the natural athlete in him.

We also managed to rise above an unsavoury incident that had happened during a vital match at West Brom in 1972. Leeds had been awarded a penalty, but, as an injured player was receiving treatment, there was a lull before I could take the kick. Allan Clarke was standing beside me at the penalty spot when John approached and tried to psyche me out with a joke, 'How much is it worth to let it in?' he said.

'The day I have to pay you to let a penalty in, is the day I'll pack it all in,' I said. Or words to that effect.

There were a few other lads at West Brom with whom I'd exchanged some unkind words over the years. Apart from calling Tony Brown a 'lazy bastard' and watching him taking the league title away from Leeds with the help of Ray Tinkler and the temporary abandonment of the offside rule, I'd had plenty of verbals over the years with John Wile and Ally Robertson. I had also taken a punch from Alan Merrick, for which I exacted full retribution. But as I got to know them, they turned out to be a terrific bunch, and I had two of my happiest years in football with them.

I was also greatly helped in the settling-in process by Roger Newman, a friend of the chairman Bert Millichip, who had been asked by Bert to help me find a house in the Birmingham area. I got on really well with Roger and we are still the best of friends.

Michael had just done his 11-plus, so schools were also a big consideration and, because of Roger's tireless efforts on our behalf, we found what we were looking for in Edgbaston, near the cricket ground.

As regards settling in to the player-manager role, all I knew was what I had learned with the Republic, which was enough to suggest to me that I could make it work. A few people I respected in the game, including Noel Cantwell, contacted me to say I was mad to do it. But I figured that, as a player, I wasn't going to be taking on any more responsibility on the pitch than I had been doing, and, as a manager I felt could do the job if I was able to establish certain principles. For example, regardless of how I played, I had to have the authority to tell the other players what they were doing wrong. Luckily, I had a group of lads at West Brom who accepted that.

But we started poorly. As player-manager, I wasn't playing well and I wasn't managing well. I think I had preconceived ideas about a lot of the players. I didn't know them well enough, so

I kept changing the team. I put some of my knowledge to good use when I bought a couple of Irish players who made a real difference. Mick Martin was playing for Manchester United under Tommy Docherty, and he was a steal at £20,000. Paddy Mulligan was even better value, being out of favour at Crystal Palace under Malcolm Allison, and available on a free transfer. They were good, intelligent players, as valuable to me at West Brom as they had been in the Ireland team.

If you made a point to them, you only had to make it once. In general, I believed that if I was making a point to a player, I should keep it as simple as I possibly could. Some players would tell me they'd got it the first time, and it would turn out that they hadn't. So I would make the point again. And maybe they'd get it this time, or they'd just tell me that they had. But if I had to make the point more than three times, and it still hadn't got through, I would give up on the player. With Paddy and Mick I would make the point once, they would tell me they'd got it, and it would turn out that they really had got it, first time. They became big favourites at the Hawthorns that season. The following season, there would be four Irishmen including myself playing for West Brom, when Ray Treacy joined us from Preston North End, bringing his usual commitment to all-round entertainment, and, while he was at it, scoring a few important goals for us. Ray was as quick on the uptake as Paddy and Mick, an excellent header of the ball with a really good understanding of the game.

But in that first season, there was another important development when Tony Brown moved to the left side of midfield – soon the confidence started to flow.

Under Don Howe, the previous manager, the squad had lost belief in itself, but they were clearly good players. John Wile and Ally Robertson were excellent defenders who made a fine partnership. Willie Johnston was one of those about whom I had preconceived ideas, assuming him to be a lad who liked a drink and a bit of argy-bargy on and off the pitch. Turned out, he was a fitness fanatic who loved to train, was well-liked by the other players and a constructive influence in the dressing room. He liked a drink, too, it's just that he couldn't hold it. Because of his terrific form, and the success of the team, he got his dearest wish, and was recalled to the Scotland team. I was delighted for him. And there was Bryan Robson, who started badly but returned to have a superb season. Bryan played in several positions for me – left-back, centre-back, midfield. He was modest, with a top-class attitude and work ethic, and he would fulfil all that potential by becoming a great player.

Meanwhile, the complex personality of John Osborne was revealing itself. I had learned that he'd had a row with Don Howe over Don's idea that he should train with the rest of the players, instead of doing the sort of specialised goalkeeping work that John felt he needed at the time. So I told him he could do his specialised goalkeeping work.

'No no,' he said. 'I'll train with the rest of the lads.'

I also discovered that the more he complained on match days about having a touch of the flu or a problem with his fingers, the better he played. He kept twenty-one clean sheets that season, a club record. John remains one of the all-time greats among the West Brom fans, who themselves deserve the highest praise for being so patient and generous with their new player-manager in his early struggles.

If there was one game in which we turned it around, it was about ten weeks into the season, when we played Bristol City, then considered the best team in the Second Division. We outplayed them in the first half, but it was still scoreless. I told the lads at half-time that the game was there for the taking and I wanted us to take it. We won 2–0. And we never looked back.

It was still on a knife-edge coming to the last game of the season, at Boundary Park against Oldham. A win would guarantee us promotion. A draw would do us, if Bolton, our main rivals, also drew away at Charlton – if we both lost, West Brom would go up. But we didn't want to think about that. It may have been the last match, but it was also the first match of the season in which our destiny was entirely in our own hands. The situation was pressurised enough without the added burden, for me, of learning that the referee would be a certain Ray Tinkler. And that this would be his last match before retiring as a referee.

At half-time, the game was still scoreless. We didn't know how Bolton were doing, and we didn't want to know. This turned out to be a wise move because, as it happened, they were winning 4–0 at half-time and we didn't need the added pressure that that knowledge would have brought. Our attitude was: we needed to beat Oldham. End of story.

We scored midway through the second half and, with time running out, it looked like we were going up. Except it was taking quite a while for that time to run out, with Tinkler letting the game go into overtime far too long for my liking.

I was now seriously worried that Tinkler, in his last game, just couldn't bring himself to blow the full-time whistle. So I had a go at him. 'I remember you from Leeds . . . are you going to do us again?' I said.

'I remember you too,' he replied, with enough menace to make me shut up.

He seemed to be enjoying the tension of the match, the last few minutes of his career. But, for us, in that situation, every second felt like an hour. The torture continued with Oldham getting several corners, any one of which could have kept us in the Second Division for another season.

Mercifully Mr Tinkler eventually found a reason to end the match, with West Brom still winning. And the man who scored the decisive goal on the day was Tony Brown – the same Tony Brown who helped to deny Leeds the championship back in 1971. So maybe there is some poetic justice out there.

Tony and I had been able to laugh about that offside debacle at Elland Road, though he probably laughed just a bit more than

I did. He said that the West Brom lads found it particularly funny because they always expected a hammering at Leeds, and they invariably got one – until that day. I found that the man who had done much to deprive me of that league winners' medal was a wonderful player and wonderful lad all round, and he did a terrific job for me, making a huge contribution to the cause in that promotion season.

Tony scored a record 279 goals in 720 appearances for West Brom, and, in all seriousness, I think they should put up a statue to him in West Bromwich – with no mention, not even in small print, of a certain match against Leeds United a long time ago.

So I had brought West Brom up to the First Division. As a manager, I was on my way. I was, as they say, on the ladder. Yet, by the start of the next season, I would have decided that I couldn't continue to do the job at West Brom, under the system that was regarded as normal at that time, and that I was getting out of football management altogether.

In the first board meeting after promotion, I expected the directors to ask me what I needed to take the club forward. This did not happen. The previous season, during our run for promotion, they told me repeatedly that what we needed most of all was a good striker. Now, during the close season, I became aware that Brian Kidd was available from Arsenal for £100,000, which I believed would be a good buy for us. The directors agreed to the fee, but dismissed his wages of £200 a week out of hand. They also dismissed out of hand a proposal for a fairer bonus system for the players, indeed one of them was strongly against the bonus system already in place. I was devastated.

When I got home I said to Anne, 'We've just had a great season. Imagine what it would have been like if we'd had a bad one?'

After a sleepless night, I phoned Ronnie Teeman, who advised me to tell the club secretary Alan Everiss, with whom I had a good relationship, that I was going on holidays. And that I'd review my position when I got back. This brought Bert Millichip down to the ground to meet me later that day, and Bert put it like this. 'John, I can assure you that wherever you go in the game, you will get the same treatment.'

I told him in that case I was finished.

'You can't do that,' he said.

'Nobody can stop me finishing,' I said.

Bert wasn't being nasty about it, and actually he was telling me the truth – wherever I went in the game, I would have got the same treatment. But he was still shocked that I would simply pull the plug. Apparently, this had never been done before. And, to this day, I believe I am the only manager ever to leave a successful club, just like that – or at least to hand in my notice. I eventually decided to postpone my departure for another season, because of the close relationship I had with the players, and because pre-season training was about to start, making it difficult to find a suitable replacement.

Despite all my experience as a player, I had still been naive in the workings of the game. I believed the manager would have control over a number of important areas, such as the players coming in and going out, and the appointment of his staff, and that he could agree terms with the players without the approval of the board, spending his agreed budget as he wished.

This seemed to me like common sense, but I was now discovering that it didn't work like that at all. And it had never worked like that, which explains why Bert, with whom I got on well on a personal level, was so taken aback at my reaction.

To understand it, you need to go back to the early days of the game, when the secretary and the directors were in charge of team matters, and the ex-pros, who actually knew about football, were merely trainers. Over time, managers got more respect and authority but, ultimately, they were subservient to the directors. Or, at least, the manager faced a constant struggle to get the conditions needed for success.

The way that culture worked was again confirmed to me by Bill Nicholson, who had been treated so shabbily by Spurs, and who came up to West Brom with a Spurs youth team to play a friendly around the time that news of my discontent had reached the papers.

Bill was obviously curious about it, and when I told him what was troubling me, he too was surprised.

'John, you've got to put up with that type of thing,' he said.

From then, until the time I left West Brom at the end of the next season, as I had promised, nothing happened to dissuade me from my belief that I couldn't function within this ludicrous system. The case of Paul Mariner illustrates perfectly how it worked. He was playing for Plymouth at the time, and available for £200,000. One of the directors, Tom Silk, said he'd be a good player for us, and I agreed, but added that as we supposedly didn't have the money, there was no point talking about it.

'I think we could raise the money,' Tom said.

I thought about it.

'Hang on a minute,' I said. 'What you're actually saying is, if I rate a player and you don't, we have no money. But if you rate a player, we can raise the money.'

Tom just laughed and left the office. In the end, we didn't get Mariner.

But we did get Laurie Cunningham and Cyrille Regis. In fact the £110,000 we paid to bring Laurie from Leyton Orient to West Brom was by far the biggest fee ever paid in British football for a black player. Right up until the mid-70s, there was a widespread view in the English game that the black players 'didn't have the bottle'.

I always felt this was wrong, and obviously wrong. Pelé, for example, and Garrincha and Jairzinho had the bottle, and a lot more besides. So this was a cultural problem, borne out by the fact that at clubs such as Everton and Liverpool and Newcastle United, where they knew their football, and knew that some of the great players happened to be black, there was still an unspoken ban until the likes of John Barnes and Andy Cole came through.

It was Ronnie Allen who recommended Laurie Cunningham to me, and I went to see him a couple of times at Orient. It was clear that he could really play, and that he lacked no bottle whatsoever. He would become one of the first black players to be capped for England, and would eventually be sold to Real Madrid for about a million.

With my time at West Brom drawing to a close, Ronnie Allen also spotted Cyrille Regis, who was playing non-league football for Hayes. We signed him for five grand. Cyrille was a very intelligent lad, and he would become a hero with the West Brom fans. It was a pleasure to meet him again in 2010 at the launch of his own book.

With the team going well in the First Division, Bert again raised the possibility of me staying beyond that season, so I gave him the conditions under which I would be happy to stay. I wanted control over all incoming and outgoing players and coaching staff, the power to agree terms with players without reference to the board, a £250,000 transfer budget and a long-term contract. I decided not to include my own financial terms with the list, so that if negotiations broke down, it couldn't be blamed on my personal demands. After a few weeks Bert came back to me to say that the board wouldn't agree to these terms.

'Anyway,' he said, 'if I give you all these conditions, I would only be a puppet in the club.'

'So you want me to be the puppet instead,' I said.

Right until the end, I think they believed I'd change my mind and stay. But I couldn't do it. It was sad for me to leave the job too, because it had extended my playing career by two precious years. And I really liked West Brom, and the supporters and players who had done so well for me. In fact I can't speak highly enough of them, because we were there around the time of the

Birmingham bombings, done in the name of Ireland. So I had direct experience of that famous English tolerance.

About seven years later, feeling that things were changing in the English game, I accepted the invitation of Sid Lucas to manage West Brom again. Unfortunately, I had been away in Ireland and Canada for too long, and I wasn't as familiar with the English game as I needed to be. Because I'd always had that good relationship with the West Brom supporters, I regret not doing as well the second time around. This time I wasn't playing and instead of people doubting the wisdom of my dual role as player and manager, they'd say, 'It's a pity you can't get out there and show them how it's done.' I'd laugh at that, but pretty soon I realised that it just wasn't going to work, whatever I did. I resigned but, this time, everyone agreed it was the right thing to do.

We still live in that part of the world, and I am still patiently waiting for that statue of Tony Brown to be erected in the high street of West Bromwich.

Just because something has always been done a certain way, doesn't make it right. I wouldn't accept this notion of responsibility without power, just because it had always been done that way. So the logical conclusion was that the manager had to be as powerful as the directors, or be a shareholder.

Back in Dublin, the Kilcoyne family had bought Shamrock Rovers and Louis Kilcoyne, who was my brother-in-law, was president of the club. When things didn't work out with West Brom, Louis brought up an idea he had suggested before, that I should come to Rovers, where I could have an option on 50 per cent of the shares.

It seemed logical. We could create a youth policy, persuading some players to stay in Ireland, rather than moving to clubs in England as they had traditionally done. We could give them the right football and educational environment, and if and when they were transferred to an English club, they would be guaranteed

20 per cent of the transfer fee. I knew it hadn't been done before and it would be difficult, but I was still optimistic. Perhaps I should have listened more carefully to Ronnie Teeman, who had reservations about it on a business level.

But I thought I could make it work. I would bring in men such as Ray Treacy and Eamon Dunphy who would have much to contribute to the development of young footballers as players and as people, and who were similarly enthused about the project. Ultimately, we felt we could build Shamrock Rovers into a club that could compete in Europe – hadn't Ireland always produced players of the highest class?

In the first season, we were delighted to win the FAI Cup with an experienced team. But I made the mistake of bringing the young players through too quickly. I was looking to the future, but the future was now. The Rovers supporters, quite rightly, became impatient. It also quickly became apparent to me, that because of the expense of running the project, the idea of me being a 50 per cent owner was just impossible.

From the press, I got an attitude which could be best summed up in the line: 'Who does this little bollix think he is?' I think they preferred the old style of Irish soccer hero, the player who was exploited and abused and who had ended up virtually down and out. I had always had a dread of ending up like that and I spent a lot of my career fighting against the system that, for generations, had treated some of the great players like dirt. I wanted to be independent, even if the Manny Cussins' of this world didn't think I was entitled to it. In certain quarters, they seemed more comfortable with that idea, than with the likes of me coming in with my big plans.

And I think the mood in Ireland had darkened against me after my testimonial match. It had been awarded to me by the FAI during that hectic season when West Brom were promoted, at the end of which I genuinely thought that I was no longer able to continue combining the two playing jobs. So at thirty-five, I decided to announce my retirement from the international team. The testimonial, against a Don Revie X1, was meant to be my last game for Ireland.

But I had a really good rest that summer and, by the time the following season came around, I found that I was playing really well. My assistant Alan Kelly saw me scoring at Anfield in a League Cup match, and was convinced that I should play in a forth-coming friendly against England at Wembley. You only get one playing career and, besides, I felt I still had an obligation to play, unless there was anyone better out there – and it was generally accepted that there wasn't. So I played against England, and played well, in a 1–1 draw, but there was now a public percep-tion that I had pulled a stroke, announcing my retirement to boost the attendance at my testimonial.

There would also be comical suggestions that I was 'giving myself another cap', as if I needed one, and that it all confirmed the notion that I was the money-grabbing type. It was put about so much, I have to remind myself sometimes that I was never paid more than £6,000 a year by the FAI as player-manager of the Republic, with responsibility for the under-18s and under-21s throw in. It also didn't help my popularity when it was announced that I was getting an increase of £3,000 – which was reported mischievously as 'a 50 per cent rise'. And I never did get that '50 per cent rise' because, in 1980, after seven years in the job, I resigned before the increase came through.

But any of these mere facts that I might use in my defence were far outweighed by the nonsense that was flying around. For example, at the end of my first season with Rovers, I went to Philadelphia to play for half a season, which might seem a reason-able enough thing for a professional footballer to do, but which was seen as more evidence that I was only in it for the money.

At the next home international match against Northern Ireland, I could feel the hostility from the crowd. Against Bulgaria, though I didn't hear it myself, my kids were able to tell me that when my name was announced, I was booed.

I always knew that if the Republic could qualify for a major tournament, the reaction would be as great as it actually turned out to be, when we qualified with Jack. All my efforts over the years had been directed towards that, and we had made huge progress. The people I felt I was doing it for, were the very ones who were booing my name. So when Anne wondered why I was still doing that job, I couldn't really think of a good answer.

I will freely admit that my media skills were terrible. My negative attitude to journalists seeped into their overall coverage of the side, helping to create the party line that the team was negative on the pitch, even though the two things were completely unconnected. And we surely demonstrated that we weren't negative by scoring three against the USSR and Denmark, and four against Turkey.

Ray Treacy marvelled at how bad I was at basic public relations – if someone came up to me and asked me nicely if I remembered them, I would treat it as a straight question requiring a straight answer, and often I would simply say 'no'. I didn't intend to be rude, but people might be forgiven for taking it that way.

Ray would also say, 'People who knew John well, were loyal friends of his. But the problem was, there weren't many people who knew John well.'

Even at Leeds, I didn't have the sort of rapport with the fans that some of the other lads had. In fact, in all the time I was at Elland Road, I was never chosen in the top three in the fans' Player of the Year competition. This was completely irrelevant to me, the ultimate rapport, for me, was not to be found kissing the badge or clapping the crowd after losing 3–0 when I hadn't tried a leg. I was looking for a different kind of rapport, the ultimate kind of rapport, which comes from helping the team to win matches, ultimately to win the league or the cup. Which is what we were all looking for, players and fans alike. That's the rapport I wanted.

I was never a 'character', which helps to explain why I wasn't the most popular guy during my career in Ireland, as a player and a manager.

But we never lost a competitive match in Dublin while I was player-manager of the Republic, having taken over when we hadn't won at home for six years. We beat the Soviet Union, France, Denmark and Switzerland. Our ranking went up significantly, which, in itself, was an important boost at a time when only one team would qualify from a group for the major tournaments. And yet there would be more muttering about the style of football we were playing, how we were hitting it back and forth to each other for no real reason, something that was apparently far too boring for those who had enjoyed all those endless defeats played in the proper style.

Probably my happiest memory of the League of Ireland actually took place in Argentina. Louis Kilcoyne, who was a brilliant organiser of such things, set up a match between a League of Ireland team and an Argentina team just before the 1978 World Cup. As manager, I was ably assisted by Shay Brennan, my old friend from Manchester United, then with Waterford.

We thought we were playing a selection from the local Argentinian league, but in Buenos Aires we gradually learned that we'd be playing the full national team, with Ardiles, Kempes, Passarella and Luque, who would all become world famous in a few weeks' time.

We came up from a tunnel into the ground, a packed stadium with flags, bunting and tickertape, like Christians to the slaughter in the Coliseum. I have never been more frightened in my life as a manager about the result of a game.

When the match started, we did OK for a while. Ray Treacy was playing up front and he thought he'd detected a tragic flaw in their defence. The guy he was marking was small for a central defender. Unfortunately, as it turned out, his name was Daniel Passarella, who could leap as if he had springs on his heels, one of the best headers of the ball I have even seen. So sending the ball up to Ray wasn't working. We were 2–0 down at half-time. And I had to come off injured. I would have to watch the horror unfolding, helpless to intervene.

Then early in the second half, they made it three. We were on course for a hiding of historic proportions. At which point, out of nowhere, Synan Braddish who played with Dundalk, got the ball about thirty-five yards out, and hit a screamer into the back of the net. Suddenly, the whole mindset of the Argentinians seemed to change. Instead of proceeding with the slaughter, they decided to hold on to what they had, and it ended 3–1.

It was both a stunning example of the unpredictability of football, and probably one of the best results I've had in my life – they won the World Cup final against Holland by the same score.

A lot of the good results the Republic got were undermined by the mysterious refereeing decisions which are now part of Irish football folklore. Partly, I suppose, it was because we were still regarded as second-class citizens, or even third-class citizens, as suckers who should never be given an even break. And partly, I think, we just got 'done' by dismal officials.

There was an equaliser in Sofia that I scored from just outside the box that was disallowed for no reason at all. In fact, I had been to see France playing Bulgaria in Sofia, when Michel Platini had been taken down for an obvious penalty that wasn't given. Let us just say that Bulgaria had an unbelievably good home record.

And we, in turn, had a bad night in Paris, when Liam Brady got to the by-line and crossed to Frank Stapleton to head a goal which would have made it 1–1, if it had been given. Needless to add, it wasn't. And to this day, no one has the faintest idea why.

For years, the Irish supporters were reluctant to celebrate a goal until the ball was back at the centre-circle and the game had restarted, confirming beyond doubt that an Ireland goal had indeed been allowed to stand. And some of them still wouldn't believe it until they saw it confirmed in the paper the next morning. I suppose we can laugh about it now.

I would continue playing until I was forty years of age. My last match was for Shamrock Rovers against UCD at Milltown, though I hadn't known it was going to be my last match, so there was no big deal about it. In my late thirties, I had gone to play in the North American Soccer League for Philadelphia Fury, a club partly owned by musicians such as Rick Wakeman, Peter Frampton and Paul Simon. The league had seen players of the stature of Pelé, Beckenbauer and Carlos Alberto; in Philadelphia, we had Peter Osgood and Alan Ball. It was quite glamorous at the time. I have a vague memory of talking to Charlie Watts of The Rolling Stones after a match in New York. But I wouldn't have known much about those guys.

And I particularly enjoyed the time I spent as player-manager of the Vancouver Whitecaps, when we lived for three years in one of the most beautiful cities in the world.

Again the standard was surprisingly high. We bought the twenty-year-old Peter Beardsley from Carlisle for £250,000 – and we didn't have any competition from English clubs for Peter's signature.

I was voted North American Soccer League Coach of the Year, which wasn't put to the popular vote, but was decided by other coaches in the league – otherwise I probably wouldn't have had a prayer.

I wasn't a character in Canada either, but then my father was enough of a character for both of us. In 1978, I was in Copenhagen with the Republic, playing a Denmark team that was just starting to come good. I knew that my father had travelled for the match, still enjoying my career more than I enjoyed it myself.

When I was player-manager, I would usually be up to my eyes

at all times, but especially at half-time, which was just ten minutes back then. I would always try to get off the pitch before any of the other players, to settle myself in the dressing room and sort myself out and then figure out what to say to the lads. As I made my way to the dressing room on this occasion, I was very pleased with the way things were going. Without Liam Brady, who had carried an injury into Arsenal's defeat to Ipswich Town in the FA cup final and, against all expectations, we were leading 2–1.

And then all the happiness drained out of me. Because there, at the dressing room door, stood my father. As soon as I saw him, I felt there could only be one possible explanation for his desire to speak to me at that moment. Clearly, someone had died – almost certainly my mother. All these dreadful scenarios went racing through my head in a matter of seconds. It would have to be a death in the family, because I figured it would have been just too difficult for him to get through all the security and the stewards without getting special permission – the sort of permission you only get, if something terrible has happened.

I nodded to him, like a condemned man accepting my fate, bracing myself for the bad news. He cleared his throat. 'This fucking team is made for offside,' he said.

For a few moments I was dazed. I couldn't quite take it all in. At one level, I was enormously relieved that it wasn't bad news after all, and, at another, I was trying to come to terms with the fact that my father was standing there telling me, not that my mother had died, but that, as he saw it, Denmark was playing in such a way that they would be vulnerable to the offside trap. That he had made his way – somehow – through all the barriers that must have been in his way, in a stadium in a foreign country, to tell me, not that five members of our family had been killed in an accident, but that the Danes were 'made for offside'.

I can't remember my exact words to him, all I know is that he got the hell out of there very, very quickly. I was player-manager of the Republic of Ireland. I had played for Manchester

United and Leeds United and I had won most of the major honours of the game at least once, but in some part of his head I was still playing for Stella on a Sunday morning, and he was sharing his knowledge with me.

I should add that the Danes were indeed 'made for offside'.

He was right.

EPILOGUE

I SOMETIMES say that the main feeling I had at the end of my career was one of relief.

Which sounds a bit downbeat, but I don't mean it that way. It is like the feeling you have after a long journey, a feeling of satisfaction that you've done what you meant to do.

I had a gift, and I could look back and say that I was true to that gift. But I had always seen it as a big responsibility that demanded that I do my best all the time. I had dreams and they came true, but it hadn't happened just because I wanted it. I wasn't like the fellow at home in bed who dreams of scoring the winning goal in the cup final, and then leaves it at that. I had to go out and do it.

I had a long playing career, but there comes a time you want another life as well. And hopefully you're happy to go when the time comes. I think I was.

To this day, I would say that the people I am most comfortable with are the old Leeds players. I always wanted to play for a team like Leeds. A team that stuck together through the dark days, making the victories when they came all the sweeter.

After all these years, we are completely relaxed in each other's company. It is unusual for players still to have that bond, because the culture of football dictates that we are mostly ships in the night. But we still meet from time to time, usually at some event that is organised for us at Elland Road. I stay with Peter Lorimer, the man with whom I drank in the empty banqueting hall in the Queen's Hotel, on the night we lost the league at Wolves, Peter who never let a defeat get him down, and who was right.

Paul Madeley comes along, Paul who didn't look like he'd make it at the start, and who finished up playing in every position except goalkeeper – and maybe we should have tried him in there too. There's Terry Cooper, always in the mind's eye making some brilliant overlapping run, and the other full-back Paul Reaney, who could keep George Best quiet.

Norman Hunter, the man loved by Don as if he was his own son, is always there, and so are Allan Clarke and Mick Jones who scored so many goals for us, such different personalities. Mick Bates, as ever, is there or thereabouts. And so are Eddie and Frankie Gray. Then we have the younger lads, Gordon McQueen and Joe Jordan and Terry Yorath, and from the early days Rod Belfitt and, of course, Big Jack.

Despite being the victim of some very cruel jokes over the years, Jack is comfortable with us. These days Jack doesn't have to be berating Sprakey, whose long-suffering understudy David Harvey sometimes makes it down from his farm in the Orkneys. We remember Billy, who led us out so many times, and who died at the age of fifty-four, and we remember Don. We might talk about odd things known only to us, like that horse that was hired by the lads to carry their colours, the slowest horse in the history of racing. Or maybe a game in Ankara that no one else remembers, when some little Turkish fellow kicked us all night.

It was good to play in that team, with those lads.

No, it was great.

Declan Lynch

Declan Lynch began his writing career at the age of seventeen with Ireland's rock and roll magazine *Hot Press* and now writes for the *Sunday Independent*. He is the author of several works of fiction and non-fiction including the acclaimed novel *The Rooms*.